WASH 'N' DRY MURDER

When she opened the lid of the washer, a sudden thought stopped her.

"Fred, look at these. They're wet."

"You expected dry?"

"I'm serious."

"You'd better tell me." A certain I'm-being-patient-with-this-nonsense tone.

"Fred, this tells us she was still alive about forty minutes ago."

The respect was missing from his raised eyebrows this time.

"Sure," she insisted. "I used to have almost the twin of this machine. Set like this, it takes about forty minutes from start to finish. I heard it when I came in and I told you just now when it went off."

Now he was nodding. He reached into the washer and bore the wet things off. Joan sighed. She knew something didn't make sense.

———————— ★ ————————

Murder in C Major

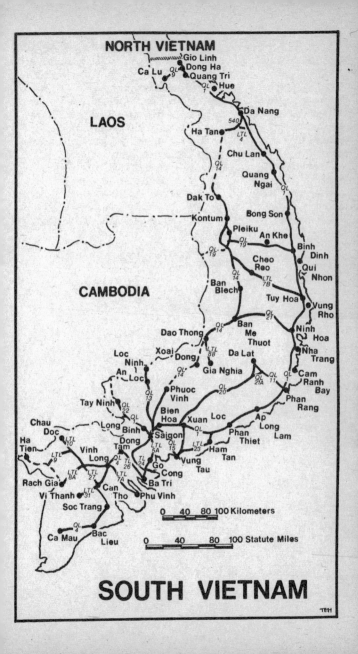

PROLOGUE

As I write this book, we are at the close of another conflict. Most of the DESERT STORM warriors have come home, and we have begun to forget that some are still there cleaning up. People have asked me if I resent the homecoming given the men of DESERT STORM. My reply is, "No, they won their war!" I am proud that this time we have not let our fighting men come home unappreciated. I felt a warm feeling inside as I watched General Schwarzkopf conduct a soldier's war. If I were to resent anything, it would be that those of us who fought in Vietnam were not allowed to win our war. Anyone who believes that American fighting men were defeated in Vietnam is wrong; they were defeated at home.

This book is a tribute to the courage of the men who fought in Vietnam. While I do not wish to detract from the efforts put forth by my brave comrades at arms in Saudi, it is important to remember that the soldiers, sailors, airmen, and Marines who made their sacrifice in the jungles, offices, airfields, and hospitals of Vietnam also did so with great courage, dedication and patriotism. Men who were shot at daily still realized that the people they called REMFs were doing what they were assigned to do. Many who went did so accompanied by the ridicule of their peers, and returned the same way. Still, they fought with a courage and tenacity of which they can be proud. There were those who did not want to go but, nevertheless, brought home Silver Stars, and many who did not believe in the cause, but won Distinguished Service Crosses or Navy Crosses. I saw acts of courage that deserved Medals of Honor but were rewarded with less. I saw daily acts of courage that went unnoticed and unrewarded.

I once heard the TV show "Tour of Duty" criticized for having too many heroic acts performed by a single sergeant. While the show intended to be a representation of all acts of courage, I know of former paratroopers of the 101st Airborne Division who could say, "What's so special about what they do on 'Tour of Duty?' "

I believe that the Vietnam veterans' gift to the DESERT STORM veterans is the support and the homecoming they were given. Many Vietnam veterans have worked hard to see that "it" did not happen again. Maybe the hoopla has been overdone, as has been suggested. Well, the Vietnam veterans can smile with pride about the overkill on this one, for I believe the excess belongs to them. It is the guilt of a nation ashamed, making up for the last time.

Vietnam veterans have their own special heritage. It comes from the way they were received at home. There is a bond that I believe is stronger than veterans of other wars share. It is a bond that lets us make a phone call twenty-two years later and find a friend on the other end of the connection. It is bond that says it doesn't matter if there wasn't a parade, we have each other. It is a bond that gives us membership in an exclusive club, and those who didn't care can never belong.

I was privileged to serve with the paratroopers of the 101st Airborne Division. In the face of all the reasons they were given to perform poorly, they fought with a courage and intensity that put them on a equal footing with their brothers in Bastogne. These Screaming Eagles faced the protesters, the press, and all their detractors and said "Nuts" with their actions.

The motto of the Kingsmen was *Opera Non Verba*, "Actions not words." On a daily basis, the crews of the 17th Assault Helicopter Company lived up to that motto. Even as they became B Company, 101st Aviation Battalion, the commander took pride in picking up the phone and hearing, "We need help. Can you send me a Kingsman?"

Finally, I wish to honor another hero of the Vietnam war with this book. One that was wounded many times. One that saved thousands of lives. A hero that has not received one decoration for all the times that it performed flawlessly. The Huey. The UH-1 helicopter brought many of us back alive. Ask any grunt what the most beautiful sound he heard in country was, and he'll tell you that it was that loud thump, thump, thump of the Huey's blades. Ask any pilot if he ever screwed up and had his Huey save his ass by doing things it was not built to do. Huey never complained. Huey never quit. Many times these birds continued to fly with their life's blood leaking out till the mission was complete. Many of these veterans are still flying with almost thirty years of hard service. Many still proudly wear scars that are left from their Vietnam service. They served in Grenada, Panama, and Saudi. They will continue to serve into the next century. They have indeed earned a Distinguished Flying Cross; it is worn in the hearts of the pilots that flew them.

I have tried to get the facts down as accurately as possible, but many years have passed since these events occurred. In many hours of interviews, I have found that two witnesses remember the same event differently. Five witnesses remember the same event five different ways. I have consulted the national archives and as many people as I could contact. This story is true and as accurate as I can make it. I have woven into the story some of the music that was so important to me during my tour in Vietnam. I've tried to include most of the people that I had the privilege to serve with. If I have forgotten anyone, I am truly sorry. There are some cases where I have changed the names of people with whom my experiences were not positive. This was done because it is not my purpose here to cause someone shame or embarrassment, and I realize that mine was not the only side of any disagreement which may have occurred.

I invite you now to travel back with me to 1968 and share my "Rendezvous with Destiny."

CHAPTER 1
MARCH 1968

FORT LEWIS ARMY PERSONNEL CENTER

The graduation celebration after flight school had been somewhat dampened by thoughts of our next assignment. We were well trained, at least we thought so. We were, at least, prepared to learn how to be combat pilots. The next phase of training would be the most important. In the next ninety days, we would be become very good or, in the harshest grading of all, would not survive.

My orders read that port-call information would arrive while I was on leave. When it came, I was notified that I was to report to the Fort Lewis Overseas Replacement Station on Wednesday, 20 March, at 1200 hours. So much for hopes that they would forget me while I was on leave.

Fort Lewis was like a class reunion. Jerry Foster, Pat McCrady, Clyde Hackler, Gene Gillenwater, and I went to the club for dinner and proceeded to get smashed on our last night in the World. Some bar hopping would be just the thing to help us forget the plane that was leaving at 1600 hours the next evening.

21 March 1968 (364 days to go). That was when the count of days began, though, at the time, I did not know how important the count would become. We did know that our time started counting down as soon as we left the States. Once the wheels of the plane left the runway at Seattle-Tacoma Airport, our tour had begun. The days remaining on one's tour established the unofficial pecking order. It was your mark of status among your peers. Many times, it would, in fact, supersede military rank. No one counted the days he had already accumulated. The days that remained were all that mattered. The smaller your number, the more important you became. A short-timer was the symbol of survival. When you saw someone going home, it meant that you might survive your tour, as well. Later on, I would find out that there was actually a bonus day. You did not have to count the last day, since you left before it ended. It counted simply as a "wake-up." All you had to do that final day was to wake up and get on the "freedom bird" for the ride home.

The plane was full of soldiers who had been out-processed at Fort Lewis. Most were young. Many wore the blue rope of the infantry. Their rank varied, but none in the group seemed to be in charge. No one seemed to want to take charge. We moved along like cattle to the slaughterhouse, calm, unaware, and cooperative. The NCOs from the replacement station got us on the buses, then to the airport, and finally on the plane. They watched somberly as we departed. We were to stop for fuel in Yokota, Japan. They told us in the replacement station to hope for plane trouble during the fuel stop, because if we got stuck in Japan, the time spent there would come off our tour.

My feelings were mixed. I certainly agreed that a day spent in Japan was a day that I was not likely to be shot. But then, how did I get this far in the first place? I must have been marching to the beat of a different drummer than my friends in high school and college. Many of the guys I knew in my high school graduating class had gone on to college to major in education so that they would be eligible for a teacher's deferment when they graduated. Many claimed to be opposed to the war. I wonder now if any of them still teach. If so, I feel sorry for their students. They must be some very unhappy teachers, for none of that group ever expressed as their vocation a desire to nurture the flowering minds of America's youth.

There were those who enlisted in the air force and navy, selecting job fields that they believed would keep them from going to Nam. Then there was the group that let fate take its course; they waited for the draft, hoping they could spend their two years somewhere where there were no bullets.

Finally, there were Rod Heim and W. T. Grant. Rod found out that the army would allow you to be a helicopter pilot without a college degree. Certainly the glamour of being a pilot was a prime consideration, but there could be little doubt as to the consequences; becoming an army helicopter pilot was a sure ticket to Vietnam.

It was not that I felt that I was volunteering to go. I just never considered not going to be an option. I would fight in my country's current war, just as my father had fought in Africa during World War II, as a member of the Big Red One. In a time of rebellion and "doing your own thing," the way to truly avoid conformity was to cling to the traditional values.

The most difficult part was facing those piercing green eyes of my girlfriend Jackie as I gave her the news that I was off to flight school. Those loving green eyes. I could not go off to war without being able to look into those eyes and say, "Wife."

As the landing gear thumped into the wings, I had already discovered the ache of missing her. I had a reason to count down the days even before I knew it was a required ritual.

YOKOTA, JAPAN

We stopped for fuel in Yokota, after ten hours in the air. They allowed us off the plane in the terminal only. The stretch felt good. Good news, the date line takes a day off your tour on the way over, and you get to leave by the date in Vietnam. My DEROS date ("date estimated return from overseas service") was 20 March 1969. One free day, proceed to "GO" and collect two hundred dollars. There was time to send off a postcard to Jackie; I sent love and told her we would depart 1900 hours for Cam Ranh Bay. It was 1900 hours 22 March 1968 there, and 0500 hours 21 March in New York. I had fun driving her crazy the whole tour by comparing times and dates in letters.

CAM RANH BAY

The plane landed at Cam Ranh Bay late at night. It had been a long flight, but I found it difficult to catch more than twenty minutes' sleep at a time. My excitement had increased tenfold since leaving the States. Something told me that I should be afraid, but I wasn't listening.

The wheels chirped as we touched down. We had finally reached "The Nam." It was quiet on board the plane, as each of us was left with his own thoughts. This was what we had been preparing for since basic training. For some, it had only been a matter of a few weeks. For others, like myself, that had been over a year. It was now the time to find out if we had learned anything. My biggest fear was, Can I pull my weight?

We remained silent as the plane came to a stop. As soon as the door opened, I felt the blast of hot, humid air. The pilot asked that everyone continue to remain seated. The plane seemed so isolated. The lights were on in the cabin, so it was impossible to see anything outside the aircraft. It felt like we were living an episode from the "Twilight Zone"—sitting in an island of reality in the center of a black void.

A staff sergeant stepped through the door of the plane. In his best army voice, he said, "Good evening, gentlemen. Welcome to Cam Ranh Bay, Vietnam. We are currently under a yellow alert, so please move quickly and quietly and follow instructions. There are buses waiting outside the plane. Grab your AWOL bag and move to the first bus. Your other bags will be unloaded and brought to the replacement center."

We moved to the buses and were soon on our way. The starch in my khakis had long since relaxed during the flight, and it now disappeared entirely in the sweat that drenched me. The bus was the standard-issue U.S. Army bus, a school bus with an OD (olive drab) face-lift. The notable exception was the wire mesh covering all the windows. I'm sure that my companions wanted to ask why? but like myself, they did not want to appear stupid. Finally, Gene Gillenwater, who was not easily embarrassed by anything, piped up. The staff sergeant explained in a patient tone that the mesh was to keep Charlie from throwing grenades through the windows.

I suddenly realized that I did not have a weapon. How dangerous was a yellow alert? I found myself peering into the shadows outside the bus, trying to locate the grenade thrower before he did his evil deed. It never occurred to me that if things were all that serious, the sergeant would have had a weapon and would not be wearing khakis.

From the way the bus was riding, the road had apparently turned to dirt. Now this was more like what I expected, a beat-up old bus and a dirt road. I felt like we were now in a war zone. The airport at Cam Ranh Bay had been a disappointment. Much too civilized!

We were in for a long night of in-processing. I finally got to bed around 0400 hours, woke up around 0600, and got up at 0700 because I couldn't sleep any more. The replacement center reminded me of a POW compound—long rows of barracks buildings, sandy ground. We were not allowed to go anywhere because they didn't know when we would get shipped to our units. I didn't understand, as I'd had orders to the 17th Combat Aviation Group since January. On the positive side, the replacement center had a PX, free movie, and an O club (officers club).

On Saturday the twenty-third (363 days to go), we were told there had been a change in orders. Oscar Goodman, Jerry Johnson, and I would go to the 16th Combat Aviation Group (CAG), with further assignment to the 212th Combat Support Aviation Battalion. Clyde Hackler and I went to the PX, then back to the hootch. I spent the late afternoon hanging around the club, drinking Cokes and playing the slot machines. Later, we switched to beer. I figured the beer would help me sleep.

After dinner at the mess hall, Jerry and Oscar joined us back at the club. We stayed late enough to guarantee a good night's sleep. Clyde and I had been together since Fort Wolters, but now would go our separate ways. I would not see him again.

DA NANG

The next morning at 0800 hours, Oscar, Jerry, and I were on our way to Da Nang on a C-130 transport. Riding on 130s quickly became one of my most unfavorite things in Nam. They were loud and uncomfortable, and you couldn't see where you were going. Many times you had to ride on a cargo pallet, without a seat. The C-130, when equipped for cargo, had rows of rollers along the floor. The cargo was loaded on to aluminum pallets and then rolled into the aircraft. To haul passengers, the air force simply loaded on the pallets, and everyone sat on them. I think the pilots enjoyed making short-field takeoffs and landings during these operations. On the takeoff, as the nose pointed skyward, the pallets would roll to the rear a few inches. When they stopped their roll, the passengers piled up on one another. On landing, the reaction was worse: as the pilot reversed the props and applied the brakes, the pallets slid forward, and everyone flew toward the front of the aircraft.

On this occasion, we were lucky, we had seats. They were not airline seats, just nylon sheets that are stretched taut between supports. They were similar to the passenger seats in the Huey. I wasn't fond of them either.

Monday, 25 March (360 days to go). We spent the day hanging around the 16th Combat Aviation Group (CAG), waiting for further orders. That afternoon, Oscar's and Jerry's orders were changed again. They were now going to the 174th AHC of the 14th CAB. I was beginning to think that there would be a lot more dead NVA and VC if we would spend less time changing our minds. Oscar and Jerry shipped out that afternoon. I was left in Da Nang. The old gang had been whittled down to one. Still, there was no word on my final assignment.

So far, I had not had to do any hard work out in the sun, but the heat had not been as bad as I had expected. The nights had been reasonably cool. Vietnam was starting to get really boring. I knew it was safer to wait around in the rear, but I wanted to start flying. I wrote home, but still couldn't give Jackie an address to write to me.

On the twenty-sixth, they finally told me that I'd be staying in Da Nang with the 282d Aviation Company. According to the papers, Da Nang was supposed to be one of the hottest spots in country at the time. While I hadn't seen much of the city yet, the truck ride to the 16th CAG from Da Nang Main had taken about a half hour. I'd been told it was a pretty large city. Most of the scenery was about what I had expected in a poor country in this part of the world. Palm trees, shanty houses, with some nice villas along the way. The streets all seemed to be bustling with business, making it hard to believe that a war was going on. The city was so large that an attack in one part would often go unnoticed in another part. I was anxious to get that information in a letter home so Jackie wouldn't believe I was dead every time the news reported that someone had fired a shot in Da Nang.

I had become weary of the journey. It had taken seven days to get that far; eighteen hours to travel the first ten thousand miles and six and a quarter days to cover the few hundred miles from Cam Ranh Bay to Da Nang. The boring routines of in-processing, drawing equipment, and lugging all my belongings to hell and back had worn me out. I just wanted someplace to call home for a while. I discovered that Da Nang had a mixture of army, navy, air force, and Marines.

The Black Cats were located on a Marine Corps base at Marble Mountain. Marble Mountain itself was actually a large black rock that rose up out of the sand on a peninsula on the east side of Da Nang. The mountain was located at the southern end of the peninsula, and the rest of the peninsula was occupied by the airfield, hangers, and the living areas. The peninsula made the airfield hard to reach for the enemy, and therefore, fairly secure.

The company area was full of neat little rows of light green buildings. The compound was divided into neat little blocks with concrete sidewalks around them. The hootches were of wood construction with clapboard siding. The roofs were shingled in light gray shingles. Sandy streets that were once penaprimed gave the appearance of worn-out tar roads. The whole thing resembled a beach resort where all the little houses looked the same. After I signed into the company, I found out that Gene Gillenwater, who'd left Cam Ranh Bay ahead of me, was already here and would be my roommate. Gene helped me move in, then took me over to operations, where I met the assistant ops officer, Don "Sleepy Bear" McClure. I did not have to ask why they nicknamed him Sleepy Bear—he was not real tall, stocky, with eyelids that looked as though they would close shop at any moment. Bear showed us around the company, introducing us to different people as we went. He showed us operations, maintenance, and the armament shop. As we walked, he explained that the Black Cats flew mostly VIP and ARVN missions, neither of which were likely to get us into much trouble. Bear referred to these missions as "pigs-and-rice" missions. He told us that the last Black Cat pilot that had been killed in action was over two and a half years before, and that was due to mortar fire while on the ground at a Special Forces camp. Some more good news to send home! As we approached the officers hootches, he said that the first two on the first row belonged to the gun platoon. They called themselves the "Alley Cats." My ears perked up at that. I told him that I went through gunnery training at Rucker and wanted to fly guns.

Bear said, "The Alley Cats get shot at a lot more than the rest of us, so you'd better think about that for a while. Besides, right now the Alley Cats are full up, and the Black Cats are short of peter pilots" (copilots).

I said, "I thought that since I went through gunnery training that I was supposed to fly guns."

"Relax, you'll get your chance if you really want it, just not right away. A lot of the Alley Cats are in the double digits (meaning less than one hundred days to go). When they start getting really short, Captain Weitzel will be looking for guys to fly guns." He skipped over the orderly room, since we had signed in there. The last place on the tour was the Black Cat Club. He told us that the club opened at 1300 hours each day and closed somewhere between 2000 and midnight, depending on business. Then he said, "It will be a few days before your records catch up to you so you can fly. Might as well take it easy. Go back to your hootch and get settled, take a nap or whatever. Tomorrow, I'll get a truck and take you guys to the big air force BX on the other side of the city if you want to get anything."

The next day, Gene and I split the cost on a three-foot-high Sanyo refrigerator at the big PX. After we got back to the company area, we set out to fix up our room. It looked as though it wouldn't be such a tough tour after all. The room was air-conditioned, and there was TV, radio, and running water. For a few bucks a month, hootchmaids cleaned the room, shined your boots, and did the laundry. They told us that the bunkers would take a direct hit, so we did not have to worry about rocket and mortar attacks.

I was also told that day that they didn't have my flight records, and I couldn't start flying till they got them. I thought, "Isn't the army wonderful! They send me here to be an aviator and I have to prove to them that I am." I wrote a frantic letter home to have Jackie send my copies of the flight records so I could fly.

Thursday, 28 March (357 days to go). Gene and I went to the beach and did some bodysurfing. We found out later that the navy recreation center had surfboards available. There was a big party at the club that night. So, after I got cleaned up from the beach, Gene and I went over there. As we stepped through the door, a bell rang, and everyone cheered. Wow! What a reception for a couple of FNGs (fucking new guys). Then we found out we had performed the big faux pas. Just inside the swinging saloon doors of the club, the Black Cat emblem had been inlaid in the tile of the floor. Anyone who stepped on it was required to buy a round of drinks. The Black Cat emblem was a yellow circle like the moon, with a black cat, tail up and back arched, superimposed over it. The club closed about midnight, and people who did not have to fly the next day went to different rooms to continue drinking. When the party finally broke up, I had to help two guys find their beds. It was getting harder and harder to remember that there was a war going on out there somewhere.

On 30 March, I wrote Jackie that I had been surfing for the last two days. I wrote about how strange it was to walk around the company area in swimsuits and shower shoes, and then go to the navy PX carrying a .45 pistol. Travel from one military compound to another in Da Nang required moving through civilian areas, making it necessary to carry weapons. The evening of the twenty-ninth, close enough to shake the building, outgoing artillery pounded the hell out of Charlie. But we weren't even on alert. Sleepy Bear told us that "outgoing" was a normal occurrence and not to worry about it. Yet it was only a thirty-minute helicopter flight to Khe Sanh, where the Marines were catching hell from the NVA. There was an empty spot inside me that belonged to Jackie, and it was growing bigger each day.

CHAPTER 2
APRIL 1968

The beginning of a new month brought the realization that it was going to be a long time before I would get another goodnight kiss. I found the thought depressing. I wanted to go home to my wife.

Saturday, 6 April (349 days to go). I had a short-timer's calendar made up and taped to the front of my locker. One of the most popular calendars was that of a woman's body sectioned off into 365 spaces. One to be colored in each day, the lower numbers occupying the better parts. That one was not my style, so I made my own—just row after row of little squares with the date and the number of days in each one. I colored them with colored pencils, so that it came out diagonal rows of the same color. I still have the calendar. I probably would not have saved the other one.

The sixth of April, I got the first letter from my wife. Somewhere out there, there really was a World. My letters did not fall off the end of the earth when I mailed them. Even the mail seemed strange here. Just the idea of writing the word "free" where the stamp should go made Vietnam seem all the more unreal. Jackie sent me news clippings and wrote that maybe I would like to read them if I got some spare time. I wrote back that I had nothing but spare time. I still had not flown.

7 April (348 days to go). Finally, my flight records arrived and I got to fly. The day started off with a short "currency flight" with the instructor pilot. As my left hand began to pull up on the collective control to bring the Huey to a hover, I felt a nervous twinge. I had not flown in over a month; I wondered if I would still be able to hover. When the aircraft got light on the skids, I realized that my right hand had instinctively moved the cyclic stick to the right rear; I had prepared for the bird's tendency to move to the left front coming off the ground. The machine lifted to a three-foot hover and sat there like I knew what I was doing. I hovered out to the runway as the instructor pilot (IP) made the radio calls and explained local procedures. I moved out over the runway as we were cleared for takeoff. I increased the power slightly and lowered the nose, adding some left pedal at the same time. Flying a helicopter takes frequent practice because each control input requires the adjustment of all the other controls.

The airspeed climbed to eighteen knots, and the familiar shudder traveled through the airframe as the aircraft moved through translational lift and the rotor became more efficient. The airspeed continued to climb, and the runway started to fall away below us. A warm feeling rushed through my veins; I was home again; this was what I was meant to do.

The mission was a pigs-and-rice mission, take people here, take cargo there. All the loads were light, two or three PAX (passengers), a couple hundred pounds of cargo. The UH-1D performed as well as it had in flight school. I would soon find that the D-model would not seem so powerful when serious demands were placed on it. There was a lot of shut-down-and-wait time on the mission. We logged just under two hours of flight time, it took about six hours to accomplish the task. It was probably a lot more boring than I realized, but actually having gotten to fly for the first time since February made it fun.

The UH-1 "Huey" helicopter was the latest in the army's inventory. In flight school, I had flown the A-, B-, C-, and D-models. The A-model had an engine that was temperamental, underpowered, and frequently overtemped during the start sequence. It was the first of the line, and there were none in Vietnam. The B- and C-models were used as gunships. The Charlie-model had the same L-11 engine that the D-model had, about eleven hundred horsepower. With the wide blades of the 540 rotor system, the Charlie made a pretty fair gunship.

The eighth was another exciting day of doing nothing. I had taken up poker. Nothing too serious, just a nickel-dime-quarter game to fill some of the empty hours. Sometimes I would allow myself to lose as much as five dollars, all in the same night. It didn't much matter, since it was the same four to six guys almost every night, the money would be at the table again and I had a good chance to get it back the next night.

With 346 days to go on the ninth, I found myself on standby for a flight. They told me that standby flights almost never go. We ended up with a little over an hour and a half of flight time. The mission was to fly a Vietnamese general up to Hue. We could see some of the damage from the Tet offensive. Most of it had already been cleaned up, but there were a few shiny new tin roofs. Maybe there was a war somewhere.

While I was waiting for the mission, I found out that the reason my room had been getting so messy was that the hootchmaid was on vacation. Communication had become an interesting experience. The maids spoke very little English; ours carried around a Vietnamese-English dictionary. Whenever you said something she did not understand, she would laugh. We had been told not to trust the maids 'cause they might be VC. We were cautioned not to leave anything like family addresses or mission sheets in the room. We were encouraged to burn our mail when we were through with it. The maids were all happy to tell you that the VC were "Numba Ten." They rated everything on a one-to-ten scale, with ten being the worst. "GI numba one, VC numba ten." It made you wonder how much conviction there was in all the talk. This all came home one day when one of the pilots caught a maid with a notebook, pacing off the company area. She was plotting a map for the VC to adjust mortar fire from. The pilot had drawn his .45 and was about to cure the problem when Sleepy Bear stopped him. The guy was angry with Bear for stopping him.

He said to Sleepy, "Ya shoulda let me waste the VC bitch!" It would be a while yet before I understood his hatred and frustration. In the end, she was probably worse off, because she was turned over to the Marine MPs for interrogation. Along with the outgoing artillery, this made up my total encounter with the war since my arrival in country.

By Thursday, 11 April (344 days to go), I had accumulated a grand total of two hours and thirty-five minutes of flight time. My attitude was beginning to change. I wrote home that I saw a sign in the finance office.

THE UNWILLING
LED BY THE UNQUALIFIED

TO DO THE UNNECESSARY
FOR THE UNGRATEFUL

To me, it summed up what was going on in the war. I was still convinced that the cause was good, but we were sure screwing up the execution. The headlines said that the Marines had secured Khe Sanh. The true story was that the First Cav had gone there to relieve them. We were saying that the Cav didn't go up there after Chuck, but to see if the Marines were really there. The leadership in the Corps was still trying to fight World War II. The Marines fought bravely, but all that bayonet charge, take-the-high-ground, follow-me crap was outdated. There will never be a piece of ground that someone can take if there is a Marine on it still able to hum two bars of the Marine Corps Hymn. The higher-ups in the Corps wanted the enemy to come out and fight, but Chuck was not having any of that game. There were a lot of Marines getting chewed up because of it. The Cav and the 101st were going out and hunting the bad guys down. They were using helicopters to outmaneuver the enemy, and taking hills from the top down. Khe Sanh sat on a plateau, surrounded by high mountains. The Marines held Khe Sanh, but all the gooks were sitting on the mountaintops and in Laos and shelling and rocketing the place. When the 1st Cav came in, they took the mountaintops, and everything got quiet in a hurry. That probably did not go over well in Washington because it would look too much like a victory, and it was becoming obvious that we had not been sent there to kick ass.

As the month of April wore on, I flew occasionally and came to understand the popular toast in the Black Cat Club. "What War?" The missions quickly became as boring as the days I didn't fly. Most of the time, we flew fifteen- or twenty-minute legs, and then shut down to wait for the next sortie. One day while at an ARVN compound, I spotted a guy wearing a cowboy hat, western shirt, jeans, and western boots. His ensemble was topped off with an olive drab pistol belt with U.S. holster and .45 automatic. When I asked the AC (pilot, aircraft commander) about him, he said, "Don't point, and pretend you don't see him. He works for the Company and they like to pretend that they are not here." The big thrill of the day, I had seen my first CIA man. Well, the first that I was able to recognize as such anyway. Later on, I would learn that the silver, gray, and blue painted Hueys belonged to Air America, the CIA airline. These pilots were getting paid three and four thousand dollars a month. Army pilots flying the same kind of missions were only being paid 650 bucks a month.

Once in a while, I would get to fly with our platoon leader, Captain McClendon, a good pilot who always took the time to explain things. McClendon had been in every branch of service. He had about eighteen years in and said, "I've tried them all so I could see which one I liked the best." Captain Mac always carried his "artillery piece" around with him, an M-1 Garand. Mac was a big man. Still, this rifle was enormous and weighed about a ton and a half. The most popular personal weapon in the Black Cats was the pre-World War II vintage .45-caliber Thompson submachine gun. There were also .45-caliber grease guns, .30-caliber M-2 (automatic) carbines and M-1 (semiautomatic) carbines, but, Captain Mac's M-1 was one of a kind.

I had managed to acquire a version of the M-1 carbine for myself. The stock was cut down to a pistol grip and the barrel had been cut off just past the gas ejection port. This made it small enough to handle easily in the aircraft. But I found, when firing it, that it had a tendency to stovepipe, that is, the spent cartridge would get caught by the closing bolt before it traveled clear. The unit armorer said it was caused by insufficient gas pressure because the barrel was cut too short. But he found that the flash suppressor from an M-14 rifle would fit nicely over the end of the barrel. The small amount of machine work required was just enough to ensure a good fit. He tapped the barrel for a setscrew, and the job was complete. He told me where the practice range was and said I should go try it out.

He'd fixed the stovepiping problem; the weapon would fire as fast as I could pull the trigger. I had three 30-round magazines taped together, alternating up and down. This gave me a survival weapon, with ninety rounds available. It made for a great supplement to the issue .45.

Whenever I flew with Captain Mac to the village of Hoa An, we would go to the Marine range and shoot. Along would come Captain Mac with his M-1, and all these young Marines with their M-16s would be suppressing snickers. He would hold that big rifle on his hip and blast the hell out of a target. By the time he was through, they all wanted to try the weapon and were ready to trade in their M-16s for an M-1.

On the eighteenth, I logged 7.7 hours of flight time, my biggest day while in the 282d. That was also the day I would find out the UH-1D was not up to the task of supporting combat operations in Vietnam. I was flying with Captain Mac, who informed me right off that the bird we were flying was the company dog. We landed at a small village southwest of Da Nang to pick up some passengers. The pad we landed on was surrounded by two rows of concertina wire, a barrier about five-feet wide. With a thousand pounds of fuel on board, we picked up four passengers at the pad. Captain Mac gave me the controls and said, "You make the takeoff."

I picked the Huey off the ground and started to take off. Almost immediately, the electronic whoop of the RPM warning sounded, in company with the illumination of the bright red RPM warning light on the instrument panel. I set the aircraft down. Captain Mac was grinning. He said, "I have the controls."

The captain picked the aircraft up to a low hover and lowered the nose and took off. As he cleared the wire, the RPM had bled off to about 6400 RPM, but the audio remained silent. As he flew toward the north, he explained that I had been overcontrolling the aircraft. I recalled that back at Fort Wolters, during primary flight training, I had landed an OH-23 in a confined area. Try as I might, every time I tried to take off using full throttle, I could not clear the trees; the instructor would take the controls, and we would sail over the trees with no problem. It took seven tries before I made it out on my own. Captain McClendon was teaching me the same lesson that day. In this environment, it suddenly made much more sense.

As we passed through the Hi Van Pass headed north, Captain Mac explained that we were headed for Fire Support Base Bastogne. The captain made his approach from high overhead. The "tactical approach" was a technique I had been taught in flight school. The idea was to drop faster than the enemy could shoot you down. From fifteen hundred feet up, the fire base looked barely big enough to accept the Huey. I found myself clutching at the sides of my seat. I was sure that this pig of an aircraft would not have the power to stop us at the bottom of his approach. It seemed to me that we were falling faster than we would be in autorotation. In fact, we were. At the bottom, Captain Mac leveled the aircraft and flared, and we landed as gently as a butterfly alighting on a flower. I had ridden through my first truly tactical approach since arriving in country. Captain Mac let me do most of the flying for the rest of the day. He coached and corrected till I was able to fly the weak aircraft without setting off the audio when we had a load.

We didn't have it hard in the Black Cats, but news of classmates was making death far less a stranger. When I got back to the room after the day's flight, Gene Gillenwater told me he'd just found out that on one of Oscar Goodman's first missions, he had the entire crew shot out from under him. He had to fly back to the base camp with the rest of the crew dead.

Gene said, "They told me he wouldn't talk to anybody when he got back. Even to tell operations what happened."

I shook my head, "I hope he'll be all right."

Gene said, "Can you imagine being so new that you are not sure how to get back to base, and then having everybody on board killed. They say he seems to be doing all right now, but it's not an experience that I'd like to have."

The nineteenth rolled around (336 days to go). I had been at war for an entire month, logging just over twenty-six hours of flight time, and nobody had even bothered to shoot at me. The next day became the highlight of my tour thus far. I got to fly "chase ship" for General Westmoreland, meaning that I flew empty, following the VIP's aircraft, to pick him up and continue the mission if his bird went down. We also flew a Vietnamese three star, another man who lessened my opinion of the people of Vietnam. He would ball up his fist and beat on the back of the pilot's flight helmet when he wanted to say something. Each time he did it, I got a little closer to blowing my top.

Finally the crew chief said to me, "Relax, sir, he used to rap on the pilot's helmet with his swagger stick."

"If the son of a bitch did that to me, I'd break his swagger stick and throw it out the window!" I replied.

"Sir, that's why he doesn't do it anymore," the crew chief said. "One day, Mr. Springston did just that."

The room Gene and I shared was new and had not seen any improvements to the original decor. We didn't mind, and we had big plans for a bar, closets, and tile flooring. We had already scrounged up five bar stools. We had a stereo system on order at the PX. Vietnam could be an amazing place to fight a war. We had paid for the refrigerator, but all the lumber and tile we had acquired through scrounging. I had discovered that the Seabees were not allowed to have any booze. It was amazing the amount of carpentry and electrical work you could get done for a two-dollar bottle of bourbon.

Many of the things Gene and I had learned about how to get by in our strange new world, we had learned from CW2 Tom Springston. Tom had extended his tour for six months and was in

his fourteenth month in country. Tom knew all the ropes and enjoyed showing off for the new guys. He was a skilled aviator, a
poker player, folk singer, and generally just fun to be around. If
something interesting was going to happen, you could almost bet
that Tom Springston would be in the middle of it.

Late at night after the club had closed, he would take out his
guitar and sing folk songs. His fee was a constant supply of
beer. Sometimes it was his beer, sometimes it was yours; either
way, you did the fetching.

Tom had his own version of Barry Sadler's "The Ballad of
the Green Berets." I don't know if he wrote it himself or borrowed it from someone else, but it was one of our favorites.

> Silver wings upon my chest
> I fly my chopper above the rest
> Cause I make more dough that way
> And I don't need no green beret
>
> Out in the jungle
> Is where the Green Berets belong
> Out in the jungle a writin' song
> Tonight a hundred men must take the test
> While I fly home
> And take a rest
>
> When my little boy is grown
> Please don't leave him out there alone
> Just give him wings
> And give him pay
> And he won't need no green beret
>
> And when my little boy is old
> His wings of silver all lined with gold
> He can wear a green beret
> In the big parade
> St. Patrick's Day

On Sunday the twenty-first, I had a hydraulic failure while
flying and made a running landing. After we shut down at Marble Mountain and started looking over the aircraft, there was little doubt that it was caused by a broken line. There was
hydraulic fluid everywhere.

On the twenty-fourth, the weather closed in, and I got stuck in a Special Forces camp for a couple of hours. There was always the fear that the enemy would take advantage of the bad weather and attack. The attack never came, and the weather broke. Such was life in the Black Cats. All the real excitement was in the club.

By 25 April (328 days to go), I had pretty much settled in for the year. The plans for fixing up the room were coming along well. I had gotten into a routine. I wrote home almost every day. Some days there really was not enough news to make a letter worthwhile, so I'd continue the letter into the next day. I was always anxious to tell Jackie what was going on. Since so little happened, I was glad to tell her so she would not worry so much.

The mail came daily, at 1030 and 1530 hours. When I wasn't flying, I was at the mail room when it arrived, hoping for another prized letter from Jackie. One letter said that an old boyfriend had been calling her up! If I could have gotten on a plane home, he would have been a paraplegic. I trusted Jackie, but the thought of some asshole trying to play Jodie really pissed me off. I wrote back that she should tell him to make sure that his hospitalization was paid up, 'cause when I got home, he was in for beaucoup broken bones.

The twenty-sixth of April began my busiest time in the Black Cats. In eight days from the twenty-sixth to the third, I flew 20.4 hours. In the not too distant future, I would not find it unusual to fly that much in two days. During this period, I flew General Westmoreland and President Thieu of Vietnam. Thieu made a much better impression on me than his generals had. He seemed to be considerate of those around him. It was beginning to sink in that we flew an awful lot of VIP flights, and that those people did not go where the bullets were. I had begun pestering to be moved to the gun platoon. The life of the Alley Cats seemed far more appealing than chauffeuring VIPs.

Saturday the twenty-seventh. The news reported that 87,000 demonstrators marched against the war in New York City. It was good to know that the folks back home were solidly behind us. I could feel my attitude changing, I had begun to ask myself why I was there. The frustration had begun to mount. The war was being protested at home, Jodie was after my wife, and I wasn't even getting to take it out on the enemy. The Alley Cats had to be the answer.

CHAPTER 3
MAY 1968

Friday, 3 May (321 days to go). Finally the bad guys discovered that I was in country. We were flying far too high to be hit, and the only way I knew about it was that the crew chief saw the muzzle flashes. Nonetheless, it was a significant event for me.

We were mortared—first time for me—on the fourth; nothing came close, but the powers that be had us sleeping in our bunkers on the fifth just in case of a repeat performance. The sense of urgency it brought on would later seem pretty silly at Camp Eagle.

Gene and I had started building a superbunker like those Bob Leeper and some of the others had constructed. The bunker we had was okay, but in Da Nang they had a tendency to make you sleep in the bunker if there was any possibility of an attack. A superbunker consisted of two conex containers buried completely under the ground and covered with about six feet of sandbags. The conex containers were steel shipping boxes that measured about six feet by eight feet, and were about six feet tall. Two of them made a very large bunker that was quite comfortable if you had to spend a lot of time in it. Putting bunk beds at both ends made it a very nice four-man bunker.

When there was no flying to be done, getting into mischief was a popular pastime. One morning, while I was flying, Leeper was showing off for some of the new guys. He made the statement that you could get away with anything in the military, if you have a clipboard and a big enough pair of balls. To emphasize his point, he announced that he would prove his theory that very afternoon. He got a truck, with two of the enlisted guys and one of us "wobbly ones." WO1s were frequently called "wobbly ones" from the WO abbreviation for warrant officer. As they left the Marble Mountain compound, he explained to the new guy what he wanted him to do.

"Take this clipboard," he ordered. "When we get where we are going, just follow me around, and whatever I say or do, just keep writing. Do you understand?" he asked.

The new guy said, "Yes . . . But what are . . ."

Bob cut him off with, "Don't ask questions; the less you know, the better you'll do!"

Soon they arrived at a gate with a sign that read NAVAL SUPPLY POINT, and in smaller letters AUTHORIZED PERSONNEL ONLY. The Marine sentry snapped to attention and saluted as they drove through the gate. Bob returned his salute. Once inside they parked the truck near a warehouse and got out. Bob said to the two spec fives, "You guys know what to do, give us a couple minutes after we are inside, and then get started." The new guy was now wondering if he was part of a bank heist or something.

Inside the building were three levels of crates of various sizes, awaiting distribution to units all over I Corps. Bob started mumbling and pointing at things.

The new guy said, "What?"

Bob quietly growled, "Start writing, asshole!"

He immediately complied.

The navy chief who ran the warehouse came over, reported to Bob, and asked, "Can I help you, sir?"

Bob said, "Are you in charge here?"

The chief answered, "Yes, sir."

Pointing to a large box on the third level, Bob asked, "What's in that crate up there?"

The CPO responded, "I don't know, sir."

Bob shot back, "What do you mean 'I don't know'? What kind of a warehouse are you running here?"

"Sir, I mean that I don't know off the top of my head, but I can find out for you."

"George, bring me the inventory sheets for section D8, on the double!"

Bob continued to fire off questions, checked tags on fire, extinguishers and soon had everyone in the warehouse hopping. The new guy kept writing.

After about fifteen minutes, Bob went to the latrine, peeked out the window, and saw that the three-quarter was now full of air conditioners. He went back into the warehouse and called the chief aside, put his arm around his shoulder, and said to the new guy, "Stop writing."

Then to the chief, "Look, I can see that you work hard at keeping this place straight. And, I can see that you have the government's best interest at heart. Soooo . . . I'll tell you what . . . I'm going to come back in say . . . Oh! Two weeks. If everything is squared away then . . . *that* will be my surprise inspection, and this one never happened." He winked and said, "Okay?"

The grateful chief replied, "Thank you, sir."

They got back in the truck, with the enlisted men sitting on the loot, the new guy driving, and Leeper riding shotgun. At the gate, the cherry's heart fell into his left boot when the Marine MP stopped them and asked for their requisition form. Bob calmly reached into his shirt pocket and pulled out a piece of paper and handed it across to the MP. The MP looked over the paper, handed it back, saluted, and said, "Thank you, sir".

As they drove down the road, the new guy asked, "What was that paper you gave him?"

Bob replied, "It was a requisition for aircraft parts we picked up last week. He doesn't know the difference, all he's looking for is something that looks official."

The ninth of May, I wrote home to Jackie that I was very depressed with the conduct of the war. I was beginning see that we were fighting with our hands tied behind our backs. I could support the cause, but it seemed to me that we were going about it all wrong.

On the tenth, I flew an early mission, got in two hours of flight time, and was back in the company area by about 1000 hours. I think that I was flying with Captain Mac. As we walked back from the flight line, something about the company area felt out of place. Normally, at that time of day, the whole place got kind of quiet. Those left moved about slowly, as though time was at a virtual standstill. The whole atmosphere was like siesta time in old Mexico. It was not that way today, the few who were around moved with a sense of urgency. As we walked into operations to close out our paperwork, Sleepy Bear said, "Joe Reichlin was killed this morning!"

I was stunned! This was the Black Cats, no one was supposed to get killed. That happened in the Cav, the Marines, but not here, and not to Joe. Joe was an aircraft commander (AC) with the Alley Cats, and he and I had started to spend some time together. I wanted him to know that I intended to be an Alley Cat, too. We hung around the club together swapping jokes and playing a little poker. We hadn't become great friends, we hadn't had the time yet.

Bear was still talking. ". . . they were flying gunship support for a unit the of the Americal Division out in the Vu Gia River valley, west of Firebase Rawhide."

That was the hottest area that we flew, but generally, it was considered to be ours during the day.

He continued, "They only took one hit; it came through the windshield and caught Joe in the head. The aircraft was a mess. I saw his rifle when they brought it to the armorer for cleaning. All of the Alley Cats are flying missions in that area all day. They are going to stay at it till they get a big enough body count to get even. I figure that means at least a hundred."

"I want to fly with them." It was out before I realized that I said it.

Captain McClendon said, "You can't Grant, you're not current in a B-model."

"Then I want to fly as a door gunner!"

"I can't let you do that, we can't risk losing a pilot flying door-gunner duty."

I said, "I've ridden along in the back before. I know how to use the 60."

"That was a slick mission, with gun mounts. The free guns on the gunships are a whole different ball game. Besides, they need gunners that know what they're doing."

He was right, of course. The mounts on the slicks restricted the travel of the M-60 machine guns so that you couldn't shoot up your own aircraft with it. The gunships had the 60s hung from bungee cords in the door. That setup allowed more freedom of fire, to include shooting yourself down if you got carried away.

I just knew that I wanted to help contribute to the revenge mission. After leaving operations in a huff, I found my outlet. A platoon of gunships attacking a free-fire area can use up ordnance in a hurry. The armament guys were working their asses off trying to keep up. They were glad to find someone willing to hump rockets with them.

The 2.75-inch, folding-fin aerial rocket comes packaged in cardboard tubes with metal ends. These tubes were much like the ones that draftsmen use to store their drawings. The rocket motor and the explosive warhead were packed separately. They came about a half dozen of each in a wooden crate. In order for them to be ready to fire, the wooden crate had to be opened. Then taking the rocket motor tube out of the crate, you pulled a string near the top; this opened the cardboard tube. With the top of the tube removed, the rocket motor could be taken out. The same procedure was followed with the warhead. The base of the warhead was then screwed onto the top of the motor. The rockets were then taken to the aircraft. The aircraft was grounded by attaching a grounding wire from a grounding stake to the aircraft. Then a check was done for stray voltage. This procedure was important since it only took .3 to .5 volts to ignite the rocket motor. The safety clip was then removed from the rocket motor fins, and the rocket inserted in the tube. The rocket igniter was then turned back into place. You had then loaded one rocket. This procedure was repeated thirty-seven times for the gunships that were known as "hogs." Fourteen times for those with the M-21 minigun. The M-21 system required the loading of six thousand rounds of linked 7.62mm ammunition. The six thousand rounds weighed 390 pounds; assembled, a rocket weighed 21 pounds. Firing the miniguns at eighteen hundred rounds per minute per gun meant less than two minutes of actual firing time. And the hogs could shoot all their rockets in a matter of seconds.

The Alley Cats had about ten operational gunships. They kept returning in rotation for ammunition, which made for a long, hot afternoon in the ammunition revetments. I worked with a passion. It was my contribution to getting even. It was my first real taste of fighting the war. Several times during the afternoon, the ammo NCO came over and make me take a break and drink some water. At first, I found it annoying, until I realized that the sergeant appreciated my help and was just looking out for me. I returned to my hootch when it was over, dehydrated and exhausted. But I was satisfied. I had grieved for Joe by helping retaliate. The Alley Cats confirmed about a hundred enemy KIA that afternoon, they were all for WO1 Joseph Albert Reichlin, Jr.

By the eleventh (313 days to go), being such an experienced warrior, I was now totally fed up with the way things were going. I found out from John, the Marine sergeant who tended bar in the club, that the Marines on the perimeter during the mortar attack back on the fourth had seen Charlie dropping mortars in the tube. They had not been able to get clearance to fire until it was too late! What a bullshit way to fight a war! Then the jerks in charge decided to make us sleep in the bunkers all night just because they thought there might be an attack. Even in the Cav, where they were really fighting the war, they didn't go to the bunkers unless they were actually under attack. It was no wonder we were building our bunkers into luxury condominiums. I wrote home to Jackie and told her all about it. But I made no mention of Joe or my adventures in the ammo revetments. I think it was more because I did not want to face it than my not wanting to worry her. It took me two weeks to write about it, and then I was angry. I wrote that I had come to realize that the God-mother-and-apple-pie attitude I had gone to Nam with was not going to work. During those two weeks, I made the transition from the young idealist to the soldier who was prepared kill his way home. I was determined to survive and take as many Americans home alive with me as I could. I no longer saw sense in any of us laying our lives down for a cause that no one really cared about. This new, hard-nose attitude set me up perfectly for my "Rendezvous with Destiny" and becoming a long-range-patrol pilot for the 101st Airborne.

I began to bug Captain Weitzel, the flight operations officer, daily to get moved to the Alley Cats. I figured that the more dinks I killed, the more Americans would go home alive.

On the fifteenth of May (309 days to go), I flew with Tom Springston for a total of 2.4 hours. A hard day's work completed, we headed for the club for an evening of relaxation and boozing. Neither Tom nor I were on the flight schedule for the next day, so we planned to raise some hell that night. We sat and played in the nickel-dime-quarter game till about 2000 hours.

Eventually I went to the bar to order another bourbon and coke. A group of the Alley Cats were sitting around a cluster of three tables pulled together. One of them came over to the bar and asked me to join them. I was surprised that they wanted a slick driver to sit with them. Hueys used for transport were referred to as slicks since they did not have guns and rocket tubes hanging on the sides like gunships. Most often the only interest a group of gun pilots had in a lone slick driver was harassment. Not in the mood for the slicks-are-for-kids routine, I hesitated.

He said, "Look, we heard from the armament guys about what you did the other day, and we appreciate it; we'd like to buy you a couple of drinks."

"That's not necessary. Joe was a buddy, and that's why I did it. I don't need any thanks."

"We know, and that's the real reason we want to buy you a couple drinks."

I couldn't resist that kind of logic, so I followed him back to their table. A couple of drinks turned into many. When last call came they invited me to go back to the Cat House, the Alley Cat hootch, with them. The other platoon BOQs were divided into two-man rooms, each with its own outside access. The Cat House was set up with the rooms off a central corridor with a large open room in the middle. Each Alley cat had his own room, but all shared the rec room. I enjoyed hanging out with those guys, because they were doing what I wanted to do, fly guns. The party continued until well after midnight, with plenty of war stories, lots of loud music, and, of course, gallons of cold beer. Finally, one of the Alley Cats announced that he could perform a levitation. There were many "boos" and "Ah, bullshit"s from the crowd. He said, "This is not bullshit; I can make a man hover three feet off the floor, and I'm taking bets to prove it."

Well that brought out the MPC and got it waving in the air. MPC was military payment certificates, the money that the military allowed us to use in Vietnam as a way of controlling cash flow from the United States into Vietnam. Greenbacks could be exchanged for gold. MPC could not. The price of goods on the economy was based on the form of currency. The lowest price could be obtained with greenbacks, then MPC, and then Vietnamese piasters. It made one believe that the MPC system worked. The flaw was in that while MPC could not be exchanged for gold, the "Monopoly money" could be traded on the black market for greenbacks that then could be exchanged for gold.

Bets were made all around. Then the magician announced, "Just to prove that there's no collusion on my part, I will use a neutral party for the levitation. I'll levitate Grant.

"You don't mind do you, Grant? Thanks."

I was once again a little suspicious, but drunk enough to go along anyway.

"So Grant can't be accused of helping me in any way, I will tie his hands and feet with these belts," he said.

He had me sit on the floor and secured my hands and feet with GI belts. For extra effect, he blindfolded me.

There was long pause as he recited some mumbo jumbo. Then he ripped off the blindfold, and they all poured beer over me.

"Damn it, you guys, that was certainly a waste of a lot of perfectly good beer," I announced.

They all had a big laugh, then I was untied and asked to wait for a few minutes. About the time I became worried about what would happen to me next, they returned. They told me that I had passed my initiation; I was to be the next Alley Cat. As soon as the next man went home at the end of the month, I would be moved to the gun platoon. I knew that the need had been created by Joe's death. Even so, I staggered off to bed with a warm feeling deep inside. I would get to fly guns.

The sun rose the next morning on a hung over but happy young aviator. The two weeks I had spent in aerial gunnery training were the only time that I really excelled. It was a relatively new program, and only a small percentage of the class was allowed to attend.

I sat up in the bunk, and my head began to spin. I looked over. Gene was already gone, probably off flying somewhere. I looked at my watch, it read 0730. My head told me that I would feel much better if I went back to sleep. Well, the head would just have to suffer, I had to find someone to tell the good news to. The thought occurred to me that I should write to Jackie and tell her. But I knew she would worry, so I decided against it. This was far from the last time I would protect her from knowing exactly what I was doing in Nam. Then I remembered Tom, I had left him at the club last night without telling him where I was off to; I felt bad about taking off on him with no warning.

When I got to Tom's hootch, he was up and nursing a Bloody Mary. He invited me to join him. In Vietnam there were two ways one coped with the things that were outside of one's control: booze and dope. Though it was not something I was aware of at the time, I think that Bloody Mary marked my commitment to the former. Like not shooting at bad guys who were mortaring you, guys like Joe Reichlin dying for a cause no one seemed to care about, not going after the enemy every day the way we did the day Joe was killed—many things would not make sense in the months to come.

The twenty-first of May (303 days to go) found me flying down to Cam Ranh Bay to pick up an aircraft. I flew down and back with Sleepy Bear. We took the maintenance officer down with a crew, and they flew the new aircraft back. We spent the night of the twenty-second in Nha Trang, a beautiful old city with a giant marble statue of Buddha on a hillside overlooking the city. As we tied the aircraft down at the airfield, I noticed a Huey with a camouflage paint job. It had high frequency radio antennas strung down the tail boom but no visible markings. I asked McClure about the Huey, but he said, "I don't know, and it's probably best if we don't find out."

Later, as we sat at our table in the club, I noticed a guy at the bar wearing tiger stripe fatigues. Hunched over a beer, he looked like he was carrying the weight of the world on his shoulders. There was something familiar about him. I made a trip to the latrine so I could get a closer look. As I passed him, I noticed that his uniform, like the Huey on the flight line, had no markings—no insignia of rank, no unit patches, no "U.S. Army," and no name tag. By then I realized that I would not need a name tag, because I knew him, he had been in flight school when I was there.

I went over and said, "Hi, Ulakovic! How ya doin'?"

He ignored me.

"Hey, man, don't you remember me?"

He was ignoring me, a hell of way to treat a schoolmate. We hadn't exactly been the greatest friends, but, hell, we endured flight school together, and that had to count for something.

I tried again. "Hey, man, is that your Huey out at the airfield? Must be, I see that you're dressed the same."

He looked up at me and said, "What Huey? Do I know you?"

"Ah, come on, man, what have you been up to?"

He answered, "I can't tell you, now go away!"

I came to the brilliant conclusion that he must have been doing something that he wasn't allowed to talk about. Of course, it would have been a little less obvious if he had just said, "Hi," had a beer with me, and brushed the whole thing off. Months later, after being involved in special operations myself, I better understood his reluctance to communicate.

The next day, at the Black Cats, Captain Weitzel told me that I would be transferred to the 17th AHC in Phu Bai because the 17th needed people who would DEROS in January through March of 1969, and the Black Cats had a bunch of them.

"They can't do this to me," I told him. "I'm going to the Alley Cats, I've been initiated and everything!"

"I'm sorry but the decision has been made," Captain Weitzel

said. "When you get there, go see Capt. Charlie Rake, the gun platoon leader. He's a good friend of mine. Tell him I said that he should take care of you."

"Thank you, sir." A very disappointed young aviator, I headed for my room to start packing.

I would not be alone in my journey to the 17th; Gene Gillenwater, Ron Nelson, and Ron Stutesman had gone up to Phu Bai while I was away. Lou Pulver and John Reitz would be leaving on the twenty-seventh with me. Rod Heim, whom I had gone to high school with and who had been the best man at my wedding, was also being sent to the 17th.

I wrote home to tell Jackie that she shouldn't write till I was able to give her a new address. That really depressed me. I told her that I had found out that I would be living in a tent and that there was no club yet at Phu Bai. I told her that those would be the only real differences. I was really off base on that one; I was headed for another universe.

Since President Johnson had cut back the bombing, we had been noticing that Charlie seemed to have more mortar rounds. He'd been dropping them on us like they were going out of style. They hadn't done much damage, but we were sleeping in the bunkers every other night. I figured that maybe with things starting to get so chickenshit, it was time for a change anyhow.

24 May (301 days to go). I found out that Ron Holly, another classmate, was in the 1st Cav, the grapevine there worked pretty well. I finished my flying in the Black Cats, and my records were closed out without credit for the round-trip flight to Cam Ranh Bay and back. It left me with a total of sixty-seven hours of flight time to show for the two months.

May 26 was a milestone day: 299 days to go! I finally had broken three hundred. It kind of meant that you were no longer an FNG. I wondered if going to a new unit meant I would have to start over.

When we boarded the aircraft for the flight north, Pulver, Reitz, and I had little idea of where we were going or what we were getting into. We had been told only that the 17 AHC was in Phu Bai. Well, that was close, but no one said anything about Camp Eagle. When we got dropped off on a large helipad, we noticed we were standing on a big 101st Airborne patch. There was some good news, the 17th had brand new H-model Hueys. But it didn't take too long to find out that I would be flying "about" 140 hours a month, actually it would be more like 200, but the max the regulation allowed was 140. So they called it 140.

The call sign for the new unit was Kingsmen. The guns were Lancers. They called the aircraft parking area the Castle. Camp Eagle was located between Phu Bai and Hue, just west of Highway 1. It did not take much imagination to see that the highway had been built as far west as it could be built with ease. Just on the west side were the rolling foothills. On the east side of the highway was the sandy South China Sea coast. The Castle was located on the southwest side of Camp Eagle.

The company area sat on the side of two small hills that formed a small valley between them. On the east side, the aircraft were parked in their steel-and-sandbag revetments. The hillside had been terraced to form level areas, with revetments for aircraft parking. There were three rows, each one on a different level, with a landing pad on the south end. Just north of the pad were the 1st Platoon aircraft, then 2d Platoon. Where the small valley widened out to the north end, maintenance and the gunship platoon were located along the bottom of the hills. The west slope of the valley was occupied by three rows of tents, five plywood buildings, and a row of conex containers, located between the lines of tents. Unlike the sandy ground in Da Nang, the ground here was hard and rocky. It was not impressive. Although Camp Eagle had been in existence for only three months, it already looked old and dirty. It was to be my home for the next 296 days.

One of the five buildings was the orderly room. It was framed out with plywood walls extended halfway up, then the walls were screened in to the roofline. Plywood shutters were mounted on hinges hung from the roof. They could be propped open to permit ventilation or closed to keep out wind or rain. The whole affair was topped off with a corrugated tin roof.

We signed in at the orderly room and then went across the compound to Supply, a couple of "GP" (general purpose) medium tents stretched over wooden frames. We were each issued chicken plates (bullet-proof ceramic chest-plates), a mattress, and a .38 revolver. The .38 came from a conex out behind Supply that served as the arms room. In the 101st, my cut-down M-1 carbine was an unauthorized weapon, and it would be stored in the personal weapons conex except when I came to clean it. Great! My weapon is being sent to prison, but it's all right because I'm allowed visiting privileges.

I was not very impressed with the .38. My grandfather had

carried one as a cop, and just looking at the ammo, after carrying a .45, made it seem so inadequate. I have always tried to make it a rule never to shoot anybody with anything that is only going to piss him off.

Reitz and Pulver were assigned to the 2d Flight Platoon and I was assigned to the 1st. It was beginning to seem that the army made an extra effort to make sure that you never got assigned anywhere with someone you knew. As I stumbled back to the tent with all the junk I had acquired, I was feeling a little down. After all, I was now living in a tent, they had taken away my weapon, and I was expected to sleep on a wafer-thin mattress. It was a far cry from Da Nang's air-conditioned hootches, air force beds, and real mattresses. The supply sergeant had mentioned that he normally issued two mattresses a man but he was short right then. He told us to check back in a few days.

The low feeling would not last long; the 17th was a first-class unit, full of good people who took pride in their work.

ANY MISSION, ANYTIME, ANY PLACE,
IF YOU CARE ENOUGH TO SEND THE VERY BEST
SEND A KINGSMEN

Brash mottos like that were found all through the army, from basic training on, but those guys meant it and lived by it. The unit emblem bore the motto *Opera non Verba*—Deeds not Words. It was more than a motto, it was the spirit of the Kingsmen.

When I had been shown my bunk and had dropped off my personal gear, the tent had been empty. When I came back a short time later, there was a man at the bunk next to mine. He was straightening up his wall locker. As I rolled out my mattress, he looked over with an impish smile, extended his hand, and said. "Hi, I'm The Dave."

"Hi, I'm Bill Grant. Nice to meet ya."

That handshake marked a moment that affected the rest of my tour, if not the rest of my life. I did not as yet wear the Screaming Eagle patch of the 101st, but I had made my Rendezvous with Destiny. I thought the guy was a little strange, referring to himself as "The Dave," but something about him intrigued me. I would soon discover that David Allan Poley was more than a little strange; he was a great pilot and a renowned crazy person. As I unpacked, he said, "The Dave is going to dinner. Wanna come?"

I looked down at my gear scattered about.

"Don't worry about that; it'll be here when you get back. No one will bother it . . . or put it away for you."

The rest of the plywood buildings comprised the mess hall and three separate dining rooms, one for the officers, one for the NCOs, and one for the enlisted men. The good news was that they also served as the officer, NCO, and enlisted clubs. It was a relief to find that there being no club was just a rumor.

The Dave was a LRP pilot. LRP (pronounced "lurp") was the acronym for long-range patrol. I thought at the time that what I really wanted was to fly guns. Dave Poley would soon give me another, more exciting, option.

The twenty-ninth, I flew 2.7 hours with the 1st-Platoon IP. We first did a few autos and running landings at a dirt strip in Hue. This took care of my one-hour qualification in the H-model Huey. What a difference these birds were over the D-models I had been flying. In the Black Cats, we had a D-model so under-powered that we had to limit the fuel to no more than one thousand pounds, just to take off with three or four passengers. While that particular aircraft was a dog, during the short mission we flew after my check-out, I could see how much more could be packed into the H-model. The two aircraft were the same airframe, but with an improved engine, the new H-models could be loaded more based on space than weight. Both models had a maximum allowable takeoff weight of 9,500 pounds. On a nice cool day with a little skill, the D-model would actually take off at 9,500 pounds, but cool days were few and far between in the Nam. The H-model performed so well that we would load up until it was full or we guessed that the weight was all we could haul. Then if the engine could pick the aircraft up, we would take off. It wasn't until years later, back in the World, in an air-conditioned office, that I calculated that we routinely flew those Hueys at over 12,000 pounds. A Huey with a crew of four and full load of fuel, with door guns, personal weapons, and ammunition weighs about 8,500 pounds. The cargo compartment would nicely hold 150 cases of C rations, they weighed 24.5 pounds each. That would put the whole load at just over 12,000 pounds at takeoff.

The next day, I flew with CW2 Jim Riden who had been with the Kingsmen since the old days at Fort Riley in 1967 and 1968. Jim was a little older than the rest of the pilots, most of us being twenty or twenty-one. He was about twenty-eight. With Jim's being older, he had a stabilizing influence on the rest of us. Jim and I flew a log mission and logged 11.8 hours that day. That seemed like a lot of flight time to me, but it was not unusual to the Kingsmen. I was already feeling a lot better about my situation; flying hard would make the time go faster, and my new unit had an enthusiasm that was contagious.

One of the things that really impressed me with the Kingsmen was the crew coordination. The four men on the aircraft functioned with one mind. Any time the aircraft got light on the skids, "Clear left" and "Clear right" came automatically from the crew chief and gunner in the back. The crews in the Black Cats were very professional, but in the Kingsmen, the relationship was much closer. In the 282d, the relationship had been just as the army expected it to be, two officers and two enlisted men. In the 17th that division was never forgotten, but it never got in the way either. Each crew member's life was on the line each day with every decision that the AC made. The tighter the situation got, the more input that came from the back of the aircraft. They learned to anticipate the pilot's next move and be prepared for it.

The hover-down LZs in the mountains would bring the highest peaks of coordination from the crews. Many of the LZs used to resupply units in the triple-canopy jungle of the mountains were so small that only inches of clearance kept us from knocking off tail rotors and crashing. We would hover in above the trees, and each crew member would guide the pilot flying the aircraft down.

"Bring the aircraft two feet forward."

"Turn the tail six inches to the left."

"Okay, now come down two feet, sir."

"Slide right a foot."

"Now back a couple of feet."

The instructions would continue down through 120 feet of jungle. Many times, once at the bottom, I would look up through the greenhouse window in the roof of the aircraft and not be able to see anything but trees above us!

THE OLD MAN

Maj. Daniel A. Addiss was the commanding officer of the Kingsmen. He was tall and thin, with red hair. He had the military bearing of a professional officer. And he had the unenviable job of commanding a company full of twenty-year-old aviators who had visions of Tommy McGuire and Pappy Boyington dancing in their heads. I had the feeling that he tolerated us more than approved of us. Many times, when the flight schedule got heavy and we were flying long days, there would be occasions when we did not bother to shave for two or three days. Haircuts were not very popular, and mustaches tended to get too long. Major Addiss always seemed to be able to find ways to ignore the *minor* transgressions. He avoided the club unless things got too loud. It was not long before I discovered that he took great pride in the reputation the Kingsmen had established for themselves. More than once at the end of a mission briefing for a lift, he got up to tell of calls he got in the middle of the night.

"Gentlemen, I want you to know that I was woken up by a call at 0300 hours last night. There was a unit in contact out there. The battalion commander called and said that they had an aircraft that would not take ammo in because it was a hot LZ. He asked if I could send him a Kingsmen. Keep up the good work, men."

Such statements were greeted by cheers, catcalls, and the desire for a celebration. The club was used for the briefings. Thus, the CO would wait until the end of the briefing and make his comments brief so he could leave and allow the party to get started.

31 May (294 days to go). I had been given my first "additional" duty. A common belief in the army was that no officer should be without one; consequently, jobs were frequently created just so there were enough additional duties to go around. Mine was to be the Soldiers' Deposit officer. It was an arrangement the army had at the time to encourage soldiers to save money. The army would pay 10 percent interest (tax free) on your savings. My job was to sit in the pay line and encourage unit members to utilize the Soldiers' Deposit fund, collect the money, and write receipts. It also meant that once a month I had to take the money to Da Nang and deposit it, so I got to visit my friends in the Black Cats.

I found myself starting to like it at Camp Eagle, I wasn't sure why, but I was eating better and sleeping better. The bunk sucked, the food was all the bad things I'd heard about army chow, but there was something about the unit that fit just right. The long days' flying certainly made the time pass more quickly. There was only one major drawback—missing Jackie. Most of the time, I had to force myself not to think about her, or I wouldn't have been able to do anything else. March 20, 1969, was about a hundred light years away.

CHAPTER 4
JUNE 1968

The first of June, it rained so hard that it sounded like thunder pounding the tent. The tents were surrounded by a four-foot-high wall of sandbags, designed to afford some protection in the event of mortar or rocket attack. Between the tents, part of the walls were connected by PSP (perforated steel planking) that had about three layers of sandbags over the top. This comprised the bunker system, a far cry from Da Nang. Since we were located on the side of a hill, when it rained the water backed up against the sandbag wall until it found a "weak spot"—the doorways to the tents. When it rained hard enough, a small river ran from the uphill door to the downhill door right through the middle of the tent. The water then ran to the next row of tents, repeating the process until it got to the third, and ran down the hill below the aircraft revetment. Eventually, it reached the gully between the hills, where it met a larger flow of water that surged off toward the perimeter.

During the next few days, I became much better acquainted with the twelve thousand-pound Huey. On the fourth, I had 11.5 hours, and 10.2 more on the sixth. These log missions, with the one on the thirtieth, totaled 33.5 hours of flight time and 196 sorties. In just those three days, I flew half again as much as I had flown in the previous two months in the Black Cats.

The mission of the 17th Assault Helicopter Company was to fly in combat support of the 101st Airborne Division. Logistics missions in support of the 101st were long and hard, and with good reason. The entire division was being supported by only a small number of aircraft. There were three lift companies; A Company, the "Comancheros," which was organic to the division; the 188th AHC (Assault Helicopter Company), "Black

Widows," our sister company; the 17th AHC "Kingsmen." Chinook support came from the 57th Aviation, "Pachyderms," out of Phu Bai. Each brigade had its own aviation section, with about four Hueys and six OH-6As. A total of 72 slicks, 20 C-model guns, and about 15 Chinooks (large cargo helicopters), for total of 107 aircraft. By comparison, as an airmobile division the 1st Cavalry Division had over 400 aircraft. Both divisions had similar areas of operation (AOs) and much the same mission. Even after the 101st was designated an airmobile division, only about 95 more aircraft were added before early 1969.

Log missions were simply resupply missions. An aircraft would be assigned to resupply an infantry battalion. This meant that it had to haul all the necessary food, ammunition, medical supplies, and equipment that the battalion would need until its next log bird arrived. The log bird was also required to perform the "admin" missions for the battalion—hauling the battalion commander around to visit his companies, replacement soldiers to the field, short-timers and injured soldiers to the rear. Medevac aircraft were at a premium, so slightly wounded or injured troopers sometimes had to wait for the next log bird to be taken to the rear area for treatment. Since not all the units had their resupply well planned, the mission was frequently interrupted by captain so-and-so who wanted to go here or there. Log missions were usually long and often frustrating.

5 June (287 days to go). I flew my first combat assault. The 101st had been conducting Operation NEVADA EAGLE since 17 May. The operation, involving the 1st and 2d Brigades, was initiated to protect the local rice harvest. The operation would provide a secondary benefit in that, if it was successful in its first goal, it would help to win over the local Vietnamese farmers, something the United States had been trying to accomplish since 1964. The operation also had the potential to deny the enemy a much needed local food source.

We were assigned to fly for the 2d Brigade, lifting troopers from a village named Ap Lai Tranh, in the foothills west of LZ Sally. The LZ was another ville about six klicks east of Sally. The infantry company was to sweep the village for signs of the enemy and make "nice-nice" with the villagers. They would then hang around a few days to let Chuck know that the paratroopers of the 101st Airborne Division were not going to let him screw with the rice harvest. I was flying with Jim Riden in Chalk Three. When we landed in the PZ, the troops were ready and onloaded quickly. I was already beginning to appreciate working with American Airborne soldiers. They were well organized and did not have us waiting around doing nothing, unlike the VIPs I had flown in the Black Cats. The flight took off in the usual tight formation of five aircraft and headed east. When we got to the LZ, we swung around to the south and landed to the north on the east side of the village. Jim was on the controls, so I took advantage of the opportunity to take in the scenery. The flight was landing about three hundred meters east of the village in a rice paddy. As Riden brought the nose up to lose airspeed for landing, I saw ten or twelve strobe lights flashing in the tree line over by the village. I wondered who would be using strobe lights out there, then realized that they were not strobe lights! The crew chief shouted, "We're receiving fire from the tree line, sir."

I looked back at him and saw him raise his 60 in the direction of the tree line. Amidst the noise of the Huey I heard a *swish, swish, swish* sound. Then the VHF radio came alive.

"This is Kingsmen One-Six, we are receiving fire from the tree line on the left."

"Roger, One-Six. Lancer Three-Three rollin' in hot."

Then the Fox-Mike (FM radio) sounded off, "This is Chalk Four. I'm taking hits."

It seemed to take weeks before Lead (the flight leader) got around to pulling pitch and getting the hell out of there. It was a sensation I would encounter often flying for the 101st Airborne. A hot LZ seemed to slow time almost to a standstill even though the mind continued to operate at full speed. It left you sitting in your seat, wondering why everyone else was brain dead and not doing anything.

Finally Lead pulled pitch, and we were on the go. Five called, "Lead, Trail. Flight's up!"

That meant everyone including Four was off the ground. Apparently Four had not been damaged badly enough to leave behind in a hot LZ. I looked back over my shoulder through the open cargo door and saw the tree line erupt with fire and smoke as the rockets began to rip into the vegetation. For the first time, I was seeing the war close up. For the first time, I was being shot at and didn't need to be told about it by the crew chief or the gunner. I had seen the devastating firepower of the Charlie-model gunships before, but somehow it was different now. I had fired rockets from a gunship in gunnery qualification on Matteson Range at Fort Rucker and had been impressed. But today, they had been fired at the unseen enemy in the tree line and seemed far more violent. I didn't believe that anyone could have survived in those trees. I was surprised to find that I felt no regret.

The second lift was mine to fly. Once again, we swung around to the south side of the village to land to the north in the LZ. From several klicks out, I could see the smoke rising from the tree line.

Jim pointed to the smoke and said, "That's the tree line, you can use the smoke as a marker. Just swing around the way we did the first time."

I lined up on final and slowed with the rest of the flight. Smoke was also rising from the village. Some of the thatch hootches were smoldering. I wondered if the villagers were still glad we came to protect their crops. At touchdown, I looked over at the tree line, it wasn't winking at me this time. I saw some of the paratroopers from the first lift walking in the wooded area. We finished that lift and several others without further incident. When we had returned to the Castle, we logged 2.7 hours, a pretty light day for the Kingsmen. I decided that I liked flying with Jim Riden. The whole time we flew, he had corrected, advised, and adjusted my flight technique. I never once during the flight felt like I was being talked down to. Many of the IPs at Rucker made you feel like dirt, but Jim had a way of sharing his knowledge without making you feel inferior.

As we sat waiting for the rotor to coast down, I debated about asking "the question." I didn't want to seem stupid, but I had to make sure about the *swish* sounds. "Jim, what was that *swish* sound I heard that first time in the LZ?"

He answered quickly, like he had been waiting for the question. "It was bullets passing behind us."

Specialist Ronco, the crew chief, jumped in, "Bullshit, sir. Those rounds were in front of us."

The gunner backed him up, "That's right, sir!"

I said, "No, the sound definitely came from behind us."

After several moments of argument, it finally dawned on us the that it was good that the cargo doors were open or we would have taken hits. The bullets had indeed been close. They had passed through the five feet of empty space between the cockpit and the transmission wells where the gunners sat.

I swallowed hard then asked Riden, "What does it sound like when you take a hit?"

"You haven't been hit?"

"No."

He seemed surprised. "You've been in country almost three months and haven't been hit?"

I was puzzled by his reaction. "Nope, no hits."

He said, "It sounds just like someone dropped a seat belt on the floor in the back."

By that evening, it was all over the company. Grant was still a cherry. In the infantry, one was considered a cherry until his first firefight. In aviation, you were cherry until your aircraft took a hit. The theory was that in the infantry a firefight was up close and personal. We had more opportunity to get shot at, but we were harder to hit. It had not yet happened that anyone in the Kingsmen had made it through their first month without taking a hit. It was true that I had spent two months in the 282d with much less exposure than the Kingmen were used to, but they found it unbelievable that I was still a cherry. Before long, my cherry would become a point of major discussion in the 17th AHC.

WILD BILL MEACHAM

That night in the club I was forced to endure some serious harassment over still being cherry. The abuse was beginning to get on my nerves a bit, when a lieutenant came over to where I was sitting, with a can of beer in each hand. As he sat one of the Budweisers down in front of me, he drawled, "Don't let it get to you partner, they're jus' jealous. Have a beer."

"Thank you, sir."

He extended his hand. "I'm Bill Meacham."

"W. T. Grant," was my reply as I extended mine.

I had just met a man who would become a good friend, on the way to becoming like a brother to me. As we sat having a few beers, Rod Heim came over and joined us. Meacham was deeply engaged in telling us how things were around there. He made no bones about letting us know that if we hung around him he would be glad to teach us everything we would ever need to know about anything. There were those who felt that Bill's self-confidence was a bit overbearing. I always found him to be at least entertaining, if not as educational as he claimed to be. His confidence must have been contagious, because it was not long before Rod Heim began to brag about what he was going to accomplish as a Kingsmen. Meacham just sat there and listened a while. Finally, he said, "Boy, don't tell me what you're gonna do, show me."

The comment brought Rod to a screeching halt. It may have burned at the time, but a few months later it would become obvious that they were words that he had taken to heart. Wild Bill Meacham liked to refer to himself as "just a dumb ole country boy." He was raised in North Carolina; he first lied his way into the air force at the age of sixteen. One year later, they found him out and sent him home. At eighteen, he enlisted in the army for Airborne training. He spent a few years as an enlisted man, and rose to the rank of sergeant. During that period, he completed his high school education and applied for Officer Candidate School. Upon completion of OCS, his application for flight school was approved. Arriving in Vietnam as an army aviator, Wild Bill quickly became the country philosopher of the Kingsmen.

9 June (283 days to go). I wrote home that in a little over a week I had flown fifty hours as a Kingsmen, almost as much as my first two months in country. I told Jackie I had heard about the assassination of Bobby Kennedy. I could hardly believe what was going on at home. Martin Luther King, the rioting, and then Bobby Kennedy. I wrote that maybe she would be safer in Nam with me. There were signs being put up that read,

SUPPORT OUR FIGHTING MEN IN AMERICA
RE-UP NOW!
FIGHT IN THE CITY OF YOUR CHOICE

She had written that another "friend" from our high school class had been calling her up to "see how she was doing." I was certainly glad to know so many of my friends were attempting to look after my wife while I was gone. I was determined that when I got home I would contribute my share of the violence. I was developing a fine list of names so I would be able to participate in the new American sport.

MAGNET ASS

The name Magnet Ass applies when you have a knack for attracting bullets. There were two in the Kingsmen. One was a Huey, 66-16350. The other, WO1 Phillip G. Heim. It was considered unusual for either to come back from a mission without taking hits. Rod Heim and I had gone through high school together, and Rod had told me of the Warrant Officer Flight Program in the army. We both enlisted in the army for the flight school option. It was a deal too good to pass up. The enlistment was for only two years. No bigger a gamble than the draft. If you did not make it as an aviator, you could be back on the street in no time. If you graduated, the commitment was for three years after graduation.

At the time, we gave little consideration to the fact that there might be some difficulty in surviving the three-year hitch.

Upon arriving in Vietnam, Rod was sent to the Coachmen in Phu Bai, a VIP unit. Still, Rod wasted no time at all attracting hostile fire. On one of his very first missions, Rod flew to a helipad called Hotel One right up on the DMZ. When approaching pads on the DMZ, the aircraft was brought in low and fast from the south to avoid being blasted by North Vietnamese guns on the other side of the line. Departures were made to south after spending a minimum of time on the pad. Standard procedure was never to shut down on the pad, since a hasty departure was frequently needed. When they landed, the AC got out of the bird and went into one of the bunkers for a mission briefing. He had left Rod minding the controls of the running Huey. The aircraft commander had just barely disappeared into the bunker when the 122mm rockets started arriving. Rod having been "in country all day" was slightly confused by the events. The crew chief had no such problem. He yelled, "Let's get the fuck out of here, sir!"

Rod questioned, "What about . . ."

The crew chief cut him off. "That's his problem, I say we get the fuck out of here, sir!"

Rod, ready to listen to any reasonable point of view, grabbed an armload of collective and took off, with the crew chief still standing on the skid. As they got about twenty feet in the air, a rocket landed dead center on the pad they had just vacated. Bursting under them, the rocket caused a ripple of thumps along the belly of the Huey as the shrapnel impacted. Rod checked the instruments, but everything stayed in the green. He promptly climbed to altitude and remained there—circling.

He was too new to know that flight at altitude in that neighborhood was dangerous. He was also too new in country to know that his circles were taking him into North Vietnam. When the rocket attack ended, it took a while before Rod realized the figure that was frantically waving on the ground was his aircraft commander. Such was Rod's luck for quite a long while.

Wednesday, 12 June (280 days to go). I struggled to write to Jackie in the fading light of day. The generators had been having problems and were kicking on and off. I had flown over nine hours that day and was beginning to feel the effects of the heavy flight schedule. I wrote about how I had been hearing rumors floating around about the Kingsmen moving south.

Finally, as dark fell, I could no longer see well enough to write. I put the letter away. Something made me just sit there and think. I was feeling very alone that night, maybe it was just because there were no lights. Maybe I was just plain homesick. From somewhere in the darkness, The Dave announced that he was going over the hill to the movie. He quickly had a crowd of followers. With no power, the club would be closed, and nobody could use their stereos. I decided to stay put. When the crowd had left, I pulled my boots off and stretched out on my bunk. It was warm, and the sides of the tent had been pulled up. As I lay back, I could see each star as it appeared in the everdarkening sky. I let my mind slide thirteen thousand miles away to Long Island and Jackie. I could see her face. I let myself think about how much I missed her. I felt a tear roll down my cheek, and did nothing about it. The lights were off, and I was alone in the tent. No one would see me let down my defenses. I could see her face; her hand reached out to touch my face. The thoughts made me sad, but also made me feel closer to her, so I let them envelop me. I wondered if she could feel me thinking about her in the night. I stared at the stars and enjoyed the feeling. Suddenly, it was light, and I sat up with a start wiping the tear that was no longer there so nobody would see. As I looked around, I realized that it was not the generator, but the sun. It was the thirteenth, and I had 279 days to go.

I spent the thirteenth flying an ash-and-trash mission with The Dave. We logged almost six hours. About midday, we shut down near a village to have our lunch. The folks we were hauling around had told us that they would be at that location for two or three hours. Dave Poley checked with them to make sure the area was secure. They gave us assurances that we would be safe where we were. There was a full battalion of airborne infantry in the immediate area.

Dave showed me how to make a stove from a C-ration can. The stove was made from one of the short cans that the crackers came in. The sides were vented with a can opener. The can was then filled with sand, and the sand was wetted down with JP4. The fuel was obtained by draining a small amount from the fuel drains in the belly of the aircraft. The fire could then be lit, and the fuel-soaked sand would burn for twenty or thirty minutes. It allowed more than enough time to heat the entire crew's C rations. As we opened up the boxes that contained our meals, Dave said to me, "I noticed that you wear a Saint Christopher medal."

"Yes, it was given to me by the people I worked with in the supermarket. It was a going-away present when I left to enlist in the army."

The Dave reached inside his T-shirt and pulled out his dog-tag chain. On the chain was a tarnished P-38 can opener. There were several of them contained in each case of C rations. It was small, and it folded up to make it easy to carry around. The openers even had a hole on one corner that made it convenient to put them on your dog-tag chain. He said, "This is my Saint Can Opener of the C's medal. It protects me in my travels, and it will also open my lunch."

He then took his medal and let it bite into a can of beanie weenies. My Catholic upbringing made me feel a little guilty about laughing, but I laughed anyway. It was funny.

Dave looked at me and asked, "Are you laughing about my Saint Can Opener of the C's medal? You know it's not nice to make fun of a person's beliefs."

He really sounded serious, but it was the impish gleam in his eyes that gave him away. I reached in my pocket and pulled out my beer-can opener and said, "I won't make fun of your Saint Can Opener, if you don't make fun of my church key." We both had a good laugh. Dave was the type of guy who could have fun doing almost anything. I would find that he could make light of the worst situations, and keep my spirits up when I was down.

After we finished lunch, some kids from the village started hanging around looking for handouts. The oldest, a boy about ten, asked, "GI, gibbe cigarette?"

I knew that the standards were different here, still I could not make myself give the kid a cigarette. He asked again, "Numba One GI, gibbe cigarette?" I guess he figured flattery would help.

"Cigarette numba ten for boy-san," I said.

"Bullshit, GI, gibbe cigarette," he said.

I tossed him a John Wayne bar and said, "Baby-san havey chocolate instead."

A John Wayne bar was the round, chocolate-and-rice crunch bar that came in the C rations. The kid came back with, "I no baby-san, GI." He struck out his chest and jammed his thumb against it. "Soon I be ARVN soldier."

Yeah, bullshit, kid, I thought. But I didn't say it. Scott Wilson, the crew chief, had rummaged around in the aircraft and come up with four unwanted C-ration meals to give the kid. They were all ham and lima beans. Yuck! No wonder they all grew up to be VC.

The area we had parked the aircraft in was a large sandy area just outside the village. The LZ was surrounded by palm trees on three sides. On the near side of the village, there was a bombed-out building. It was large and must have been a pagoda or meeting hall of some sort. Most of the roof was gone, but some of the building was under cover. The number of antennas sticking up from within the walls indicated that it must be in use as the battalion TOC. There was, in fact, enough roof to give all the staffers a dry place to sleep. Once our passengers had disappeared inside the building, there was no sign of any Americans around. Even though I knew there was a battalion out there, it made me feel very alone with no one in sight.

After lunch was over, we knew it would be a long wait yet for our pax. Dave got his chicken plate and propped it against the front crosstube for the helicopter's skids. I got mine and did the same against the skid-toe cap. It made a convenient recliner to stretch out in the warm sand and relax for awhile.

Poley asked me, "When is your DEROS date?"

I answered, "Twenty March."

Dave then said, "Gee, that means in couple days, you'll have your ninety days in country and can get to fly LRPs."

Scotty Wilson was sitting on the bench seat in the back of the aircraft, sharpening his knife. Scott said, "Here it comes; watch your ass, Mr. Grant."

Dave looked back at Wilson, "Scotty, are you tryin' to cheat W. T. here out of the opportunity to be a cut above the rest?"

Wilson ignored him and said, "Just remember what they told us in basic, Mr. Grant, 'Never volunteer for anything!' "

They were both smiling, so I was not too sure how to take any of this. Dave began again, "L-R-P stands for long-range patrol. They are six-man teams that go out looking for bad guys.

It's a good mission, and they treat us well. They are some bad muthas. It gives us an opportunity to kick some real ass."

"Just remember to wear your bullet-proof underwear," Wilson chimed in.

Poley put on a lisp, "Oh Scotty! You are jus' thuch a big putthy."

"Yeah, and you can get to be one, too, Mr. G, when this lunatic takes you out and gets your dick shot off," the gunner tossed out.

It seemed that I was the only one that did not think getting my dick shot off was funny. The rest of the crew was having a good laugh for themselves. Now I may have only been in Nam "all day," but I wasn't born yesterday. I smelled a rat here. "Dave, just why am I being offered this fabulous opportunity?"

"Cuz Saint Can Opener called you."

"What?"

"Saint Can Opener came to me in a vision last night and said, 'Grant should be a LRP pilot.' He is right. Believe me, The Dave knows about these things."

I had been to see Capt. Charlie Rake about flying guns as soon as I had gotten signed into the Kingsmen. He told me that he would look into it. When he got back to me, he told me that the 17th was short of peter pilots for the slicks. Therefore, I would have to wait. Once again I had been put on hold for flying gunships. Could it be that God was trying to tell me that my Rendezvous with Destiny lay elsewhere?

I grinned at Dave, "When one is called by a saint, one should answer right away. When do I start?"

Dave answered, "I'll check with Captain Senita and operations; I'll let you know."

The warm afternoon sun felt so good that I was soon sound asleep. I had flown over a hundred hours in the last fifteen days. Using a helicopter skid and a chicken plate for a pillow was getting easier.

The day closed out with us logging 5.9 hours of flight time. The Dave and I trudged up the hill to our tent and put our helmets and chicken plates in our lockers. We arrived at the mess hall on the late side of dinner. I wandered over to the club and got us a couple of beers to wash down dinner. I was feeling unusually tired. Poley went to operations and came back announcing that he and I would be flying together again the next day. We would not be taking off until around eleven. That was really good news; they had been flying me pretty hard. Of course, I'd been transferred because the Kingsmen were short of peter pilots. I was fresh meat, and they were making the most of it. I sat and talked with Dave until about 2100. We drank some beer, and Poley continued his LRP sales pitch, which was not necessary; I'd already decided I was going to try it. But I was having trouble paying attention. Finally I excused myself, "Dave, I'm really trashed. I'm going to hit the sack."

Poley said, "That's cool; I'm about ready myself."

I slept through breakfast, dragging up from my bunk about nine. I had slept for about eleven hours and was still tired. The Dave was stretched out on his bunk, reading a book. He looked over at me and said, "Relax, W. T., the mission has been put off until after lunch. The Dave has already done the preflight, so we are all set to go."

I said, "I'm sorry, you should have woke me."

Poley said, "Nope, The Dave could tell last night that you needed the rest."

The mission was an administrative move of a unit from a hilltop to a large LZ in the valley below. The operation would be conducted with five aircraft. Since the hilltop would only accommodate one aircraft, it had been decided that the flight would daisy chain from the PZ to the LZ. The spacing was to be thirty seconds between aircraft. It was a secure move, no worries about hot LZs. The flight had been planned for about twenty sorties to move the battalion.

It was turning into a hot afternoon as we set up a rectangular traffic pattern from the PZ to the LZ. Poley and I alternated on the controls and starting trying to make perfect traffic patterns. There was not much opportunity in Nam for that kind of flying. We began trying to fly exactly eighty knots on downwind, lose exactly three hundred feet turning base while slowing to sixty knots. It was about the sixth pass, and I had nailed the airspeed at eighty knots on the downwind leg, and the altitude had been just right. I made the right turn to the base leg as smooth as I knew how. I was working at the chance to impress Poley. I was concentrating on losing the right amount of altitude and speed. The approach was coming together nicely.

Suddenly Poley said, "What in the fuck are you doing?"

My eyes sprung open, the airspeed had instantly gone from seventy knots to zero. The vertical speed indicator was pointed straight down. I lowered the nose and pulled in power as Dave took the controls away from me. I must have fallen asleep, but I hadn't even felt sleepy. My mind and body had stopped functioning as though someone had pulled my plug from a wall socket. Poley flew the rest of the mission. I kept apologizing and saying that I did not know what was wrong with me. Dave said, "Don't worry about it. How much have you flown since you got here?"

I replied, "I don't know for sure, around a hundred hours, I think."

We finished the lift and returned to the Castle. The Dave set the aircraft down in the revetment smoothly and softly. This was no small feat. The revetments were walled on three sides. The right was cut out of the hill and covered with steel planking as a retaining wall. The front and left side were made with steel planking that covered a two-foot-thick wall of sandbags. The revetments were to prevent damage to the aircraft from shrapnel during mortar and rocket attacks. When an aircraft was hovered into the revetment, the rotor wash would blow against the three walls and back to the bird. It created a great deal of turbulence and made it hard to set the aircraft down. Once on the ground, Dave rolled the throttle back flight idle and waited for the engine temperature to stabilize for the required two minutes prior to shut down. As the rotor blades coasted to a stop, Dave filled out the log book for our 2.6 hours. While he wrote, he said, "I'm going up to ops and complete the afteraction reports. You go to the hootch and I'll meet you there."

I was more than a little concerned he was going have them pull me off flight status or something. I helped the crew chief and gunner put the bird to bed and headed up the hill. I sat on my bunk, listening to my stereo, while I waited for The Dave.

He walked into the tent and came over and said, "You have flown 135.7 hours in the last seventeen days. I'm surprised you're still alive."

An army aviator was allowed to fly ninety hours in a thirty-day period. Under the supervision of the flight surgeon, that could be extended to 110 hours. The combat emergency limit was 140 in a thirty-day period. I was almost there in seventeen days.

Dave said, "Go to the ops officer and tell him you are exhausted and need some time off. If he says no, tell him you'll go to the flight surgeon."

I did as The Dave suggested. The operations officer said, "I know we've been pushing you, but we are short of peter pilots. I can't afford to give you any time off."

I said, "I almost killed us all today; if I get back in an aircraft, I'm afraid I will kill someone."

He said, "Look, I can't spare anyone right now."

I said, "If I can't get some rest, I'll have to go to the flight surgeon and tell him how much I have really been flying."

That gave him a pause for thought. There was a large board in operations, it listed every pilot's name and thirty-one columns. Each day, the flight time for that day was added, and the time for thirty-one days ago was subtracted. That gave you a running total for the last thirty days. After my name in the column for the fourteenth it said 65.1.

He finally said, "All right, you have three days off. Don't let me catch you using it to party."

I thanked him and left.

I used the time to rest. I went to bed that night, and slept until the next afternoon. I got up, ate some C rations and drank a couple of beers, and went back to bed. I would wake up, soaked in sweat, in the heat of the day; stay up long enough to dry off, shower, and go back to bed. Sometimes I would read for an hour or so and drift back to sleep. By the third afternoon, I felt good enough to go to the PX and have laundry done. If the captain checked on me during my time off, he found me sleeping. In that three days, I slept nearly sixty hours. By the morning of the eighteenth, I felt like superman again. I had learned a valuable lesson. From then on, I would grab a nap at every opportunity, even if it meant only twenty minutes.

The next two days, I made a number of admin runs to Da Nang. I got another 13.8 hours. I felt pretty good. By the end of the month, I must have been pretty close to 200 hours. My flight records recorded 109.

I had acquired an Akai stereo tape recorder from one of the guys who was getting short. I got it at a good price after his sales pitch. He had reasoned that it was·a good idea to buy one used that I could use while in country, then sell it to someone else when I got short. I could then buy a new one through the PX and have it sent home, without it being exposed to the dust and dirt in the Nam. Maybe it was just a pitch, but it made sense, and I had a stereo system of my own. I was finding that my music was becoming more and more important. It was a link with the outside world; it meant that there was a reality out there. I would spend many evenings with the headphones on, to fall asleep relying on the automatic shutoff feature on the Akai.

The music took me away from the war, away from the strain of long days in the air.

LONG-RANGE PATROL

One of the reasons I was able stay under two hundred hours was that on the twenty-second, The Dave took me on my first LRP mission. Special Operations would entail less flight time, but far more excitement.

F Company, 58th Infantry, was a long-range patrol company. The mission was reconnaissance. This unit was airborne infantry like the rest of the division. That was where the similarity ended. The junior soldiers were mostly paratroopers who had volunteered for this duty. Many of the more senior noncommissioned officers were either Special Forces or Ranger trained, some had both qualifications. The platoons were divided, not into squads, but into six-man teams. These teams would be inserted into areas of suspected enemy activity to hunt for the enemy. The fact was that they were good at what they did. That meant they often found the enemy and would need to be extracted under less than favorable circumstances. The teams were generally placed in areas that were free of other friendly units. That meant that help on the ground was unlikely. On a typical mission, a team would be assigned a four-thousand-meter square recon zone (RZ). This RZ would have a thousand-meter buffer zone around it. No one in the division was allowed to enter the RZ without the LRPs' being aware of their presence. The RZ was a free-fire zone, where we could use air strikes or artillery at will, without having to obtain clearance to fire. A normal patrol would last five days, during which the team would have two slicks, two gunships, and artillery on twenty-four-hour standby.

My introduction to LRP flying was indicative of what my life was to be like as a LRP pilot. Flight procedures were different from those used when conducting other operations. Since we had the comfort of air superiority, the general rule was that flight fifteen hundred feet above the ground provided immunity from ground fire. This did not allow a margin of safety against fire by larger antiaircraft weapons, but did leave you fairly secure from small arms. LRP insertions and extractions were most often flown at low altitude to prevent the insertions and extractions being observed by enemy forces. The aircraft would use the terrain to mask movement to and from an area and to keep the enemy from being able to tell exactly where landings and takeoffs were made.

Insertions of six-man teams were made by placing the team on the lead bird. The number two, or chase aircraft, flew three or four hundred meters behind. When the insertion bird landed, the chase ship continued at high speed and made a pass over the insertion aircraft. The pass served two purposes. The first was to draw fire. If anybody near the LZ saw the lead bird hovering, they knew that they had an easy target. But the chase bird flying over would only be available as target momentarily. Invariably, human nature caused them to fire at the speeding chase ship. But the moving aircraft was harder to hit, and while they were shooting at it, the lead aircraft would finish its business and be moving again. The technique proved effective time and again. The second purpose was that by the time the lead landed and got going again, it would be the same distance behind as the chase bird had been to begin with. At any distance, that gave the appearance that no landing had been made. The low altitudes and the leapfrogging, coupled with false insertions, gave us a very high success rate at inserting teams undetected. Even if we were observed in the area, the enemy could only suspect where a team might have been inserted. Of course, all the sleight of hand in the world did not help when a team was inserted right on top of an enemy position or in the middle of a base camp.

We reported to the LRP pad as a flight of three, two slicks and a C & C (command and control). The Kingsmen would also provide two Charlie-model guns from the Lancers. Wild Bill Meacham was the AC of the C & C bird. The mission was to insert a team in the area just east of the A Shau Valley. Burdened with ropes and ladders, two men came to the aircraft. When they had dropped their load on the pad, Poley introduced me to SFC Doc Brubaker and Staff Sergeant Burnell. Both NCOs growled the same response as they shook my hand, "Airborne, sir!" I could tell right away that both had been formed by the army's Airborne Ranger cookie cutter. I have now known Burnell over twenty years, and I don't believe that he has ever given me any affirmative reply other than "Airborne, sir!" These two men, I soon discovered, were the models that the young paratroopers of F Company followed. They were the tools that fashioned young soldiers into hardened Rangers who would face hundred-to-one odds in the steaming jungles. These teams would not only face large numbers of enemy, but defeat them by using with great skill the fire support that was available to them.

I watched with fascination as the two Rangers quickly rigged both aircraft with McGuire rigs and ladders. The McGuire rigs were 120-foot ropes with a small nylon seat at the end. The McGuire rigging started with a floating safety ring, a nylon strap that was attached to the aircraft at four cargo tie-downs. The ropes were fastened with carabiners to the safety ring, the cargo tie-down that the ring was hooked to, and an additional cargo tie-down. Each rope was thus attached to three cargo tie-downs on the floor of the bird. Each aircraft got four of these ropes. The McGuire rigs were used to extract teams from areas where there was no LZ the helicopter could land in. The seats were dropped down through the jungle canopy so a man could get in the seat. Team members would lock arms and be hauled out of the jungle, hanging 120 feet below the helicopter. This was not the preferred method. The first reason was that only three LRPs would be extracted at once. That left the last half of the team with less firepower to protect themselves. Another reason was that McGuire rigs require a vertical takeoff of 120 feet, and normally the reason that the team could not get to an LZ was *bad guys*! It was not a good feeling to have to make a take-off straight up, into wide-open sky, under fire.

After the McGuires came the ladders. The ladders had been made for use from the back of Chinook helicopters. They had aluminum rungs and steel cable sides. They were attached to the aircraft with carabiners, just as the McGuires had been. The center of the ladder was centered in the aircraft, and the ends rolled up into the bird. This left about fifteen feet of ladder on each side that could be rolled out the door for pickups when landing was not possible. The most desirable method was an LZ that we could land in. The next was a pickup at a hover, then ladders, then McGuires. The nature of the mission was that we could not always make extractions under ideal conditions.

We were briefed and got ready to go. The team loaded on the lead aircraft. The Dave and I were to fly chase on this one. As we flew west, The Dave continued to explain the procedures. "The C & C bird will locate the LZ and guide us in. Then we will make the overflight and head back. Piece a cake."

A few miles out, Poley lowered the nose, and the airspeed began to creep up toward 110 knots. He did not add power, which caused the altimeter to start to unwind. At treetop level, he added a little torque and the aircraft skimmed along at a foot above the lush vegetation. Wild Bill Meacham vectored the lead to the LZ, and we followed. Meacham called to the insertion bird, "Two hundred meters out."

I could see the lead aircraft start to slow. The excitement started to build in me as our rate of closure increased. Our speed stayed the same. The timing of the flyover was so close that I thought that we would surely collide. As the lead aircraft dropped into the trees, we were hot on his heels. When we thundered over the LZ, I could see the team spilling out of the insertion aircraft and the lead bird start to climb out of the LZ. I could feel my heart pounding. I thought he would surely climb up into the bottom of our aircraft. The speed with which it happened made the adrenaline pump wildly. In seconds, the team was inserted, and the aircraft was climbing out behind us. We departed the immediate area and circled, waiting to hear that the team was safely on the ground and not in contact.

"Kingsmen One-Nine, this is Kingsmen Two-Five." Meacham was calling Poley.

"Two-Five, One-Nine. Go ahead."

"This is Two-Five. One of the team members has injured his leg on the insertion. We are going to extract the team. Division wants the team put in the alternate LZ as a team of five."

Normal procedure would be for the aircraft that made the insertion to make the extraction. Since this would be a turnaround insertion in the alternate LZ, we would make the pickup and the drop-off. The pickup was uneventful. I could see that the injured LRP was in real pain. He would remain on the aircraft for the flight back to Camp Eagle.

As we lined up our final approach to the new LZ, the C & C aircraft began taking fire from both sides of the valley. Meacham vectored us along a route that kept a ridgeline between the two aircraft and the enemy positions. The terrain that he had selected allowed us to maneuver to the LZ, out of sight of the enemy, and insert the team without compromising its location. We were able to get in and out again without receiving any fire. Meacham remained on station to direct air strikes on the NVA who had been so rude as to shoot at him. The strikes gave the team time to melt into the jungle on the other side of the ridgeline.

Poley let me fly the aircraft back to the pad at Eagle. We were flying 350 again, and on the way back, Scott Wilson piped up. "See, Mr. Grant, I told you he would get you in deep shit with this LRP stuff."

Poley said, "What's the big deal? We didn't even get shot at."

Wilson laughed, "That was just luck."

"Bullshit. Pure skill on the part of the AC."

We settled down on the LRP pad and until sunset were on standby. Normally, once it got dark, a team would be safe, hidden in the darkness from the enemy's prying eyes. Like their foe, the Rangers were master craftsmen of the night. At dusk, we returned to the Castle to rest. The dawn would once again find us beating the last of the night air with the rotors of the Huey. I had completed my first day as a LRP pilot.

Thursday, 20 June (273 days to go). An important part of the Kingsmen was the 3d Platoon, the guns. They called themselves the Lancers, but they were an essential part of the company. The guns generally operated as a fire team, two Charlie-model Hueys with an assortment of weapons hanging from them. A heavy fire team consisted of three gunships. One of the best fire teams we had was that of R. L. "Hootchmaid" Smith and Wild Bill Turner. Hootchmaid got his nickname when the company was located in Long Binh after it first arrived in country. It was his duty to pay and control the hootchmaids that cleaned the rooms. He got the name, and it stuck. R. L. flew the gun version known as a Hog. It had a 40mm grenade launcher mounted on the nose, and tubes for thirty-eight 2.75-inch rockets mounted on the sides. Turner's aircraft had the M-21 subsystem, which consisted of the six-barrel miniguns that fired eighteen hundred rounds per minute each. The machine guns were located on flexible mounts on the sides of the Huey. The guns could flex up, down, left, and right at the command of the pilot in the left seat. The rockets on that version consisted of two 7-shot pods mounted on the same pylons as the miniguns.

The Lancers had an excellent reputation for providing fire support. The Turner/Smith team had a reputation that even extended to the enemy—a captured document offered a 500,000-piaster reward for the head of the gun pilot known as "Hootchmaid." While flying a combat assault that day, we were flying a staggered-left formation. I was the peter pilot of Chalk Three, and the aircraft commander was flying the first lift. I was watching as R. L. Smith suppressed the right side of the LZ with rockets and forty mike-mike. As I watched, a hole appeared in the small window at the top of the pilot's door. The hole was about an eighth of inch wide and three-eighths of an inch long. There was a crack that ran to the end of the window. Later when I examined my flight helmet I discovered a three-inch-long gouge in the visor shield. A freak piece of shrapnel had hit us. No one else in the flight had been struck by anything. It was all over the company in no time at all, the ever accurate Hootchmaid had hit an aircraft.

There was an unofficial company meeting to decide if I still had my cherry. The outcome was that, since it was not enemy fire that holed the aircraft, Grant was still a cherry.

That night I took my helmet to the club. When I walked in, Smitty was at the bar. I walked up to the bar and set the flight helmet on the bar between us. Not a word was exchanged. He just pointed to the bartender, then at me. I drank free that night.

Sunday, 23 June (269 days to go). The dawn found me on the LRP pad again. The flying was uneventful. Poley and I spent the day in the company of Burnell and Brubaker. At first, I thought that we were just passing the time, but as the day wore on, I began to realize that I was being trained. In the beginning, discussion was mostly centered on the procedures the teams used in the field. They talked of each man on the team having an assigned area to scan. I learned of point men and walking slack and drag. I was told of night defensive positions and what it meant to "lay dog." The discussion turned to the duties of a downed aircrew with the team. It was then that I realized we were having more than just a bull session. The crew chief and the door gunner would become the machine gunners for the team. The peter pilot would become the assistant senior RTO. The most interesting assignment was that of the aircraft commander. The AC would become the assistant team leader. Of course, if anything ever happened to the team leader, the AC would still be the ATL. As long there was a LRP left on the team, the AC would always be the ATL.

The next two days, I logged eighteen hours of flight time, flying log missions. The twenty-fifth, I flew with Jim Riden. We supported a unit that had been in contact on and off for three days, and was desperately short of ammunition. We spent the better part of the day hauling everything they would need to sustain them for another couple of days. That was my first log mission that was important enough to be performed under fire. This battalion was operating in the Rao Trang River valley, southwest of FSB Rakkasson. Jim skillfully guided us through each sortie, carefully approaching each LZ as though it was the first time we had landed there. Each time, we approached from a different angle. Sometimes we would take off, head toward one of the units, then at the last minute, turn toward another. We received fire a number of times. Jim made sure that our flight path changed each time, and we never overflew the same spot twice. Each time that we were shot at, I noticed that Jim was not rattled or excited. He calmly and professionally continued the mission. We logged the whole battalion, to include bringing each company "hots," a hot meal prepared in the rear and sent out on the aircraft in insulated marmite cans. Jim planned around the LZs that were hot. When we were getting shot at, we only went in if the cargo was desperately needed ammo. Each time we returned, he would coordinate with the sergeant running the log pad. If a company had contact, we would delay the hots and go to one of the other companies.

I found that I had a growing admiration for the man, and I knew that there was much that I could learn from him. Each time that we were shot at, he was calm and calculating. Jim was a little older than the rest of us and gave us a calm and professional image to live up to. He showed a genuine concern for the grunts in the field and did what he could to make their life better. Sometimes it meant getting a mission extension, when we were tired, to fly some cold beer out to an LZ in the jungle. Supporting the grunts, Jim was the example of the kind of AC I wanted to be.

Jim Riden made a point of trying to help me improve my "control touch," i.e., how smoothly I manipulated the controls of the aircraft. I had a tendency to be rough on the controls; Jim Riden patiently worked with me to overcome that. Overcontrolling causes the rotors to be less efficient and lose lift. I believe it was Jim who showed me that you could actually set a loaded Huey on the ground from a hover simply by overcontrolling the cyclic stick. He would overcontrol, and the bird would settle to the ground. He would then hold the cyclic still and the aircraft would pop back up to a three-foot hover. All this without changing the amount of power that the engine delivered to the rotor system. I was amazed. These lessons were valuable when we had to fly aircraft over their allowed gross weight. They were even more valuable when I used the same skills to extract LRPs from thick jungle canopy on the end of a 120-foot rope.

I closed out the month of June on the Acid pad, flying LRPs. I flew several hours of VRs, some unexciting insertions and extractions. That is, I was allowed to sit there and watch Wild Bill Meacham make some insertions and extractions. I was quickly learning that if a peter pilot was going to gain flight experience, he was not going to get it while on LRP missions. The ACs did most of the flying. The standby hours were filled by my new mentors Burnell and Brubaker. I was run through immediate-action drills and squad tactics. They had even started making me sneak around the company area with a rifle. Burnell would jump all over me every time I moved fast enough to make the gravel crunch under my feet. At times, I felt like I was back in basic training, yet I realized that they were teaching me skills that would help insure my survival if I was ever shot down. It would not matter if I was flying LRPs at the time; these were the skills of jungle warfare. I was being taught by some of the best in business. I ended the month of June with 203 flying hours. So much for Army Regulation 95-1.

CHAPTER 5
JULY 1968

The first of July (261 days to go). Jackie and I had been married for a whole 365 days. I'd spent 104 of them in this shithole. I had been carefully planning a celebration of my first wedding anniversary. It would not be the way I wanted to celebrate, but would have to do. I had come up with a case of champagne. I had the club reserved. The Kingsmen would help dispose of the case, and then I would run a tab. I flew a short flight in the morning and was back on the ground by lunchtime. It was about 1400 hours when I was told that the battalion had preempted me for the club, and I would have to take my party elsewhere. I was livid. The only thing I could to do was to postpone or cancel the party. The word quickly spread through the company as the crews returned from the day's missions. I had carefully planned the party and had begged operations to make sure that I would not fly late that day. I was heartbroken. The army had not only made sure that I could not be with my wife, but now they had ruined my makeshift celebration. Slowly but surely, the company area emptied as the Kingsmen sought other forms of entertainment for the evening. It was not long before the Castle became as quiet as the graveyard it had once been.

I had decided that I would stick around and see just what kind of party the lifers had planned. And find out what was so important that they had to screw up my anniversary. At least with everyone off to other places, I knew that I would have the shower all to myself. Small luxuries were becoming more and more important. Privacy and a quiet moment to yourself were really hard to come by. On the way to the shower, I slipped going over the lip of one of the grave mounds that were in the company area. The flip-flop on my left foot got sideways, and I smashed a toe as I fell. As I sat on the ground looking over the scraped and bleeding toe, I thought that it was the topper to the ruined celebration of my anniversary.

Later, I limped over to flight operations to see what Rick Haines was up to. On the way, I saw the first sergeant going into the orderly room. I was surprised to see him going to work at that hour. I looked at my watch, and the time was 1815. Normally Top was long in a club somewhere by then. I noticed that the NCO and enlisted clubs were both quiet also. When the lifers invade the company area, all the working soldiers find someplace else to go.

Just as I raised the flap of the operations tent, I heard a Huey coming in. I turned and saw a 2d-Platoon aircraft heading toward its revetment. I ducked into the tent and could hear the radio break squelch. "Kingsmen Operations, this is Kingsman Two-Five. I'm down at the Castle, destination, termination."

It was L T (pronounced el tee) Meacham completing the day's flying. Rick Haines responded. "Roger, Two-Five. I show you down at one seven past the hour."

Rick looked up at me. "Hey, what's up? You look really pissed."

"Just that bullshit with having to cancel my party so the battalion lifers could have the club."

"Didn't you hear? They canceled."

"You got to be kidding!"

Rick said, "No, they called about a half hour ago and said they weren't coming."

"Son of a bitch!"

Rick said, "That's right—I forgot about your party. Well, you can have it now."

I told him, "No I can't. Everybody has split. The muthafuckers have ruined the party."

"*Xin loi.*" (The Vietnamese equivalent of "tough shit.")

"Thanks a lot, asshole."

Rick shrugged and gave me a helpless smile.

A few minutes later, Bill Meacham and Sir James Thompson came into operations to fill out their aftermission report. After the paperwork was settled, I explained to everyone what had happened. Meacham said, "I don't see what the problem is, partner."

I said, "Well, you seem to have missed the point that everybody has left the neighborhood."

"Look, you dumb-assed wobbly one, you are an assistant club officer, are you not?" (I had taken on another additional duty as an assistant club officer. I had figured since I was spending so much time there, I might as well work there. Besides, it would give me two additional duties and keep them off my back with some other job that might be a lot less pleasant. It also meant an occasional trip to Da Nang to buy booze and visit my friends in the Black Cats.)

I answered, "Yes."

"And you have the keys to the club, do you not?"

"Yes."

"And the case of champagne is paid for, is it not?"

"Yes."

"And you have me, Sir James, and Rick here to help you drink it, do you not?"

Rick jumped in with, "I have a poker game over at the Comancheros."

"All right, you have me and Sir James here to help you drink it, do you not?"

"Yes."

"Well, no problem. Let us get rid of our flight gear and get down to business."

It was not quite what I had planned, but it seemed that it would have to do. Jim and I had been through basic and flight school together and always got along well. I was finding that I really liked this lieutenant. No problem was ever complicated as far as Wild Bill Meacham was concerned. Bill and Jim headed off to their hootch to lose their gear, and I went to the club to open up. On the way I stuck my head into the orderly room and invited the first sergeant to join us. That one act caused that night to become renowned in Kingsmen folklore.

I opened up the club and broke out the champagne. It took us till about two in the morning, but the four of us drank all twelve bottles. I then ran up my tab for another couple of hours. Just as we were about to turn out the lights and lock the door, I looked at my wrist, and all four watches on it said that it was almost four o'clock. I put the padlock on the door and turned to see where the others were. I realized immediately that it was a good thing that I still had a grip on the padlock. The bright silver glow of the moon had painted everything silver gray. I had to grip the lock tighter to keep from falling off the step in front of the club. The entire country of South Vietnam was spinning around the club at about forty miles per hour. The rocky ground was just a blur as it went by. North Vietnam might have been spinning too, but I couldn't see far enough to be able to tell. Magically, Wild Bill, Sir James, and Top (who were about ten feet from the step on which I was standing) were not whirling with the ground. I gripped the lock just a little tighter. I could see the spinning had affected my companions because Top had fallen down, and Sir James was standing on one of the first sergeant's hands to keep him from whirling away. Wild Bill was desperately trying to help Top up. Every time he bent over and reached down to the first sergeant, he would lose his balance on the speeding ground and stumble two or three steps backward. Jim had to keep his arms out to the sides to be able to balance on Top's hand. The scene was making me dizzy. I had to look away.

While I regained my equilibrium, I wondered if this phenomenon occurred often. When I looked back again, I could see that Sir James was having difficulty holding Top in place. He was swaying back and forth; I knew that if he fell, he would get some nasty scrapes, as fast as the ground was moving. It was then that I realized that the step in front of the club had begun to tilt. I would not be able to hold onto the lock much longer. It didn't matter, I had to help my friends get Top off the spinning earth. I let go of the lock and stumbled across the unstable ground. Unable to stop when I got there, I stepped in the middle of Top's back and collided with Wild Bill, who was stumbling backwards. We both collapsed in a heap. Bill and I clawed our way across the ground and grabbed Top just as Jim fell off his hand. We were just in time.

Finally, we all struggled to our feet. As we stood there holding each other up, we decided that we should get the first sergeant to bed before he was swept away with the spinning ground. When we got to the first sergeant's tent and started to get him to bed, we noticed that his dentures were hanging half out of his mouth. After a quick discussion, it occurred to us that he might choke on the teeth if we left them in. Finally, after much debate, we determined the best place to put the teeth. A place where they would be safe, and he would certainly be able to find them in the morning, was in his boot.

How the rest of us got to bed that night, I'm not really sure.

I know that it took all six legs, six arms holding on, and the determined will of three clouded minds just to be able to stand up. When I became conscious the next day, the bells of St. Mary's were what woke me. I started to get up and go look around for the bell tower when the pain in my head told me exactly where the bells were located. I looked down at my feet and saw that I had only managed to remove one boot and one pants leg. Years of training at home were evident. The foot with the boot on it was still on the floor. "Don't you put your shoes on the furniture!" What amazed me was that the pants leg that had been removed was the right leg, and it was the right foot that still had on its boot.

Late morning had me and the bells flying a couple of combat assaults. After that, I had the rest of the day to sit around and recover. I got word that day of the death of a classmate from flight school. WO1 Jerry Hampton Johnson was killed in a mid-air collision with an air force fixed-wing aircraft. I wrote home to Jackie that I thought it was ironic that Jerry should be killed in that way. Jerry and I had talked of war, and Jerry was very concerned that he might one day have to order his gunner to kill somebody. With war all around him, Jerry was taken by an accident. Nothing seemed to make sense in this place.

The rumors of the Kingsmen moving continued to persist. The rumor now had a place. They said we would be moving to Bien Hoa, just north of Saigon. The letters home were getting harder to write. I didn't want to write of the war and how often I was now getting shot at; that left news hard to come by. I wrote about the toe I had smashed the night before on the way to the shower. It was swollen and probably broken. I told her how much I loved her and missed her, but the war news was only of cold LZs.

While rinsing the remaining cobwebs out of my head with Budweiser that night in the club, I sat down at Bill Meacham's table. I said to him, "Wild Bill, how did we get to bed last night? I remember putting Top to bed, but I can't remember which of us put the others to bed."

He leaned over and put his arm around my back, patted me on the shoulder, and said, "Partner, the Lord looks out for drunks and dumb animals. You and I qualify on both counts." Clearly he did not know how we got to bed either. I would hear that statement many times before Wild Bill went home, and many times in the years that followed.

Meacham said, "Do you know that Top is really pissed at us?"

"No. Why?"

"Cause he damn near bit off his foot this morning."

We all had a good laugh over that.

Bill said, "He's especially pissed at you."

"Why?"

"Cause it was your idea to put the teeth in his boot."

I asked, "How'd he know that? He was passed out."

" 'Cause I told 'im," Meacham replied, with an ear-to-ear grin.

We had an audience of about ten pilots who all had a good laugh now. The cat was out of the bag. The story of Top trying to bite off his foot spread throughout the Kingsmen. The first sergeant refused to drink with us again.

Charlie Rake came by and asked me if I was still interested in flying guns. I told him, "Yes."

He said that he would look into it. I was not yet quite addicted to F Company, 58th Infantry.

3 July (260 days to go). During the course of seven hours of flying with Jim Riden, we had the opportunity to evac some patients to the hospital ship *Repose.* Jim let me fly out to the ship. As we got close, he contacted them on the frequency that we had been given.

"Roger, Kingsmen One-Eight, this is Repose. We are making fifteen knots. Winds are zero six zero at twenty. The deck is clear. You are cleared to land."

I thought it was kind of strange the wind had picked up so much, but I turned to zero six zero and tried to line up with the deck. The ship was headed south. It kept sliding away as I would try to line up. After three attempts, I saw that Jim was sitting there laughing his ass off. He finally explained that the navy gave the wind direction relative to the ship. I had assumed the reported winds were by compass direction as on land. I then succeeded in making the landing. Four sailors immediately scrambled out and chained us down to the deck. The way Jim had presented the subject, I would be sure to remember; I would only be able to use the lesson a few times during my tour.

That night, the gooks decided that it would be a grand idea to provide us with some fireworks in preparation for the Fourth of July. They crawled through the wire and took out one of the perimeter bunkers—with a little help from the guys on the bunker, who had smoked enough weed to get their throats cut. Then the sappers worked around behind the next two bunkers and took them out quietly. Once in control of three bunkers, the sappers sent out invitations to all their friends, and the party began. The NVA set up an eighty-one millimeter on the 1st Brigade helipad and began pumping mortar shells all over Camp Eagle. The breach in the wire was over the hill, about five hundred yards from the Castle.

"Chuck" (from "Victor Charlie," for the VC) had apparently decided to make a serious attempt to overrun Eagle. The enemy had probably figured that most of the hard-core infantry was out in the field. He was right. However, all the gunships were at home, and before long all of them were in the air. The guns circled over Camp Eagle taking turns at the gooks who were coming through the wire. Many of the crew members were flying in underwear and shower shoes. It was a turkey shoot for the guns—confined troops in the open.

Many Kingsmen, officer and enlisted alike, were gathered on the last tent row, watching the hill for signs of the enemy. The revetments where the aircraft were parked were between our position and the crest of the hill. The sandbag walls around the tents would be our cover if we became involved in a firefight. We sat with weapons ready. We were also well equipped with beer and wine. We sat there, drinking and cheering on the guns. The gunners had gotten out all the 60s and their M-16s. Any enemy that had come over the hill would have been silhouetted by the flares and the explosions on the other side. With all the firepower we had, they wouldn't have had a chance. Of course, the way we'd been drinking, our aircraft would have been in great danger, as well.

Friday, 5 July (257 days to go). I had the day off, so I slept as late as the heat would allow. When I woke, I was drenched in sweat, and surrounded by the kind of heat that makes you feel like the air is burning your lungs with each breath. I peeked out of the tent. The sun was so bright that it made the rocky, light brown dirt outside look white. It hurt my eyes all the way to the back of my head. I looked down at my watch, and it read four thirty. The damn thing had stopped again. Timex had not designed the ten-dollar timepiece for the local dust and humidity. That day was unusual. Many of my days off were occupied with trips to Da Nang, to restock the club with booze or to deposit soldiers' savings. But that day, I had absolutely nothing to do. I'd hike over to the PX and replace the latest casualty of the Vietnam conflict.

At the PX, I found a Seiko watch for twenty-six dollars, a lot of money for me to spend on a watch. As a teenage hot-rodder, I had gotten in the habit buying inexpensive watches because too many found their end smashed against the side of an engine block when I forgot to take them off while working on some-one's car. The watch was waterproof, self-winding, and most important, had the day and date, which were hard to keep track of. Besides I had not seen any 327s or 409s since I had been in country, so the watch would be fairly safe from misplaced en-gine blocks. Every self-respecting aviator had to have a big watch. This one fit the bill nicely.

On the way back to the Castle, I noticed a fenced-off area alongside the road where several German shepherd dogs were running around. Thinking at first that it was a high-security area, I stopped and looked. I began to take in the surroundings, and I realized that there were kennels and other dogs. It had to be where the K-9 dogs were kept. It soon became apparent that the running dogs were being exercised by the one soldier in the compound. I stood there engrossed, thinking about my German shepherd at home. The specialist-four handler noticed me watch-ing and came to the fence. "Can I help you, sir?"

I was busy watching the dogs and hadn't noticed him. Sur-prised I said, "I . . . er, uh . . . no, I . . . uh was just watching." I sure he must have been impressed with my suave and con-trolled officer's demeanor.

"Sir, if you'd like to come down by the gate, you can come in for a while."

My head came back from home. "That's okay, I was just thinking about my shepherd at home."

The specialist four said, "It's not a problem, sir. Actually I'm on my own here, and if you would like to help exercise the dogs, you'd be doing me a favor."

I spent the next two hours throwing sticks and balls. As the dogs ran back and forth, they kicked up the red dust of the rocky ground. I didn't notice the dust; I was somewhere else. These dogs had delivered me from the war. As I got more com-fortable with the animals, I wrestled one of them, roughhousing and allowing the dog to chew on my arm the way I did with my own dog. As I playfully slapped the dog on the snoot, I asked the specialist, "What are these dogs used for?"

He replied, "Mostly tracking and booby-trap detecting."

"Are any of them attack trained?"

He smiled. "The one you been smacking around for the last ten minutes."

I paused in playing with the dog for a moment; then it dawned on me that if this dog was going to eat me, he would've done so long ago. We talked about the dogs some more. I found out that the army kept 201 files on the dogs just as for human soldiers. One of the dogs, a booby-trap dog that had not been trained for attack, had even been awarded the Silver Star for valor. He and his handler were walking point. As they turned a corner in the trail, they came on a gook, and the handler's M-16 misfired. While the dog handler ejected the bad round and tried to chamber a new one, the NVA turned and raised his AK-47, but the dog sensed the danger to his handler and leaped, knocking the NVA's weapon out of his hands and ferociously chewing on the enemy's face. In the meantime, the handler pulled a knife and came to the dog's assistance. The dog was decorated for saving his handler's life. The dog didn't care. He was just taking care of his buddy. By the time the year was over, many of us would be just like the dog, unable to understand about awards given out for taking care of our buddies.

I left the K-9 compound, dusty, sweaty, and smelling like a German shepherd. I loved it. I was determined to go back at every opportunity; I had found another way to forget about the war besides the club.

7 July (255 days to go). Another day of standby for combat assaults. We spent the morning moving 750 ARVNs into an LZ in the foothills, just west of Hue. It was a cold lift; they usually were with Marvin the ARVN. It was a good opportunity to see Spec Four Ronco in action. Ronco was a crew chief, and a good one, one of those kids who put the first rounds on target from fifteen hundred feet and a hundred knots. After we had pre-flighted and each crew member was getting his own equipment ready for the flight, I looked over at Ronco, who was checking a pole that he had wedged between the bench seat and his seat in the transmission well. About three feet long and an inch in diameter, the pole appeared to made of oak or some other hardwood. I just had to ask, "Hey, Ronco, what's the stick for?"

He replied, "That's my fuckin' translator, sir!"

I knew I was being led down the path. "Translator?"

"Yes, sir. Ya see sometimes—only sometimes, mind you—when we fly Marvin the ARVN, he's a little reluctant to get out of the helicopter. Now when that happens, it is usually a hot LZ, and we don't want to stick around while I get the message across, so I yell, 'Get the fuck outta my helicopter, dickhead!' "

He continued, "Now Marvin don't speak English so good. So he doesn't understand, but when I beat him about the head and shoulders with my translator, he knows what 'Get the fuck outta my helicopter, dickhead' means."

Ronco wore thick glasses that looked like they were made out of bottle bottoms. The army issued him both sunglasses and clear glasses, but he hated night flying and somehow something bad always seemed to happen to the clear glasses. They would get stepped on or get caught in the slipstream and blow out of the helicopter. Operations eventually gave up and only scheduled him on day flights.

We cranked up and took off. We landed at the PZ and had to hold while everything came together. Airmobile operations took a lot of coordination of air strikes, artillery, gunships, slicks, and the grunts. It could not have been too difficult for the bad guys to figure out that someone was coming to visit. The operation would start with an air strike, the size of which would be determined by what intelligence estimated the enemy forces to be. The minimum would be a pair of F-4 fighters dropping their considerable ordnance. The air strike was followed by a coordinated artillery barrage, the idea being that the arty would be lifted just before the arrival of the helicopters. The gunships would generally make one pass along the approach path before the slicks landed. The gunships would then make another pass as the first lift landed. Then, as a finale, the door gunners would suppress the tree lines as the slicks were on short final. Of course, after all that ordnance was expended, many times the LZ was still hot.

This time the LZ was cold. However, all the fireworks did not raise Marvin's enthusiasm for getting out in this LZ. The AC was flying the approach. As we got on short final, I looked over to see Ronco suppressing the tree line with his M-60 with his left hand. His right hand, meantime, was making effective use of the translator. As the heels of the skids touched down ARVNs were leaving the aircraft as fast as American paratroopers would have.

During that afternoon, I wrote home to Jackie. I was so hot that I had to keep a towel handy to wipe the sweat from my forehead or the paper would be soaked. Rumors of our move south persisted. We had high hopes that it would bring air-conditioned hootches. It would be great not to have red dust in everything I owned.

That night in the club, Charlie Rake came over to the bar and ordered a beer. He looked as weary as all the other pilots in the company. I had found myself noticing who looked really tired ever since my nap at the controls. There was no escaping it, a day off only got you a little extra sleep and a chance to get your laundry done. Still, there was no way to erase the damage done by the constant ups and downs of adrenaline highs. The long missions under stressful conditions took much more away from a pilot than the long hours worked. Charlie Rake was one platoon leader who truly cared about his people. That added to his stress.

Captain Rake said, "Grant, I am afraid that I have some news for you that you're not going to like."

"I bet I can guess."

"I am sorry, W. T., but they say that they are too short of peter pilots to let you go to the Lancers."

"I should have known."

Charlie said, "I'll keep an ear out for you and let you know if the situation changes."

I said, "Thanks, I'll be around for awhile, about two hundred and fifty-five days."

I was disappointed, but there was not a lot I could do about it. I wanted badly to fly guns. I still had thoughts of getting even for Joe Reichlin and a list of flight school classmates who would not be going home that grew almost weekly. Maybe there was something to Poley's vision of St. Can Opener.

Wednesday, 10 July (252 days to go). Once again I found myself on the Acid pad flying LRPs. This time, with Wild Bill Meacham as the AC. I had figured out the best way to learn from Wild Bill was to watch the demonstration, because my getting hold of the controls when flying with Bill was rare. We made one insertion, and the other aircraft made one. Those two teams were out, and one other that had been inserted a couple of days earlier. Most of the day was spent on standby waiting for a team to get into trouble.

During the time I spent sitting around, I suddenly realized that six weeks had passed since I had arrived at Camp Eagle. It seemed that it was just yesterday, until I started thinking about all that had occurred since my arrival—I had more than doubled my total flight time. Not just the time I had flown since I got to Vietnam, but flight school as well. I had over five hundred hours and was starting feel like I was really in control when I flew. The aircraft commanders were sounding less and less like flight instructors. There was no longer a constant stream of chatter coming from the other seat. I had learned what was expected of me, and to anticipate the next task without being batted over the head. I had started to feel like a pilot, not like a student pilot attending graduate training. I was learning to sleep on the ground, on the metal floor of a helicopter, or while standing in the chow line. Camp Eagle was a very different place, indeed, from Da Nang. There was no sleeping in bunkers at Eagle. About once a week, someone would throw a couple of mortars or rockets into the perimeter. Many times we were so tired from the heavy flight schedule that we would just roll off the bunk and onto the floor and pull the mattress over us for cover.

Getting shot at had become a routine, almost daily, experience. Almost every day a Kingsmen or a Lancer came home with some new ventilation in his aircraft and sheet-metal work for maintenance. The maintenance guys were amazing. It was not surprising for a Huey to land at 1600 hours, with several holes in it, and be patched up and flyable again the next morning.

Thursday, 11 July (251 days to go). I logged total of .5 hours and two landings for the day. One landing on the Acid pad and one back at the Castle. We touched down on the pad at first light. The sky to the east was just beginning to get that golden glow as the sun rose from the ocean. As I sat in the right seat, still half-asleep, I noticed a tall, lanky soldier, dressed in tiger stripes, working his way down the hill to the pad. He was obviously headed to the aircraft to speak to us. He had a canteen cup in his hand. In the early light, I could see the steam rising from the hot coffee in the cup. I wanted a cup so bad that I could almost taste the coffee from inside the aircraft. There was something oddly familiar about the way he moved. We still had over a minute to go on the cooldown before the throttle could be shut off. In nonemergency situations, the Huey's turbine engine was allowed a full two minutes at idle for the temperature to stabilize before shutdown. Wild Bill looked over and said, "You baby-sit the bird, partner. I'll go see what he wants. Don't shut down till I give you the signal."

Meacham was going to make sure that they did not want us to fly right away before he let me shut the aircraft down. I just nodded and watched him crawl out of his seat. The guy he was talking to was definitely familiar, but I couldn't place him. After a short conversation, Wild Bill turned to me and drew his open hand across his throat. I looked at the clock in the panel, and there was another ten seconds to go till the cooldown was complete. As the second hand pointed straight up, I reached down, pushed the idle/stop button, and closed the throttle. Meacham's Huey 66-17121 responded immediately. The loud whine of the engine came to a rapid halt, the tachometers all started dropping toward zero. I turned the fuel switch off, then the inverters. Starting with the left side of the pedestal between the pilot seats, I turned off each of the radios in the prescribed order. I then checked to make sure that the N1 and N2 tachs were reading zero. Then the exhaust-gas temperature gauge to make sure that the fire was out in the combustion chamber of the engine. Then, as the rotor coasted down, I set up the "shotgun load." Gunships, LRP birds, and medevacs were always left ready to start in case of a scramble. Emergencies came often in all three categories.

Start generator switch - Start position.
Main Fuel - On.
Start Fuel - On.
Throttle - Full Open.
        - Check Flight Idle Stop.
        - Full Closed.
        - Flight Idle.
        - Set for Start.
Battery - Off.

The other AC had joined Bill and the lanky guy. The three turned back up the hill toward the operations building. Just as the crew chief hooked up the main rotor to tie it down, it hit me like a thunderbolt. I stuck my head out of the door and yelled, "Burford, you asshole."

The lanky guy in tigers turned, with violence in his eyes, and looked at the aircraft. I struggled with my seat belt. It finally came free, and I stumbled out of the bird, half leaping, half falling to the ground. Burford threw down his canteen cup and charged down the hill. Time had slowed almost like in a hot LZ. Meacham and the other AC turned to see what was going on. I got my feet solidly under just as Burford reached the pad. He grabbed me around the shoulders, and I grabbed him the same way. We spun and danced around in circles calling each other names.

"You dipshit."

"You maggot."

"You shithead."

"You candyass."

"You . . . you . . . candidate."

Just like being back in flight school.

John Burford and I had been classmates in flight school. We were part of one of the first of the really big classes, but the army wasn't so desperate as to give up its 40-percent or better washout rate. They took the best qualified young applicants, then gave them as tough a time as possible in flight school and eliminated almost half of them. Only the very best were to survive to become army aviators. As we came to the end of the primary phase of flight training, a major difference of opinion occurred between our flight commander and the pilots who gave the end-of-phase check rides. The result was a lot of us failed check rides. Some of us were allowed to continue after being set back a class, some were eliminated. After much deliberation, John decided that he was not meant to fly. When a soldier left flight training, it was the same as in all the old World War II movies: the powers that be simply made him disappear. At the end of the day, his belongings, his mattress, and all evidence that he had ever been there had disappeared. So it was with John. We were told that he had made the decision, but he was not even allowed to say good-bye.

Finding him again was great. I had liked him in flight school. His giant laugh and great sense of humor had helped all of us get through the harassment of preflight. John was a prior-service soldier. That meant that he had been in the army prior to coming to flight school. Most of our classmates had enlisted in the army for the purpose of attending flight school. John had already been through infantry AIT and jump school and spent some time soldiering in a nonschool environment before flight school. It was the prior-service guys who helped many of us to keep up our spirits and thus get through the tough times.

John said to me, "This is great, son! From now on I want you to be the pilot who inserts and extracts my team."

"John, you're crazy, you don't know if I'm worth a shit as a pilot."

"It doesn't matter, man, you're my pilot, and that's the way it's got to be."

The rest of the day was spent on standby, waiting for a call that a team was in trouble. It was different than the long hours spent waiting for passengers when I was with the Black Cats. Here I was doing something, here someone really needed our help. I looked in on training that was being given for some of the members of F Company. I watched immediate-action drills; I learned how the Australian peel was used for a team to break contact with the enemy. The training ended around noon, and I went down to the aircraft to get some C rations for lunch. I was about to open the box when some LRPs came down the hill. One of them was John. He came over to the aircraft and held out a dark gray plastic pouch and said, "Son, don't eat that shit. Try this."

It was my first LRP ration, a dehydrated meal that was packaged in a plastic bag. John cut open the outer bag and handed me the clear plastic bag from the inside. It felt hard and looked very unappetizing. I handed it back and said, "No thanks, I gave up sand for Lent."

John laughed. "It's dehydrated, dummy. You have to prepare it."

He opened a canteen and poured water into a Coke can that had the top cut out of it. As we talked, we moved over to the side of the pad away from the aircraft. The two LRPs with him filled Coke cans with water, also. Then John took a small block of C-4 plastic explosive from his pocket.

"Wait a minute, John, I don't think I want to eat anything that has to be blown up first."

John handed out small balls of the explosive, each about the size of dime. He then wrapped his belt around the top of the can to form a handle. He lit the C-4 and held the can of water over the flame until the water started to boil—it only took about thirty seconds. He poured the water into the bag, gave it to me with a plastic spoon. He said, "Stir the water in good, and you'll have chicken and rice."

While John prepared his own lunch, he introduced the other two LRPs. "These ugly characters here are John Sours and Ray Zoschak. If y'all shake hands with them, count your fingers afterward."

I shook hands anyway. We talked as we ate. Sours was taller than Zoschak and had reddish blond hair. Ray had brown hair and boyish good looks that hid a wild man and very professional soldier. I quickly found that I liked both of them. We talked of long-range patrols. They told me of their business in the jungle. This was not another training session; I had begun to find acceptance among these soldiers. The chicken and rice was quite tasty. I was glad that I had not insisted on eating the C rations. Apparently, in the field, the LRPs not only ate the meals cold, but dry as well. A team could not dare to light a fire in the jungle, for fear of compromising their position.

The next day was filled with visual recons of a number of areas in the AO. The recons were in preparation for a larger operation coming up.

Friday, 12 July (250 days to go). I was flying with The Dave. The other bird was flown by Wild Bill Meacham and Lou Pulver. We were briefed that the day's mission would be to extract all three LRP teams. The first team would be extracted by Meacham and Pulver. The second by Poley and me. The last would belong to Meacham's crew.

The first extraction went off smoothly. We were on the way back to the Acid pad when the radio call came.

"Windy Guard Six, this Windy Guard One-Three." The RTO sounded out of breath, and he was not whispering.

"Guard One-Three, this is Six. Go ahead."

The response sounded as if the mike was moving back and forth past the radio operator's mouth as he talked. "Windy Guard Six this is One-Three. We have been compromised and are being chased by an estimated company-size force. We are *di-di*ing for the planned PZ; requesting immediate extraction."

Poley called, "Breaking left!"

The crew chief automatically called, "Clear left, sir!"

Meacham answered, "Roger, One-Nine. We'll drop off our team and come out to back you up."

As Wild Bill spoke, Dave Poley smoothly laid the aircraft over in a ninety-degree bank. We would race with time back out into the AO to pick up the team. I looked over at Dave, and I could see the ground beyond his window. His windshield was green, and mine was blue. Hootchmaid Smith called on the VHF radio. "This is Lancer Three-Three. We are doing a one-eighty to the right. Will meet you at the PZ."

The slower moving Charlie-models had only followed us part of the way back to Eagle since we had more extractions to make. The Lancers had been circling in the vicinity of Nui Khe. It looked as though they would have some work to do on this one. The tension was mounting as we rushed to the rescue. The routine procedure I had been taught for two-ship extractions would not come into play that afternoon; Meacham and Pulver would just be departing Eagle as we made the extraction.

The Fox Mike (FM radio) came alive again. "This is Windy Guard One-Three . . . (pant, pant) ETA PZ (pant . . . pant) zero three mikes."

I could almost hear the jungle boots pounding the ground and the thrashing of the jungle as the team broke brush. I pictured them being followed by a horde of little khaki-clad gooks with pith helmets. The guns were out ahead of us. They would arrive about the same time as we would. The pith helmets had better have on their bullet-proof skivvies or they were going to get their asses shot off. Poley keyed the mike, "This is Kingsman One-Nine. We will be in the PZ in zero three mikes."

Dave dropped the nose a little lower to insure that we could keep his promise. Ahead, I could see the ridgeline that the PZ was on. We were rapidly gaining on the guns. Dave made a slight turn to the left to line us up on final. I finally had something I could contribute. I scanned the instruments and called out, "Sixty-six hundred, everything's in the green, no caution or warning lights, prelanding check complete."

Dave lowered the collective and moved the cyclic imperceptibly to the rear. The airspeed began to drop as we settled toward the ridge. The Huey belted out its familiar song of popping blades. I could see the PZ.

Hootchmaid called the team, "This here's Lancer Three-Three. Where y'all want my fire."

When the RTO keyed the mike, the staccato of automatic weapons sounded in the background. "We're (pant) about thirty (pant . . . pant) meters west of the PZ, (pant . . . pant . . . pant) kill everything west of that."

Hootchmaid's response was as fast as the radio. As he answered, we heard the woosh of the rockets leaving the tubes. "Roger kill everything." The familiar Texas drawl was reassuring. I looked out to the right where the thin smoke trails of the rockets headed for their targets. The ridgeline to the west began exploding in orange flame and black smoke as the rockets impacted. We continued to slow as we crossed over the tree line into the PZ. "Clear left" and "clear right" sounded from the crew chief and gunner in the back. The PZ was a good-size one for a change.

As we settled to a hover, the team broke cover from the jungle. What timing, what luck. The M-60s on both sides of the aircraft began chattering at the same time. On the right side, the tracers were passing a few feet over the heads of the LRPs and spraying the area behind them. I could hear the distinctive crack of AK-47s firing back. Six tiger-clad figures dove for the cargo door. I looked up, and to the rear, I could see the belly of Hootchmaid's Charlie-model as he broke right. Bill Turner was covering his break by hosing the ridge with minigun fire and rockets. As the last LRP was climbing from the skid to the floor of the bird, the gunner called, "We're up, sir!"

The aircraft was already rising as Poley said, "On the go."

I called out the torque readings during the climb out. Dave stopped at fifty pounds and dropped the nose and let the airspeed build. When we were well clear of the PZ, Scott Wilson said, "See, Mr. Grant, I warned you about the company you've been keeping." There were six smiling, camouflaged faces sitting on the floor in the back. The Dave pointed at me and said, "Home, James." I eagerly grabbed the controls and headed for Camp Eagle.

That night, there were no teams left in the field. Dave Poley and I helped the crew chief and gunner put the bird to bed. After the paperwork and dinner were done, we went back to the tent. Poley said to me, "The Dave is going over to the LRPs. Want to come along?"

"What's doing over there?"

"Nothin' special, just the Ranger Lounge."

"They got a pretty good club?"

"Nope, sometimes the beer isn't even cold, and if you want bourbon, you'll have to bring your own."

"Then why go?"

"The company is good, and the LRPs like to buy us beer."

"Okay, let's go."

We had to walk. It was a hike I would make many times in the future. As we walked, neither Poley nor I had much to say. In the Ranger lounge that night, we drank with Burford, Sours, and Zoschak. Each time another LRP came in, one of them would introduce him. I met Don Harris, Kenn Miller, Frank Souza, and others. I was finding that the more I got know these guys, the better I liked being around them. These troopers had volunteered more than once to get where they were. First, they had enlisted rather than be drafted. Next, they volunteered for Airborne, then LRPs. They were enthusiastic about their mission. Oh, you heard the usual soldier-bitching, the complaints about lifers and such. But these were men who took pride in what they were doing. Most had some college, some had degrees. Yet, every one was a hard-core, cut-your-throat-in-the-night warrior.

As I drank not-quite-cold beer, I found that night marked a turning point for me. Flying LRPs began to be more than just a mission. I was beginning to feel as much a part of F Company as I was a part of the Kingsmen. I had already developed a deep respect for the courage these guys had. The job of a LRP was to go among the enemy, collect his secrets, and leave undetected. They often were successful in the first two parts, the third was not as easy. Hot extractions happened as often as cold ones. These men were special. Not everyone could handle the stress of it, there were LRPs who went out on only one mission. Once in the jungle, the realization of how alone they were came to them like a black shadow. Sometimes a guy would freak out, and the team would have to be extracted; more often he would quietly go to the company commander and ask for a transfer to a line unit. Such requests were always honored. LRPs was a volunteer assignment; it had to remain a volunteer assignment.

In the Kingsmen, flying LRPs was a volunteer mission. Some of the Kingsmen wanted no part of the LRPs; some would fly the mission occasionally. Then there were the regulars. The ones who flew special operations as often as they could. I did not know it then, but I was being groomed to be a regular, like Poley and Meacham. The two had seen something in me that made them feel that I would enjoy sticking my ass in a meat grinder. I later came to realize that not every pilot got special attention from Brubaker and Burnell.

While Poley and I wandered back to the Castle, I thought about the hot extraction. I had not been really scared. Actually, it had been kind of exciting. We passed division headquarters and neared the PX area. Poley stopped in the middle of the road turned and said, "Well what do you think?"

I came to a halt like I had been caught in a net. What? I thought, The Dave is kind of weird, could he have read my mind?

Poley said, "What do you think about LRPs? Do you want to fly more?"

"Yeah it was fun . . . ah . . . kind of different, and yeah, I want to do it again."

I smiled at Poley and started walking again. I said over my shoulder, "Besides, Saint Can Opener of the Cs came to me in a vision last night and said I should keep an eye on The Dave."

I smiled to myself as The Dave had to hurry to catch up again.

Saturday, 13 July (249 days to go). A quiet day with no teams out. The Dave and I flew some VRs (visual reconnaissance) for coming missions. That night, Jim Riden called me to his area of the tent and told me to have a seat in his lawn chair. He was putting some polish on his boots, which we did on occasion to keep them from drying out. I looked down at mine, and the toes were all rough, light brown. The flight school spit shine was long gone. These were no longer the boots of an FNG. I liked the thought.

Jim seemed to be gathering his thoughts. Finally he said, "Grant, do you know what you're getting into? I mean, I know that Poley is a fun kind of crazy guy. Do you know that this LRP stuff is some serious shit?"

"Yeah, that's part of why I want to do it. I wanted to fly guns, but they won't let me. If I am going to be here, I want to contribute something. This war is so fucked up with all the stupid rules on who you can shoot and who you can't. LRPs are the only thing that has made sense since I got in country. We are here to kick someone's ass, aren't we?"

He laughed, "I think so; I just wanted to make sure that Poley wasn't doing your thinking for you."

"Thanks for caring, but I think I know what I'm doing—or maybe I'm just crazy like Poley."

"Okay, I think maybe you are." His mouth turned up in a warm smile and he said, "Let's go get a beer after I finish my boots."

I looked down at mine and said, "I think mine could use some Kiwi too."

I stood up, and there was a warm feeling inside me. This was not a conversation he would have had with an FNG. He would have simply decided what was best for me and seen to it that the platoon leader acted on it. I was now considered a fellow pilot by at least one of the ACs. And one whom I respected a great deal. It meant a great deal to me that he had taken the time. Jim only had about forty-six days left. I guess he was making sure that he didn't depart without giving the best he had to offer. I also realized that I did not mind blackening my boots, because I no longer felt like a fucking new guy. It had taken longer than it should have for me to shake that feeling, because of the change in units. In a lot of units, I would have already been an aircraft commander.

As I slopped some polish on my boots, I said to Jim, "Would you mind If I took your call sign when you leave?"

"No, I don't mind. Why mine?"

"You've taught me a lot, and I like your style."

"Well, I'm not sure if I like the idea of my call sign in the hands of a lunatic, but I guess it's okay."

We had a good laugh and headed for the club.

The next day was filled with resupply missions to various firebases. It was a fairly easy and secure mission, with no LZs, just the pads at fire support bases. Flying log to FSBs meant heavy loads and full days, but not much contact with the enemy. When we landed on the pad in the rear at Eagle, I noticed a large knife lying in the corner of the pad. I recognized it as a K-bar. When the sergeant in charge of the pad stepped up on the skid to tell me where that load was to be taken, I asked if it was his knife.

He replied, "It's just an old knife we use on the pad for cutting boxes open. Why? You want it, sir?"

"No, I don't want to take your knife, Sarge." Most of these guys would give a helicopter crew the shirt off their backs because they felt indebted. Therefore, one had to careful when scrounging not to appear interested in something that might mean too large a sacrifice.

"Really, sir, it ain't worth much, but if you want it it's yours."

He did not wait for a response; he just hopped off the skid and went over and got me the knife. He was right. It was in pretty sad shape. There was a chip out of the blade, and the blade was worn down about three-eighths of an inch from repeated sharpenings. The leather rings of the handle were dried out and shrunken from baking in the sun. But now it was mine, and a little TLC would make it functional again.

Jim smiled over at me and said, "Anybody who hangs around with LRPs should have himself a big knife. Next thing, you'll be running around in the jungle with them."

I just gave him my best big evil grin. He shook his head back and forth sadly, like a parent trying but failing to understand a teenager. He rolled the throttle back to operating RPM, pulled up on the collective, and took off for FSB Veghel. That left me scrambling to get the radio call off. He had done it on purpose.

We finished early enough for me to get to the little gook shop outside the PX and buy a sheath for the knife. I borrowed a file from maintenance and filed the blade down to remove the nick. I then sharpened it and taped the handle after oiling the leather in an attempt to repair the damage done by the weather. Though well-worn, it was a good knife, and I carried it my entire tour.

The more I became known as a LRP pilot, the more I noticed that I was treated differently around the company area. People had started to act around me the way people act if a patient with a violent history is released from a mental hospital. It didn't help much that I had decided that carrying the issue .38 was not a good idea because it had so little stopping power. The crew chief and the gunner had their M-16 and an M-60. I knew that if we went down, they were not going to take both. I would take whichever they left. In the end, I would only carry the .38 on Special Forces missions. Then it would be useful for shooting out the radios if we were shot down.

To many of my fellow Kingsmen, that sealed my fate—no gun, carries a big knife, definitely nuts. Leave Grant alone.

Richard A. Burnell has always been my idea of the ultimate warrior. He didn't make war because he loved it. He didn't make war because he was paid for it. Uncle Burnie made war because he was a soldier. He was a soldier because he was so damn good at it. Staff Sergeant Burnell has become a legend among Rangers in the army. The story most frequently told is of him teaching survival rations in the Ranger course. It is known as A Chicken To Go. The Ranger instructor holds up a live chicken, wrings its neck, bites off the head, and drinks the blood. He then eats some of the raw meat. The purpose is to demonstrate to the students that in the event they are isolated and desperate for food and water, this technique would be effective for survival. It is said that Uncle Burnie never bothered to wring the chicken's neck first.

Over the years, I have heard many stories about Burnell and his exploits. I feel that I have had the privilege to be witness to the best. I was flying with Wild Bill Meacham. We had made a two-ship insertion of a double ("heavy") team, twelve LRPs, into an LZ in the mountain jungles, about fifteen miles west southwest of Eagle. Burnell was the TL. The mission was to observe and report on enemy activity in the area. The insertion was uneventful, and no problems occurred on the first day. The next morning, Meacham and I landed with a second aircraft on the Acid pad and shut down to begin the day's standby. After shutdown, we walked up the hill to LRP operations to check in. We were told by L T Williams that Burnell's team had heard significant movement during the night. The team was moving in the direction of the noise to determine the size and makeup of the enemy unit. We waited, something that we did a lot of on LRP missions.

Late that afternoon, we once again found ourselves in operations. Burnell called in at a whisper as the LRPs always did.

"Windy Guard Six, this is Windy Guard One-Six."

L T Williams answered, "One-Six, this is Guard Three. Go ahead."

"This is One-Six. We have located a battalion-sized force of NVA regulars."

"Thank you, One-Six. We have your location plotted."

Captain Fitts walked in just as the next transmission came in. Burnell whispered, "Should I hit 'em?"

Williams whispered back, "What?" at the same time looking at the rest of us with a puzzled look.

The radio hissed, "I have them surrounded; I want to know if I should hit 'em."

Meacham looked at me and said, "Let's go."

Captain Fitts had just crossed the room and taken the mike from L T Williams, turned and said to Bill, "Where are you going?"

Bill, matter-of-factly, said. "Out to pick Burnell up, hot."

Fitts said, "Are you crazy? They only have twelve men, and an NVA battalion is about 550, I'm not going to let him hit them!"

Meacham said, "Captain Fitts, that's Burnell out there. You only have two choices. One is you can tell him to hit them, and then we will have to pick him up hot. Two, you can tell him not to hit them, and in five minutes, he will call you and tell you that he has been spotted and is in contact."

Meacham looked at me again and said, "Let's get ready."

We went down the hill to the pad and got the two aircraft untied. We strapped in and put our helmets on. I reached up and turned the battery switch on to check the "shotgun load."

Starter generator in the start position.

Fuel on.

Throttle set, just below the flight idle detent.

Battery off.

I knew it was set, just like it always was, but it was something to do while we waited. It had only been two minutes. Three minutes passed. Then four. Five ticked off, and nothing happened, maybe, just maybe . . . Captain Fitts then ran out of the door to the LRP TOC; he raised his hand over his head, index finger pointed skyward, and moved the arm around in a circle. The signal to crank. Burnell was in contact!

Battery on.

Starter trigger engaged.

I could hear the *tick, tick, tick* of the ignitors, then the *whoosh* as the fire started in the engine.

Battery voltage good.

Exhaust gas temperature climbing.

Rotor blades starting to turn at about 8 percent N1 speed.

Forty percent N1 speed release the starter.

Start fuel off.

Throttle flight idle.

Attitude indicator cage.

Inverter on.

The oil pressures are good. The hell with the rest. Bill took the controls and finished the run-up. I turned on the radios. The peter pilot's task was to have the radios on by the time we got the thing in the air. I didn't need to talk to the other aircraft; they knew that we'd go first since we were parked closest to the direction of takeoff. I made our call, "Eagle tower, Kingsman Two-Five. Flight of two on the go . . . Acid pad." There were only two situations when the tower would tolerate an aircraft's taking off and then calling that it was "on the go." One was Dustoff (Medevac helicopter), and they had learned to tolerate it from the LRP pad. We were trying to keep Eagle Dustoff's business down.

As we gained altitude, I looked to the south to see the Charlie-models climbing out from the Castle. They were always notified as soon as a team came in contact, so they could be in the air with us. It was good when the guns could get the jump on us; the Charlie-models were just not as fast as the slicks because of the weight of the armament they had to carry. They could hang with us in level flight but to climb and build airspeed at the same time, there was just no way they could keep up.

It took us about eight minutes to fly out to rescue them. The NVA, not Burnell. He did not need rescuing. The team had wasted about 130 of them by the time we got there, then the guns took over. As the Lancers kept Mr. Charles busy, the team *di di mau*ed (ran) to the PZ, and we extracted them. The final KIA count of the bad guys was somewhere around 360. No losses for the LRPs.

* * *

Monday, 15 July (248 days to go). The sun rose bright and hot, just like every other morning. I stumbled from the tent for my first visit of the day at the local piss tube, a 105mm howitzer casing dug into ground at an angle. The Castle looked no different than it had yesterday. There were still the tent rows, revetments, and buildings. The grave mounds and the rocky orange soil were still the same. I felt just as tired as I did each morning when I got up. But now all the real estate was part of the 101st Airborne. The Kingsmen were now officially declared Screaming Eagles by a piece of paper that someone had signed somewhere. The rebellious nature of the warrant officer told us that we shouldn't accept this without a protest.

As I made my way around the company area that morning, I noticed that the warrants had not stayed up late last night changing the chicken-with-a-sword-up-its-ass patch for a puking buzzard patch. The captains and the CO had. Looking back it was pretty comical, the way we resisted putting on a patch that we knew we would be proud to wear. Maybe we were just afraid that someone might expect us to jump out of a perfectly good aircraft. To an aviator, parachutes should only be used for the purpose of unassing a machine that would not fly any longer. Helicopter pilots did not wear parachutes, and were at peace with the idea of riding that puppy all the way down. About the only thing that we did not have an emergency procedure to cope with was the big fan on top stopping its rotation. That was a remote possibility. In that case, most of us agreed that the best thing to do was to drop your pants and sit on the cyclic stick. The impact with the ground would drive the cyclic up your ass and out your mouth. Since you were going to die anyway, you might as well give the accident investigation board something to wonder about.

The conversion of the 101st to an airmobile division had begun with the formation of the 160th Aviation Group on 14 June 1968. The group commander was Col. Ted Crozier, who managed to induce both fear and pride in the aviators of the group. It did not take long for us to learn that when we were right, he would back us to hell and back. On the flip side, he was not so in love with his pilots that he was hesitant to collect a pound or two of ass when the need arose. A rumor circulated that there was a captain on his staff whose only job was to carry a small scissors around. When the colonel saw a handlebar moustache, he would just point, and the captain would run over and hand the offending aviator the scissors. The pilot would then cut off the curls without a word being spoken. That ended the problem. No more would be said about the incident if the aviator complied promptly.

The rumors of the move south had dissipated with the news that the 101st Airborne Division was to become airmobile. That announcement also brought the news that the 17th Assault Helicopter Company would be redesignated B Company, 101st Aviation Battalion. The reaction from the Kingsmen was one of resistance. Though all of us had the deepest respect for the paratroopers of the 101st, our general feeling was that we did not want to be one of them; being "Airborne" was associated with being a lifer. None of us wanted to be forced into the Airborne mold. Another reason was that the 17th AHC was part of the 1st Aviation Brigade; that gave us an aviation identity, which we did not want to lose. We took as much pride in our aviation identity as the paratroopers took in their Airborne identity. Of course, that's all in the past; there are none among us today who do not take pride in being a Screaming Eagle.

17 July (245 days to go). It was a big day for flying LRPs. We inserted four heavy teams, i.e., teams made up of two six-man teams. Even F Company's two lieutenants went out, leaving the company area practically deserted. The purpose of the mission was to set up ambushes in an area suspected of heavy enemy activity and a possible base camp. Two companies of regular infantry were used as a sweeping force for the operation. They would drive the bad guys to the turkey shoot the LRPs had set up. The teams would have to stay in close communication, as they were to be operating close together. The first day was quiet.

When I got back to the hootch, three letters were waiting for me on my bed. That brightened my day. After reading my mail, I wrote to Jackie. It had started to rain. The cool moisture in the air was a welcome relief. It had been very hot all day. I knew that the rain only meant that it would be more humid tomorrow, but for the moment, it made the oscillating fan I had bought feel like an air conditioner. Don Harris, who lived in my hootch, had picked up a new Turtles tape for me at the PX in Da Nang. I sat on my bunk, having a beer and writing, and letting the music take me back to Jackie.

I closed my eyes and let the music fill my head, and the war went away. The wounded soldiers, the hungry civilians, the greedy politicians, the unseen enemy all disappeared. For a short time, I was alone with Jackie, and there were no smelly clothes that never got quite clean, no days without a shower. Just the two of us alone and far away. Then Poley came by and kicked the leg of my bed. When I sat up, ready to fight whoever had so rudely brought me back, he said, "You, me, 350, LRPs tomorrow."

The good feeling wouldn't come back, so I decided to get to bed after I sucked down another beer or two.

That night, Mike Ware woke up and found a large rat sitting on the end of his bunk, calmly nibbling on his big toe. Mike was introduced to the rabies series of shots the next day. Fourteen days, one shot a day, in the stomach.

During the eighteenth, two of the teams made contact and sprung their ambushes. Burnell's team got three, and Burford's team got six. No other contact occurred. So much for heavy enemy activity.

Friday, 19 July (243 days to go). A much welcomed day off after flying thirteen straight. The heavy teams would be pulled that day, and although I wanted to be part of it, rest was important. I wanted no more of my body shutting down on me. I slept late and hung around the hootch, taking it easy. I read some and drifted off to sleep again. Covered in sweat, I woke up midafternoon. As my mind clawed its way back up from the depths, I had this crawling sensation. I looked down at my chest and I was covered with hundreds of nasty, little red ants. I leaped to my feet and stomped around, managing to get rid of them and getting only a few bites. I shook out my bedding and went to supply and got some bug spray.

20 July (242 days to go). I put in for R & R in Hawaii in December. By that time, I would have served over eight months of my tour; it would be an easy haul after that. The shorter you got, the higher the priority they gave to awarding you the R & R you wanted. And I didn't want to be disappointed.

I had an easy day. I flew four hours in the morning and was finished by noon. I found out that the EM tents were going through a shakedown inspection for some morphine that had been stolen. I was glad that I had not been tapped to help with the shakedown. I would be more than glad to see anyone who was using morphine get nailed, but I did not want to be part of working over our own enlisted men. Too many things might be found that I would not want to see one of our guys get in trou-

ble for. Imagine if they found out that one of them had a
weapon that had not been issued to him. He might use it to kill
some VC or NVA. Worse yet, they might find that an enlisted
man had a bottle of hard liquor all his very own. Still worse, I
might have been the one who bought him the booze.

I got a letter from Jackie. She confessed that she had forgotten to remove my Huey model from the car before summer. I
had mounted it on the rear shelf of our '68 Camaro. In the July
sun, it experienced a meltdown. I wrote back that I would never
forgive her since I had given her specific instructions to remove
it before it got hot. She would know that I was only teasing.

Sunday, 21 July (241 days to go). I was assigned to fly as peter pilot on the Mass run for the Catholic chaplain. It was not
an exciting mission or even a mission where you got a lot of
flight time, but it was a mission I liked to fly occasionally. Mass
was said in the Kingsmen officers club every Sunday at 1800
hours. The club was also the officers' dining facility. As soon as
everyone had finished the evening meal, the chaplain would set
up his portable altar and say Mass for the dozen or so Catholics
in the company who actually attended Mass. I had noticed that
attendance was often in proportion to the number of aircraft that
had been shot up during the particular week. On the way to
Mass, I often received a lot of comments from my fellow pilots
about telling the chaplain to be brief so the club could open up.
Because of missions, there were times that I would miss the
chance to attend Mass. The Mass run meant that we took the
chaplain out to the many firebases, shut down, and waited while
he said Mass for the paratroopers on the firebase. I would attend
each of the Masses he said, and it made me feel as if I had
made up for any that I missed. In fact, operations was considerate of those who went to the various services and tried to schedule them on early missions on Sundays. Some guys attended the
services just because it made one day different from the rest.

It was Dave Poley who told me of the mission assignment. I
asked, "Who's the AC?"

"I am," Dave replied.

I fell out of my lawn chair, laughing.

He inquired, "What's so fucking funny?" He tried his best to
look cross.

I couldn't control my laughter. I kept hearing all the little
wisecracks Dave would make to me about Catholics. Each one
I remembered sent new convulsions of laughter reeling through

my body. Dave just stood there with his hands on his hips, looking down at me with that famous Poley devilish grin. I finally gained enough control to say, "I hope St. Can Opener will find it in his heart to forgive you." When I burst into laughter again, The Dave joined me.

The mission turned out to be an opportunity to witness an act of faith and courage that I will remember the rest of my life. We flew the chaplain from firebase to firebase. Poley surprised me by sitting next to me through each Mass. We landed at FSB Jack, which was located just west of Camp Evans. The chaplain set up for the service in front of rows of benches that had been set up for movies and other such assemblies, lined up on the side of a hill. The slope ran up from rear to front. Soldiers began to trickle into the seats. The priest had no sooner gotten started with his service than the rockets started landing. The crew chief sprang to work getting the blades untied, Poley and I stood, and turned toward the aircraft. Then we noticed that the chaplain was still saying Mass. Dave and I looked at each other and sat down again. We both sat there entranced. This priest had no intention of abandoning his congregation. None of the soldiers bolted for the nearby bunkers. They sat and watched as the chaplain continued the service. The rockets continued to fall. The chaplain proceeded quickly, but did not rush. He finished the service. A number of rockets landed in and around the firebase. None landed near the worshippers. Neither Dave nor I said a word, but we respected the courage we had seen displayed. My own faith was impacted. The fact that no rockets came close to us was not lost on me.

24 July (238 days to go). After two days of log missions, I was scheduled for combat assaults. We were to lift a battalion of ARVNs into an area known as the Salad Bowl, just south of Highway 547 between FSBs Birmingham and Bastogne, and was known for frequent NVA activity. As the operations officer briefed the mission, there were a number of snickers from the pilots gathered in the club for the briefing. The Salad Bowl had received the attention of a battalion of 101st Airborne paratroopers only a week before. Once again, Marvin was headed for another sure-skate operation.

The Salad Bowl's round valley opened to the north. From above it looked like someone had cut a ball in half to form it. The vegetation was thick, lush jungle, hence, the name.

I was flying with Jim Riden in Chalk Three. The PZ was to

east of Phu Bai. We got our load and headed for the LZ. Jim flew the first sortie. The first landing was always the most tense since there was no way to know if the LZ would turn hot. This one was cold. I pulled pitch and took off, trying my best to use as little torque as Jim had on his takeoff.

We were on short final when lead called, "Kingsman One-Six, receiving fire, receiving fire."

All the door guns began seeking targets, but nobody was able to identify a target. Then suddenly as we touched down the firing stopped. When we took off again the shooting started again.

"Two is receiving fire."

Another voice chimed in, "Its fuckin' Marvin, the damn gooks are shooting at us."

"Lead is hit, I'm going down."

I could just make out Captain Senita's aircraft as he kicked the right pedal and dove the Huey back under the flight into the LZ.

Hootchmaid's calm Texas drawl came over the radio, "Lancers are rolling in hot."

A frantic voice from the American adviser on the ground called, "Don't shoot. Don't shoot, that's friendly fire."

Hootchmaid's response was unexcited and immediate, "Roger returning friendly fire."

He held the mike open so every one could hear the whooshing sound of each rocket as it left the tube, further cementing our relationship with our allies. The remaining lifts were cold.

Captain Senita had done a fantastic job of getting the Huey back down on the ground without crashing. On looking over the bird, the crew chief found a grenade wedged under the platoon leader's seat, with the pin pulled. Had they not been shot down, it would have vibrated loose and blown the aircraft up. It gave me one more reason to be glad that I was no longer in the Black Cats. In the Kingsmen, our dealings with Vietnamese were rare.

27 July (231 days to go). F Company, 58th Infantry, got a new company commander. Captain Sheperd assumed command late in the afternoon of the twenty-seventh. Rumor had it that he had been transferred from the line company he commanded because his troops had put out a contract on him. He immediately announced his new rules. It seemed to me a bit unwise to treat these hardened soldiers like basic trainees. Morning PT? Mandatory formations three times a day? Passes to leave the company area? This captain was one "beaucoup *dien cai dau*" (very crazy) mutha. By the time the first formation was over, Ho Chi Minh had a better chance of succeeding Johnson as president than Captain Sheperd would have had if the LRPs had anything to say about it. By sundown, they hated the bastard.

Monday 29 July (233 days to go). I wrote to Jackie for the first time since the twentieth. The days had slipped by with fifty hours of flight time and some long days on log missions. As I wrote, I listened to my stereo with a set of headphones. I was having more and more trouble writing. There was not much difficulty in telling her how I felt about missing her. But real news of what was going on was full of things I did not want her to know; it would just cause her to worry. As I felt my eyes begin to fill with tears, I had to find something else to write about. It would not do for the hard-core LRP pilot to be seen with tears running down his cheeks. I wrote that I had been flying twenty-six of the last twenty-nine days and how the days were running to twelve to fourteen hours of duty time. I was getting used to constant exhaustion. I would drag out of bed each morning to face another long day of having little people trying to blow my ass away. I had gotten into the habit of going to sleep at night with the headphones on and relying on the auto shutoff on the tape recorder.

Jackie had gone to visit Canada, with a friend. I told her that I hoped that she did not decide to stay in order to beat the draft.

31 July (231 days to go). We got word that, during the night, Captain Sheperd, the new LRP company commander, had stepped on a toe popper (a small antipersonnel mine) in the doorway to his tent. His foot was badly mangled, and he would surely be sent home. Dave Poley told me that they were looking for an officer to hold PT formations for the LRPs while Captain Sheperd was laid up. He asked, "Would you like to volunteer, W. T.?"

Dave then recounted the tales of the CID investigation. Apparently, to a man, the response to CID inquiries had been, "Can I help it if the dumb son of a btich put his tent in a minefield?"

Some of the LRPs were a little more direct in their responses. Ray Zoschak told them, "I'm surprised the motherfucker lasted three days." A young private named Linderer was asked if he liked Captain Sheperd. He responded, "I doubt very much if

Captain Sheperd's mother likes him." The investigator then asked Linderer if he had placed the mine in his company commander's tent. "No, I didn't. I wanted to, sir, but I don't like standing in long lines."

By the end of the day, it became apparent to the CID investigators that even the seniors NCOs were not likely to cooperate in the investigation. If anyone knew who the perpetrator was, they were not going to tell. The next day the first sergeant announced that the CID had concluded that at least 40 percent of the men in F Company were psychotic. Another 40 percent suffered delusions of grandeur, and the rest were criminally insane. It made me proud that they considered me one of their own.

The month ended for me with a total of more than two hundred hours of flight time. I had flown on all but three of the thirty-one days. My flight records reflected only the 134.6-hour total that was on the scheduling board. That was the price for threatening to squeal to the flight surgeon.

I found that as the days passed, my attitude became more hardened. In my zombielike state, many times I'd rather sit alone with my music than participate in the partying in the club. I'd noticed that lately my tastes in music were leaning more to the Jefferson Airplane than the Beach Boys. The surfing safaris of Da Nang were getting farther behind me.

That night I wrote home.

Dear Jackie,

Here before me lies another dark and lonely night with the love I hold so dear to me far away.
"And the beat goes on . . ."
For tomorrow I face another day the same as the one that preceded it. And so it goes for another 230 days after that, longing for the love I crave, the love, that this cruel world has torn me away from. My whole existence is in a state of suspended animation, in a cocoon, waiting for the day it is returned to you. So the beautiful butterfly of love can emerge and flutter about the world oblivious to the misery all around it, cause it is protected by an aura of complete love and joy . . .

CHAPTER 6
AUGUST 1968

Thursday, 1 August (230 days to go). We had known for a couple of weeks that our welcome gift from the 101st was going to be a large assault into the A Shau valley. Most of us were very apprehensive about it; the 1st Cav had gotten twenty aircraft a day shot down in April, when they went into the valley. A number of those were blown from the sky by antiaircraft weapons that were inside Laos.

I was assigned to fly with Jim Riden that day. Jim was now under thirty days to go, so I was glad to get any opportunity to learn from him. Jim and I were assigned to fly the C & C ship for the 2d Brigade commander that day. In the back of the command-and-control bird was a console that contained several FM radios, which enabled a ground commander and his staff to fly above the battle and communicate on several different frequencies at once. From one of those birds, a battalion or brigade commander could sit high in the air and run the battle by remote control. The grunts hated those birds for that reason. While these aircraft did allow a commander greater mobility, flexibility, and visibility, the commander who did not get out on the ground with his troops earned little respect, being viewed as sitting up there out of small-arms range with his shined boots on, ordering men to take chances that could cost them their lives. Just because they were in the infantry didn't mean the troops weren't perceptive.

When we landed at LZ Sally on the brigade pad, a captain came out to brief us on the mission and check out the console radios. He climbed in the back and put on a headset. "Good morning, gentlemen. The mission for today is to take the colonel out for a visual recon of the A Shau valley."

I thought, "Oh shit! The A Shau, no guns and single-ship." I began to visualize all those 1st Cav birds being blown out of the sky in huge black and orange fireballs. I reached up to my neck as I realized that I had forgotten to put on my Saint Christopher medal that morning. My fingers confirmed my fears when I realized that there was no chain there. The medal was only meant to be a symbol of my beliefs; I knew in my heart that the Lord was not going to look out for me any more or less just because I had been absentminded when dressing that morning. I recalled Bill Meacham's words about drunks and dumb animals, but the thoughts of the A Shau were still there.

The captain's radio checks had been going well. Then one by one the radios in the console began to fail. Jim turned the controls over to me and got out and went in the back to try for himself. It was no use, the radios were out. The captain said that he knew that the colonel wouldn't want to fly without the radios working. The mission would have to be postponed. Jim said that he was sorry, but they were working when we preflighted.

"That's okay, Mr. Riden, I know these things happen sometimes. Go get the console fixed, and we'll go when you get back."

"We'll be back as soon as we can, sir."

Riden climbed back into his seat. He plugged in his helmet and said, "Let's go."

He finished strapping in as I rolled the throttle back to operating RPM. I lifted the Huey to a hover, turned, and departed the pad to north. The airspeed climbed, and I turned toward Highway 1. I kept the bird low-level and headed south toward Camp Eagle. Jim looked over at me when I didn't continue to climb. He did not say anything, he just smiled and shook his head. During the flight back no one said much, and I thought about the amazing odds of all three console radios failing at one time.

When we were clear of the Hue citadel, I heard the electric tone of the UHF cycling frequencies. Riden announced, "You are up on two." That meant he had turned the radio and put my selector on UHF.

"Eagle tower, Kingsman One-Eight. Hue, southbound on One, Lima Lima, for the Castle." I had informed them that I was inbound, low-level, from Hue on Highway 1 and wanted to land at the Castle. Jim's call sign sounded good to me now that I knew it would be my own before long.

"Roger, One-Eight. Report a right base for the Castle, landing to the north. Winds calm, altimeter three zero two one."

"One-Eight, three zero two one. Roger."

On the east side of Eagle, with just the thought of moving the cyclic toward the rear, the airspeed dropped from a hundred knots down to ninety. The Huey responded by popping up to about a hundred feet. I turned to the west on the south side of Eagle and was about to key the mike when tower called.

"One-Eight this is Eagle tower I have you in sight. Cleared to land at the Castle."

I was very pleased with myself for the smoothness of the landing in the revetment. Jim called operations. "Kingsmen ops this is One-Eight down at the Castle, waiting on maintenance."

I rolled the throttle to idle and said, "I'll be right back."

Jim gave me a thumbs-up. I undid my seat belts and bolted from the aircraft for the hootch. I found the medal hanging from the corner of the desk I had built from used ammo boxes. I headed back to the revetment, feeling safe and secure. The avionics guy had just finished replacing all three fox mike radios in the console when I arrived. As I slid my helmet on, I heard Riden asking the repairman what the problem was. He just shrugged.

On the way back to Sally, Jim asked if I had the shits or something the way I had shot from the aircraft. I explained what I was doing and what I thought the problem with the radios had been. Nobody said anything. They either accepted my story or thought I was nuts. There was more and more of that going around lately. The rest of the mission went off without a hitch.

My first view of the A Shau surprised the hell out of me. It was beautiful. It was hard to believe that so much death and destruction occurred here. The valley floor was covered with lush green grass. The only sign of war was the bomb craters that pockmarked the valley floor. We reconned the valley for LZs, at low altitude to avoid the antiaircraft guns on the Laotian side of the boarder. The entire time in the valley was tense. I waited for the volumes of fire that I knew were waiting for us. They never came.

The villages of the valley were A Sap, A Shau, and A Leui, all of which had long since been destroyed. There were the remains of two dirt airstrips, Ta Bat and A Leui, but you had to know that they were there in order to recognize them for what they were. Colonel Hoefling had come on the flight with just the captain who had first met us on the pad. He had shown us the areas he wanted to see on the map. He asked Jim what he thought about how to conduct the recon and asked that we do it without any circling. During the mission, we took no fire and saw no enemy activity.

During the flight back to LZ Sally, I was on the controls. I looked out at the jungles below, and then I got the "feeling." It had happened often when I was in flight school. It occurred less with the more flight experience I got. It seemed to me, though, that as I became a more experienced pilot, the feeling was far more intense when it happened. It is mostly a sense of awe and wonder. You look outside the aircraft and realize it's flying. Then you look down at your hands on the controls and realize that it is you that's making it fly. There is something in man that has caused him to try to fly since before he learned to draw on cave walls. For those of us who have had the opportunity to conquer the skies, that "something" comes out on occasion and causes the feeling. It makes you warm inside and gives you a great sense of power. It amazes and mystifies, yet there is still something in the feeling that makes you feel small and insignificant. Even after thousands of hours in the air, it still returns to remind an aviator of the joy of flying.

When we dropped him at LZ Sally, the colonel reminded us that we should not discuss the areas we had looked at with anyone, not even the other pilots. He wanted no chance of his area of interest getting back to the enemy.

Sunday, 4 August (227 days to go). Right after the chaplain was through with the club that evening, we were told that there would be a mission briefing for all pilots in the company. The CO would conduct the briefing himself. Slowly all the pilots shuffled into the small club. It reminded me of the briefing scenes from the old World War II movies. The club quickly became stuffy from all the warm bodies and cigarette smoke. Rick Haines came in and set up an easel with a cover over it and hurried back out. We knew this must be a big deal because normally only those flying an assault would be required to attend the briefing.

Major Addiss (the CO) walked in briskly and stood by the easel that was in front of the bar.

"Gentlemen, tomorrow we will participate in the insertions that will signal the start of Operation SOMERSET PLAIN. The assault of the A Shau Valley. I will be as brief as possible."

Murder in C Major

SARA HOSKINSON FROMMER

*to Rebecca Carr —
whose family I
enjoyed, too! —
all best wishes,
Sara Hoskinson Frommer*

WORLDWIDE®

TORONTO · NEW YORK · LONDON · PARIS
AMSTERDAM · STOCKHOLM · HAMBURG
ATHENS · MILAN · TOKYO · SYDNEY

With special thanks to Gabe,
to Marcia, and to Captain Charles Brown
of the Bloomington Police Department

MURDER IN C MAJOR

A Worldwide Mystery/December 1988

First published by St. Martin's Press Incorporated.

ISBN 0-373-26017-2

For Fritz Jauch
1921-1983

and to honor my father and mother

ONE

IRONING FOR A CORPSE wasn't Joan Spencer's idea of fun. She hitched up her jeans, tested the iron's sizzle with two wet fingers, and creased the first shirt she touched.

Coming back to live in Oliver should have felt like old home week, but it was turning into pure murder. And something didn't make sense. Ignoring the crease as she jabbed the iron's point fiercely between the buttons, she thought back to that first orchestra rehearsal—had it really been less than two weeks ago?

JOAN RESTED HER VIOLA CASE on the gravel in the dark parking lot and searched the shadows for a way in. The sprawling new Alcorn County Consolidated School dwarfed the limestone Oliver School building she remembered from so many years earlier.

"Thank heaven for small mercies—there's a bass."

Some twenty feet away, a minuscule Toyota was being delivered of a string bass and a long-legged stool by a short, round man who had to be going her way. Joan picked up her instrument and concentrated on catching up with him before he reached his destination.

She made it in time to open the suddenly obvious door for him. Encumbered by an instrument bigger than he was and pointing the stool awkwardly ahead, the little man nodded his thanks and struggled down a long corridor without a word.

She followed, bothered by her sudden shyness. All I have to do is introduce myself, she thought, but she couldn't make the words come.

Her fingertips felt too cold to play.

Suddenly the little bass player stormed a door with the legs of his stool and Joan was enveloped in the cacophony of an orchestra warming up. The bassist was already lugging his burdens up some side steps to the stage of the small auditorium. Balancing her case across two armrests, Joan added it to the others already littering the empty seats. She took out her viola, stretched the shoulder rest across the back, tightened the bow, and gave it a few quick swipes with the rosin. It couldn't need much, as little as she had been playing.

She climbed to the stage and paused, uncertain whether to find a seat or speak to the conductor first. But he didn't seem to have arrived yet. Most of the orchestra was seated, although a string of violinists stood laughing and talking along one side. The first stand of violas had its complement of players. At the second, a balding man with a cheerful face sat alone.

"May I sit here? I don't know how you do things."

"Sure, happy to have you. There are never enough of us."

Joan settled into fourth chair in time to see the concertmaster gesture to the first oboe for an A. She was grateful to discover that this orchestra tuned winds and strings separately, and not a bit surprised when the winds started noodling again before she'd brought her recalcitrant C string under control. Some things, she thought wearily, are the same everywhere.

She realized why she hadn't found the conductor when a woman—about five feet tall, round, and ruddy-faced—hefted herself onto the podium, laid a score on the stand, and picked up the baton. Alex Campbell was her name, Joan knew from the publicity she'd seen about this first rehearsal of the Oliver Civic Symphony season. It hadn't occurred to her that Alex was one of those names.

"Welcome back, everyone," Alex was saying, "and a special welcome to the new people. It looks as if we'll need to schedule some auditions. I'd like to hear all new winds during the coming week. For tonight, please double parts. I prefer to mix strong players all through the string section, but if you care where you sit, sign up for an audition. Yoichi Nakamura, our manager, has the sign-up sheets. Yoichi, do you want to say anything?"

A young Japanese man stood, violin in hand, among the seconds. His eyes danced, and his pointy smile reminded Joan of the delightful *haniwa* figures she had seen only in pictures. When he spoke, his barely discernible accent marked him as foreign born.

"Thank you. Please remember to fill out the registration cards on your stands. Write your name as you want it to appear on the concert program. I will have the sign-up sheets for auditions at the door for you. Also the sign-out sheets for borrowing music. That is very important. We must know where to find the music, especially after a concert. We paid two hundred dollars for missing rental parts last year. Next week I will bring you a personnel list and the rehearsal and concert schedules for the whole year. Thank you very much."

He didn't quite bow as he sat down, but Joan thought his quick look at his chair was not altogether to see if it was still there. She wondered whether he was one of the Suzuki-trained violinists now beginning to pepper American orchestras.

"Are we tuned? Yes?" asked Alex. "Then we'll begin with the Schubert."

The Schubert turned out to be the Great C Major Symphony. They read straight through the first three movements, interrupting only when a whole section of players was hopelessly lost. The beginning wobbled as September beginnings do among musicians who spend more of their summer in swimming pools than in practice rooms. But when the oboe solo danced over the violas' pom-pom-pom-pom at the beginning of the second movement, Joan began to rejoice. By intermission she was very glad she had screwed up the courage to come.

Her stand partner introduced himself as John Hocking, an engineer for one of the two electronics firms in Oliver. His daughter, he said, was over in the back of the second fiddles.

"I'm Joan Spencer. I've just come back to Indiana, but I lived here a long time ago. In fact, I've been wondering if I might know anybody in the orchestra."

"You might. Some of these folks go back as far as you possibly could. Don't let me keep you. I'm a recent arrival, myself. Over there by the punch and cookies you could run into almost anyone."

"I wonder if I'd recognize anybody after all this time," she said, getting up. "Can I bring you anything?"

"Thanks, but I'm trying to pretend I don't want any."

Joan grinned and laid her loosened bow on the stand. With the viola tucked under her arm, she threaded her way between cello stands to a table in the wings of the stage behind the basses. There she accepted a Styrofoam cup and a cookie from a woman whose tailored elegance and coiffure called for formal afternoon tea. Looking ruefully at her own scuffed sneakers, Joan wished she had a free hand to tuck up the hair she felt straggling down her neck.

The only good thing to be said for the nondescript fruit drink was that it was wet and cold. Could she have been shivering only an hour ago? But that had been jitters. An hour's vigorous playing had warmed her from fingertips to sodden underarms.

The cookie, homemade and lacy around the edges, proclaimed at least one sheep among the goats of the refreshment committee.

All around her, old friends were greeting each other. Except for the horns, who were taking advantage of the break to work on a chorale that nibbled at the edges of her memory, and the inevitable trumpet showing off his triple tonguing, the players seemed thoroughly jumbled. Many had left their instruments behind. Only a few of the fiddle players bore the rough, red brand of the chin rest beneath their jaws, battle scar of long hours of practice. Some were too young to have achieved one, but more, she suspected, were amateurs like her, who played for pleasure and stopped short of pain.

Paying the teenagers scant attention, Joan concentrated on people her age or older. No one looked familiar. Hardly surprising, after almost thirty years, but a disappointment nonetheless.

To her annoyance, the shyness had come creeping back. An inner voice needled, You don't belong here. You'll never feel at home again. With a now-or-never feeling, she introduced herself to a white-haired man standing alone.

"Hello. I'm Joan Spencer and I'm new."

"Elmer Rush. So am I."

"New to Oliver, or just the orchestra?"

"Both. My daughter and her family moved here this summer. Then her husband died, and I came to be with her and the children."

Joan blinked. "I'm sure that's a help."

"She makes me feel welcome. And one of the children needs a lot of special care."

She smiled. "Mine didn't, but at times during the past few years I would have sold my soul for someone to help me yell at them."

Elmer nodded. "How old are they now?"

"Pretty well grown. My daughter's on her own, with her first real job, and my son's in high school."

"You're still busy, then."

"Oh, I don't know. Actually, I don't see that much of Andrew. Not that I'd want him in my lap all the time. Generally, I'm glad he's so independent."

They moved back into the orchestra. Elmer crossed behind her to the bassoon section. He would have to audition later in the week, Joan remembered. She wished him luck.

Just as she reached her seat, she felt a hand on her shoulder.

"Joan Zimmerman! Is that really you? What are you doing here?"

It took her a moment to recognize in the rounded features of the tall woman beside her a member of Miss Duffy's sixth-grade class. Then it was easy. Nancy Krebs was now a dead ringer for her own mother.

"Nancy! I wondered what happened to you, but I didn't know how to find out."

"I almost didn't speak. I hardly knew you without your chipmunk cheeks. My dear, you have bones! You must tell me how you do it. Your hair's darker than I remembered, too—or do you help it a little? Skinned back like that, it reminds me of when you wore pigtails. Remember?"

Joan remembered efficient fingers catching every last strand of her hair in french braids so tight they stretched the corners of her eyes. Her own sloppy twist was skewered at the top with a wooden pin and felt in imminent danger of coming undone. She chuckled at the thought of working to cover the occasional gray strands she'd been seeing recently.

It was fun, though, that Nancy noticed how streamlined she was these days.

"I always expected to see you at a class reunion," Nancy rattled on.

"Why? The high school never knew me."

"Never mind, You're here now. Look we've got to catch up on each other. I'd offer you a ride home tonight if I hadn't ridden with another trombone player."

"Nancy, I can drive if you'll tell me where to go. I'd love to talk. You can't believe how good it feels to see someone I know."

"Great. I'll find you after rehearsal." She scuttled back to the trombones. The conductor was already tapping for order.

Joan's stand partner was grinning. "Looks as if you know the one person in this bunch who can tell you more about what goes on in Oliver than the rest of us put together—and I bet she will."

Joan thought back. Even at twelve, Nancy Krebs had known everyone else's business. *I wonder if I've changed as little as that,* she mused.

The rest of the rehearsal dragged. Partly it was because she was eager for the kind of conversation she'd expected ever since arriving in Oliver a month earlier, but partly it was because Alex Campbell apparently thought half a rehearsal was enough for warming up to the music. In this half, she was beginning to work on it, often with individual sections. She began with the long-short-longs of the first movement. The concertmaster and principal second violin debated separate bows and hooking, and Alex concentrated on exact eighth notes, rather than the triplets into which they tended to slide. Then she and the violins attacked the written triplets that rose into the stratosphere at the end of the Andante section.

Looking around, Joan realized that this must be the pattern of Alex's rehearsals. Other people were prepared for it. Several players had books in their laps. A couple of students were bent over homework. The oboists to her right were making new reeds—or were they improving the ones they had? A visibly pregnant cellist was furrowing her brow over intricate knitting. John Hocking had borrowed the music from the first stand of violas to pencil in their bowings.

Unoccupied, Joan found it hard to keep from dozing off. In spite of the long wait, however, or maybe because it gave her a chance to listen, she found her admiration increasing for the musical results Alex was achieving with few words and slight gestures. She made a mental note to practice the tricky places before the next rehearsal. She certainly didn't look forward to evoking audible groans like those she heard from the oboist during the violins' most ragged struggles. She winced at his *sotto voce* comments when the first bassoon dragged behind and hit repeated sour notes in the woodwind choir's answer to the horns.

"Lumbering elephant," he muttered, just too loudly to be misunderstood.

At last the violas—and everyone else—were invited back into the fray, and the first movement concluded in relative triumph.

"Not bad, for the first rehearsal," Alex pronounced. "We'll read the last movement next week, I think, and work on the second. We might even get to the overture."

The discipline of rehearsal dissolved into general chatter and packing up. Yoichi meandered from stand to stand picking up registration cards and the music folders of the confident few who weren't signing them out.

"Do we need to do anything about stands and seats?" Joan asked her partner.

"Audition? Sure, if you want to. I'm not going to bother. Alex knows how I sound, and I have no ambition to sit first."

"No, I'm happy. I meant the chairs themselves."

"Just leave 'em. I don't know how long it's been since anyone here has had to help set up. Some people are even beginning to agitate for pay."

"Maybe I'm out of my league."

"You're fine. I was listening. Say, could you take the music this week and let me have it next time? I know I won't get a chance between now and next Wednesday."

"Thanks. I was hoping I could."

The stage was clearing rapidly, but at the narrow steps Joan recognized the string bass player whose descent was causing a minor traffic jam.

"Come on, shorty, move it," said a curly-headed man holding a small case and patting his foot. It was the supercritical first oboe player. Below him, the little man stopped dead, set down the bass, and looked up.

"Just go, will you?" snapped the oboist. "Maybe you ought to take up the piccolo. Then we'd all get home on time."

Jaw clenched, the pudgy bassist shoved his stool aside at the bottom of the stairs to clear the path. Joan stood speechless as the oboe player hurried down the steps and out the door.

At her shoulder, Alex Campbell said quietly, "If I auditioned on any basis but music, he'd be out. In fact, if *he* played piccolo, I wouldn't put up with him. But a good oboe isn't easy to come by."

"It's really true, isn't it? An oboe is an ill wind that nobody blows good."

Alex groaned. "I haven't heard that one in years. And I haven't met you."

"Don't hold it against me, please. I'm Joan Spencer. I play viola."

"Don't worry. We're almost as short of violas this year as we are of oboes. I hope you won't let this keep you away. He's a fine musician, but tact is not his long suit."

"It won't matter. He's not conducting. I did enjoy this evening. It's been a while since I've had a place to play."

Below them, the bassist had recovered his equilibrium. Joan remembered that she owed him something and went down to thank him for guiding her in. "If it hadn't been for you, I don't think I'd have made the first half."

"I wondered if you were new," he said.

"New? She lived here before you knew where Oliver was on the map." It was Nancy. "Harold Williams, this is Joan Zimmerman. We're old friends."

"It's Joan Spencer now, Nancy."

"Of course. And I'm not a Krebs anymore. I'll tell you all about it."

TWO

By THE TIME THEY SETTLED DOWN in Nancy's roomy kitchen, they had covered most of the vital statistics. Nancy's husband, a quiet professor, retreated into his study as soon as he could without open insult. Joan wondered whether her son Andrew would ever take a course from him at Oliver College, but she knew better than to mention the possibility.

Cats dominated the childless household. A flat-faced, gray longhair blanketed the top of the refrigerator and a tabby kitten wound back and forth between them, rubbing against their legs. A calico that had materialized from somewhere now lay on the newspaper abandoned by the professor. Nancy complained about them in the tones of a doting mother. "Emily over there is death on newspapers. Makes it hard to check my work."

"You write for the paper?"

"No, don't you remember? I draw—always did. I have a nice little business doing local advertising art. Everything from nightgowns to canoes. Not the kind of thing you'd hang on your wall, but it pays well, and I'm good, if I do say so."

"I'm job hunting, myself. No talent, I'm afraid. Just dull capability. I keep hoping someone will recognize it."

Joan could see the wheels begin to turn. Well, fine, although she hadn't meant to hint.

"Don't worry about it, Nancy. Tell me about people. It feels so strange to be back in a place I was sure I'd never forget and not to see a soul I know. Even the elm trees have disappeared, and the old school. What's the same?''

"Everything. It's the same old town, only older. Miss Duffy still lives on Beech Street. She'd be tickled pink to see you.''

"And people our age?''

"They're mostly long gone. Gilbert Snarr is still here, running his dad's funeral home, and Bob Peterson works at the paper.''

"I'll bet you're the only person I'll know, except for Miss Duffy. I'll have to find her.''

"Oh, and Evelyn. Did you see her checking you out at the symphony break?''

"Evelyn?''

"You remember Evelyn Gustafson." It wasn't a question. Joan began to remember that it almost never was with Nancy, not a real one.

"No, I don't think so.''

"Oh, you can't have forgotten her. Anything she did was always better and more important than our affairs. She wore ballet slippers and crinolines to school, and she could fast dance when the rest of us were trying to figure out the box step. Made me green. Evelyn married Sam Wade from Fish Creek—well, maybe you didn't know Sam.

"Anyway, Evelyn and Sam had a thing going even in junior high. She was unbearable when he gave her his high school class ring. Don't you remember? One day she'd wrap it with blue angora yarn, and the next day it was all tape and nail polish. Anything for an excuse to wave it at the rest of us.''

"Mmm." Joan smothered a yawn.

"I knew it would come back to you. She was so smug, even then. When he was training for a chance at the Olympics, she was just like all the girls in the Charles Atlas ad, hanging around the guy with the beautiful muscles, only she had the inside track. And you should have heard her when he went away to school where he could swim outdoors all year long under some famous coach. I think maybe it's the high school Mark Spitz went to. Of course, *he* came here to Indiana for college before he won all those golds. Isn't he a dentist or something? I hear he's never swum again since. Anyway, Sam didn't last long. He dropped it, just like that, I never heard why, and went into the army or the marines, I forget which, and then to IU on the GI Bill. When he came back with a law degree, Evelyn wasn't worth speaking to—much too good for the rest of us.

"After a while, though, wills and contracts and such weren't exciting enough. It got them into the country club, though, and that's Evelyn's meat. And now that he's in politics, she's busy helping him by helping us."

"You lost me back at the wills and contracts."

"Sorry. Sam got himself elected county prosecutor and now he has his eye on a seat in Congress. Then on to bigger and better things, at least if you listen to Evelyn. She doesn't say all that, of course. But she manages to make him sound important at the same time she's putting down not only the job he has now, but the one he's going to run for next."

"What did you mean about helping us?"

"She's got herself in solid with the symphony. It doesn't matter who really licked the stamps. It always ends up looking as if Evelyn did it single-handed. You watch—at break time, she's right in there handing out all the cookies someone else baked. Didn't you recognize her tonight?"

"Not really," Joan said, stifling another yawn. "People have changed a lot since the sixth grade. I don't think I really remember them at all."

"Well, of course not. Silly of me. Sam was Giddy then."

"She sounds like the giddy one."

"No, his name was Giddy—short for Gideon. I think he started using his middle name when he decided to be a lawyer. It always embarrassed Evelyn. But I suppose she was right. Who'd want a giddy lawyer? These days I notice she has him using all three—like William Howard Taft or Norman Vincent Peale. You remember how she was."

"No, Nancy, I don't," Joan said firmly. "Most all of that must have happened after I left. I seem to have blocked Evelyn out of my life."

"Well, you can't miss her. Here we all are at our grubbiest and there she is with every hair in place. She'll fall all over you if she thinks you can do Sam some good."

"Who, me? I'll probably never even meet the man."

"Oh, I don't know about that. You're sitting next to him."

"I don't think so," Joan answered, puzzled. "The man I'm next to introduced himself and that wasn't his name. It was something to do with beer glasses."

"Beer glasses?"

"I should never have said that out loud. I'm learning so many new names right now—addresses, phone numbers—and my old memory system isn't working. He's bald, has a nice smile."

"John Hocking!"

"So much for that system."

"I didn't mean John. Sam's the oboe on your right."

"That awful man who chewed out the bassist for living? Harold somebody?"

"No, Harold's the bass. Runs Aqua Heaven. We bought our saltwater tank from him. Sam plays second oboe. The boor is George Petris. He sits first, and he's just bad news. Although some women manage to find him charming, how I don't know. His wife stuck it out almost twenty years before she couldn't take any more of his playing around, and I don't mean oboe. And last year he stole his own son's best girl. For a while it looked as if Lisa might actually end up as stepmother to her old boyfriend. But George dumped her and she took off sometime last winter—just left town. She's back now, but she not only won't speak to George—she won't give the time of day to any man. You can imagine what people are saying. The sad part is that I think those kids really cared about each other. And Daniel is all right. His mother's influence, I suppose."

"You don't like the man."

"You guessed it. Anyway, Sam's not like George at all, thank goodness. One of him is enough. Besides, Sam's much too good a politician to be rude unintentionally."

"I'll look next week. Tonight went by in a blur." Blurrier by the minute. She felt herself droop with sudden fatigue. Even Nancy noticed.

"Joan, you're tired and I'm just running on. I do remember how it feels. The last sabbatical Art took was the longest year I've ever spent. Never seeing people I knew, not even at the grocery store, just wore me out. I'd never survive in a big city. But I'll bet that after a while some of the faces on the street here will begin to ring a bell for you. And I'll be happy to tell you about people. It really helps if you know their backgrounds, don't you think?"

Joan ducked it. "Nancy, you're right, I am tired. I'll see you next week."

The chatter followed her out to the car. She started the motor and waved, pretending not to have heard the beginning of still another long story.

Soon, however, she would be wishing she could remember exactly what Nancy had told her about George Petris and his affairs.

THREE

JOAN STRUGGLED TO MATCH the oboe's ever more insistent A, but she couldn't budge the peg. Pushing with all her strength, she felt it suddenly give. The string snapped in her face, the bridge flew into a dark corner, the sound post collapsed, and the oboe rose to an unbearable wail. With her hand resisting her efforts to loosen the other strings and relieve the tension on the viola's now unsupported belly, she screamed aloud, "Stop it! I can't!"

Sudden silence. Blessed relief.

Then a voice in her ear.

"Mom, are you okay?"

Lethargy.

"Mom, wake up."

She opened her eyes. "Andrew. I was having a nightmare."

"Really. You were yelping."

Already the panic had faded. She worked to remember. "I couldn't tune my viola."

"That's a nightmare?"

"Silly, isn't it? But that oboe kept screaming at me." Probably the nasty one. George What-sis.

"Uh, Mom, I think I'm your oboe. I put the toast in the broken side of the toaster, and the smoke alarm blew while I was scrambling eggs. It took me a minute to climb up there and shut it off. I didn't think anyone could sleep through that, not even you."

"I wasn't exactly sleeping."

"Sorry. But you were really out of it. How late did you come home last night?"

"Hey, who's the parent around here?"

Andrew beetled his brows and reached down for his deepest baritone. "How late?"

"Very late—I met an old friend, and we talked our heads off. Or rather, she talked and I listened."

"Some excuse."

"No excuse. But I learned a couple of things."

"Like?"

"Oh, mostly that almost no one I used to know is still here. Except my teacher."

"From sixth grade?"

"Back in the Dark Ages. Miss Duffy's probably one of the reasons I think of Oliver as home. She was a born teacher, Andrew."

"I could use one of those."

"Oh, that's another thing I learned. My friend is Nancy Van Allen. Her husband teaches chemistry at the college."

"What's he like?"

"Smart enough to go to bed on time. He didn't sit in on all our talk. Nice enough, as far as I could tell."

"Well, Haynes won't be, if I'm late for school again. You want some cold eggs?"

"Andrew, I'm sorry."

"It's okay. I can get something later. I'll see you at suppertime. Bye, Mom."

Grateful for the how-manyeth time that this echo of his father was very much his own person, she got up to watch him bicycle off, curly head bent and long legs pumping.

She was certainly wide awake now. Cold eggs held no appeal, but the morning paper might get her moving. She scuffled into the slippers that had been a stopgap a year ago, wrapped her robe around her warmly on the way downstairs, put the teakettle on, and retrieved the *Courier* from behind the bushes. Again.

Brushing the dew-laden cobweb from her eyebrow, she plunged into the "help wanted" section. Waded in was closer to it. The bottom was so near the surface that a real dive would have flattened her. "Loving person to care for four active children in my home." "Experienced legal secretary 80 wpm." "L.P.N. for busy physician's office." "Couple to live in residential treatment center for troubled youth."

One advantage to being unemployed—you didn't have to rush breakfast. With a feeling of total self-indulgence, she scraped Andrew's eggs into the garbage and then took her time over a muffin and the funnies. After a quick call to the employment agency yielded no more leads, she set herself free for the day.

The phone book listed three Duffys—only one on Beech Street. What did M. E. stand for? She must have known once, but it wouldn't come.

"Miss Duffy? This is Joan Zimmerman. I was a pupil of yours years ago. I don't know if you'll remember... How very nice of you to say so. No, I'm not visiting. I'll be living here for a few years, I think. Could I come by to see you? Why, yes, I could easily be there at ten, if I don't get lost."

She didn't. Already she had learned that in a town the size of Oliver, she could save her gasoline money. Walking gave her time to get her bearings. And there was something even simpler. The last time she had lived there, driving hadn't been one of her options. No wonder everything looked more familiar from the sidewalk.

Halfway down a long block she recognized Miss Duffy standing on the front porch of the little house she had occupied for so many years. Feet solidly planted, she conveyed by her very posture the calm that had always given her control over rambunctious children. She had never shouted, never sent anyone to the office, never called the principal. Her snapping eyes and that steady calm had done it, plus a quick, quiet wit that stopped just short of scolding.

Miss Duffy must have spotted her, but she just waited on the porch. It fits, Joan thought. On the other hand, how would she know me? I've changed far more than she has.

"Hello," she called, turning onto the little brick path to the house. "It's me, Joan."

"Come here, Joan. Let me look at you. I'm so glad you called."

Joan returned her hug warmly.

She had visited the house on children's errands: selling Girl Scout cookies, trick-or-treating, looking for a yard to rake or a walk to shovel to augment an allowance too skimpy for a movie ticket and popcorn. Today she was welcomed as an adult. And with Margaret Duffy—the "Margaret" came easily as soon as she was invited to use it—she felt like one. The feeling that this was a person who cared about her hadn't changed it all. Yet Margaret Duffy's kind of caring didn't hover; it sat back and waited.

Somewhat to her own surprise, Joan found herself explaining about Ken's death, Andrew's interest in Oliver College, her decision to move to the little house her parents had bought years ago for the retirement they'd never been able to enjoy, and her search for a job.

"What have you done?" Margaret asked, hands folded over her ample lap, little feet crossed in the trim shoes.

"A motley assortment of things. Research assistant jobs before the children were born. A lot of volunteer work after that. Playing in the orchestra for fun, when we lived where there was one. I'm doing that here, too. And then when I had to support us, I learned about the difference between jobs that sound good and the ones that pay. You find out who your friends are when you show up in the A&P as a checker.

Some of Ken's former parishioners thought it was beneath the dignity of their minister's widow. They didn't offer to pay the bills, you understand—just fussed at me about finding something 'more suitable.' I don't think they'd have been bothered if I'd taken a part-time job in the library and starved."

"Did you put them to the test?" The eyes had their old familiar gleam.

"It crossed my mind a time or two. For one thing, my feet hurt. But finally, one of Ken's ministerial colleagues offered me a job in his church. The congregation is big enough to pay almost a living wage to the church secretary—administrative assistant, really—and they wanted someone who wouldn't carry gossip back to the members. Gossip bores me silly; he may have known that. And I suppose he thought I'd know enough about the inner workings of that situation to do a good job. He was right. It didn't occur to me that he might have any other motive, and I'm not even sure he did. I thought it would be fine. For a while, it was."

"But you're here."

"I never expected to leave. I really did like the work. It wasn't very hard, but it took an organized mind and all the diplomacy I could command to keep the nursery school out of the hair of the Tuesday morning circle meeting, and the choir director from coming to blows with the Boy Scouts."

"Mm-hmm." Still, Margaret Duffy didn't push it.

"But I'm here," Joan said wryly. "And with no job at all. It doesn't make sense, does it?"

"Do you want me to ask you why?"

"No. Yes. I don't know." And then it came rushing out, all that she had kept bottled up for months. How the minister, an old friend whose marriage had always seemed solid, had pursued her. How his attentions, at first no more than flattering, had become intolerable, until the day she had fended him off with the letter opener from the engraved desk set presented to him by the last confirmation class.

"I went home in the middle of the day, shaking. I was scared and angry—I don't think I've ever been so angry in my life."

"What did you do about it?" There was the old Miss Duffy calm.

"At first I was too upset to do anything. I paced. I must have gone up and down the stairs a dozen times in half an hour. I told myself I was making a mountain out of a molehill. I didn't tell anyone about it, not even Andrew. Least of all Andrew. Finally I thought I had it all under control. Then, the next morning, when I tried to go to work, I found I couldn't leave the house. I simply couldn't turn the doorknob. And I realized that no matter what he did the next time, I wasn't sure what I would do if I went near him—and that letter opener. So I resigned, and we moved."

"You left town without telling anyone?" Margaret spoke gently, but Joan found it difficult to respond.

"I ran. I'm not proud of that. But Margaret, that man is almost a saint in the eyes of his congregation. He's had community awards galore. No one would believe my word against his. Oh, I was angry enough to want to punish him, but it wouldn't have worked that way. The whole town would have been convinced that I was a sex-starved widow, making it up because I really wanted it to be true. And there was no way I could stay in town and not be thrown together with him—and his wife."

"You may be right."

"Right or wrong, I'm looking for a job here. I have to hang onto what's left of Ken's insurance money for Andrew's college tuition. I was counting on Social Security for some of that, but the new rules will cut him off on his eighteenth birthday."

"There aren't many jobs here," Margaret said. "Students do a lot of them. Do you have trouble because of your age?"

"My age?" A new worry she didn't even want to consider.

"It's the kind of thing you hear a lot at the Senior Citizens' Center. You know, Joan..." She paused. "Why don't you apply for the job at the center?"

"Is one open?"

"The board's been looking a week now. The director resigned suddenly, and she's given us no notice at all. We need an acting director within the week. No one who is assisting is willing or appropriate for the job, and I think you'd bring something to it that those children can't."

"Now you're discriminating on account of age."

"Not entirely, but I can't think of a better place to do it."

"I don't quite know what to say."

"How do you feel about spending time with old people?"

"Just old, or old and sick?"

"Just old. Well, we all have more creaks and leaks than we once did, but the people who come to the center are in fairly good health, at least when they come. Some of us are as sharp as we ever were and some aren't." She smiled. "Some weren't all that sharp to begin with, of course."

Going over to a neat desk, she brought Joan a mimeographed folder. "Here's a list of our programs. And I wonder... You might know one of our regulars, from the orchestra. Have you met Elmer Rush?"

"The bassoon player? He said he'd moved here to be near his daughter and grandchildren."

"That's the one. He spends all day with his granddaughter while her mother works. She's in her twenties—the granddaughter, I mean—but she's retarded. There was a water accident when she was very young, and they managed to revive her just too late, or just too soon, some people say. Sometimes he brings her to the center. It gives him a chance to talk to adults during the day. That's why a lot of people come. A husband or wife is senile or ill, or dead, and they feel lost.''

"Mm-hmm. It's lonely.'' She remembered how empty the house had felt without Ken, in spite of two active children.

"Yes,'' said Margaret, "even for people like me, who are used to living alone. Your friends keep dying. Young people arrange all the right things, but they haven't lived long enough to know what we're missing. Some of them talk to all of us as if we had lost our minds.''

"Before my husband died, I thought I knew what being widowed must be like, but you know, I had no idea at all. I'm sure I don't know what it's like to be older than everyone around me, either.''

"But you know you don't know. Just think it over. I'll be glad to dredge up an old report card, if you need a reference.'' Her mouth twitched at the corners.

Down, girl, Joan told herself. You don't even know their requirements, much less what they pay. But her relief at a real possibility outweighed any such sensible concerns. She collected herself enough to answer.

"Margaret, thank you for telling me about it. Even if it's only temporary, it could mean a lot to me and to Andrew.''

"If you're serious, I'll bring up your name tonight. Then you can apply tomorrow.''

"Oh, would you please?'' The child in Joan had already begun to celebrate. Maybe you can go home again after all, she thought.

FOUR

NANCY CLIMBED INTO the car with her mouth open. "It's been quite a week. How are you? I'm just worn out. This is the only week the painter could come, and you know how that turns everything upside down. He brings assistants and they spread out all through the house. No matter where I go to try to get something done, they've covered everything in sight. I'm putting new curtains in our room—the color is completely different. And you just can't find decent lining in Oliver, or three-inch buckram for the heading. I went all the way to Bloomington for that. They're turning out rather well, though, if I do say so. I finally told the painters they could have my sewing room or my workroom, but not both at once. That's the only way I've managed at all. Every time they give a coat of paint another day to dry, I have to switch from curtains to a big Halloween layout I'm doing."

She paused just long enough to register Joan's surprise. "September isn't early at all for Halloween. I'm already working on Christmas. Oh, and Joan, are you still looking for a job? Because I've been talking with the manager and I think I've found you at least a little one, if you'll have it."

Joan smiled, ready to share her news. "Well," she said, but Nancy cut in quickly.

"Don't say no until you've heard. It isn't much money, but it isn't much work, either, just a few hours every week, and some of them you'd be using anyway."

"Nancy, what are you talking about?"

"The librarian's job. For the orchestra. We finally have the funds to pay someone to do properly what we've been messing up b'guess and b'gosh for years. You order the music, with Alex, of course, and take charge of it when it comes. We have some of our own, but whatever we rent or borrow has to be returned on time and erased, or we're socked with fines. Someone's always losing a part. If it turns up a month later, it might as well not turn up at all. You'd need a better system than we have now. And you'd do odds and ends for Yoichi Nakamura—he's the manager. A Japanese student. He said a couple of words last week, remember? The pay's low, but after all, you're not doing anything else, and it might help some."

"It might at that. But you're wrong about one thing."

"Oh?"

"I am doing something else. Since Monday. I'm acting director at the Senior Citizens' Center." She enjoyed the look on Nancy's face.

"Well, for heaven's sake! You certainly didn't waste any time. How did you find out about it?"

"As a matter of fact, you sent me to it, when you told me Margaret Duffy was still in town. She's my insider. Nancy, it's only been three days and I have a lot to learn, but I think I'm going to like it. If I really fit in, there's a chance that I'll get to stay. On the other hand, I don't see why I couldn't do the orchestra job in the evenings. How do I apply?"

"Oh, that's easy. The orchestra has been asking around and getting no takers for about a month. Tell Alex you're willing and I'm sure it's yours."

At this rate, Joan thought, I could expect the bank presidency to fall into my lap by next month. Nancy was already back to debating wallpaper in the stairwell.

In the parking lot they pulled up beside an old green Volkswagen Rabbit. Joan recognized Elmer's shock of white hair. So he had made it past the tryouts.

"You survived."

"I did. Not only that, I'm sitting first. How's that for an old man?"

"That's great, but seventy isn't so old." She grinned at him.

"I don't remember bragging on my age to you."

"No, I peeked. Congratulations, Elmer. The new acting director of the Senior Citizens' Center is proud of you."

"Well, then, we'll have a chance to get to know each other. Congratulations to us both." He shook her hand warmly.

Onstage, congratulations were restrained at best. Earrings clinking, the former first bassoonist managed a civility that fell a few hundred yards short of cordiality. Joan hoped that Elmer could weather the miffed feelings and that his musicianship would justify a decision to bump someone with seniority in the orchestra. Amateur egos, she knew, were no less touchy then those of the pros. Maybe more so. At least professionals could soothe their wounded self-esteem with cash. Amateurs were all too likely to be donating to the very group that demoted them.

Other seating seemed to raise no eyebrows. From her vague memories of the week before, Joan thought most of the prominent players were the ones she had seen then. Nancy would know, of course, or John Hocking. She found Alex and was welcomed warmly as librarian and manager's assistant, as Nancy had predicted. The job paid a thousand dollars a season—no pittance after all. Diving right in, she helped distribute folders and barely had time to tune before the rehearsal began in earnest.

They read the breakneck last movement of the Schubert, she hoped almost up to tempo. To her chagrin, Joan found that the little practice she had managed in her hectic week of interviews and first, unexpected days at work had been spent on the wrong places. She penciled scribbly stars beside the most glaring difficulties, wondering if she'd ever be able to do them justice.

Then, back they went to the violins' problems. Books and knitting reappeared. Empty-handed again, Joan remembered that she had meant to check out the player married to her old classmate. The oboes had their reed knives and sandpaper out again. Bent to his task, Sam Wade didn't meet her eyes. No wonder the man chose a political career, she thought. That handsome face and wavy hair, graying over the temples, had to be worth at least ten percent of the vote. He'd be the bane of the political cartoonists, though. No feature was irregular enough to caricature. They'd have to label his briefcase or stick a little flag in his hand.

Beyond him she saw George Petris beginning to wind the base of his double reed. And wonder of wonders, Elmer had won him over. At least, they had their heads together and George seemed to be demonstrating his technique. Suddenly, almost fiercely, Alex tapped for quiet. George finished a sentence in full voice, but Elmer quickly leaned forward and slipped the bassoon reed he was making into a bottle to soak. He sat very still, his face reddening. Not wanting to embarrass him, Joan looked away.

Playing or waiting, she was very warm. She mopped her eyebrows with the handkerchief that kept her chin and chin rest from floating apart on a puddle of perspiration.

At intermission, even the awful punch appealed. Yoichi approached her, asking apologetically if she would pass out some new parts during the break. Crunching on an ice cube, by far the best part of the punch, she worked her way around the sections.

It was easier than passing out folders before the rehearsal, because almost everyone had left for a drink or a breath of outside air. The horn chorale haunted her again and the trumpeter was attacking a concerto. John Hocking's daughter, pointed out by her father, was working on her geometry, pencil clenched and tongue between her teeth. Joan slipped the music into her folder, but the girl didn't look up.

When Joan came past the flutes to the oboe section, where Sam Wade was drying his pads with cigarette papers slipped under the keys, her foot tangled with a chair leg and she landed almost in his lap, sending the chair and a stand crashing, music flying, and a reed bottle spinning.

"Are you hurt?" He helped her up.

"Only my dignity." She wished it were true. She hadn't changed clothes since work; one pair of stockings had just joined her stockpile for staking up tomatoes. Almost worth adding to the tomato stakers—watch it, Joan, she thought. He's married, and to a very possessive lady, if I heard Nancy right.

"What klutz dumped my music?" roared a familiar voice behind her.

"Oh, go klutz yourself," she heard herself answering. "It's all there."

Quickly, she set the stand on its foot, collected the pages, added the new ones, and stood the bottle up. She hoped its lid had protected the fragile reeds. She knew how temperamental they could be, and she could imagine what George Petris would say if one of those reeds failed him later. Without looking back at either man, she moved on with the music.

John Hocking was chuckling when she returned to her seat. "I've never seen him at a loss for words before," he told her. "He's not used to people who don't lie down and play dead."

"I'd like to see him muzzled. No one has a right to be so ugly to people." Her own indignation annoyed her. Music, she reminded herself. That's why I came.

Her annoyance increased when she realized that there would be no tuning for the second half. The break had run too long, and the concertmaster was among the laggards Yoichi was shooing in from the cool evening air. Alex didn't wait, but began with the violins and violas.

"Let's take it from the top of the second movement. There are a lot of you, but I want to hear you sound like one instrument. Be with my beat immediately and keep it steady—no accents—just like a machine. It's only piano, but I'll need a little more from the cellos and basses after the third bar." She turned to them. "That's where you have something to say."

With all the hard things in this symphony, thought Joan, here we are rehearsing pom-poms. But by the fourth time through the first few measures, she could hear why. What a simple thing, she thought, and what a difference!

"Now with everybody, please."

Pom-pom-pom-pom, pom-pom-pom-pom, steady as a rock. The cellos and basses introduced the little theme. Then, with the first oboe note, the pom-poms obediently dropped to a well-defined whisper. But the oboe was all wrong, off pitch, lagging behind the beat. Serves him right, Joan thought smugly. Abruptly, he broke off altogether.

Alex's face changed from business to concern. "George, are you all right?"

He tried to answer, but he couldn't seem to work his mouth. "Num," Joan heard him say, into silence as sudden as a General Pause. He was sitting in an odd position, holding his oboe awkwardly. As he spoke, it began to slip from his fingers. The flutist to his right caught it before it could hit the floor.

"He's sick!" she exclaimed. Sam leaned over to support him from the left.

"He needs an ambulance, fast. How far are we from the hospital?" asked Elmer, behind him.

"Not far, but the phones here are all locked up," answered John. "I'll take him."

"I'll help you," Yoichi offered.

"George, I'll take care of your oboe for you. Don't worry about a thing," the flutist told him. He managed to nod in her direction. John and Yoichi half-supported, half-carried him from the stage.

The general hubbub of concern among the remaining members of the orchestra lacked a certain warmth. No one said, "Poor George, I hope he's all right." Comments tended more toward: "He was fine during the break; I talked to him" and "Where'll we get another oboe if he's not back by the concert?" and "Looks like a stroke, or some kind of seizure, whaddya think?" Alex cut through the chatter to ask who knew George's son.

"Glenda ought to," someone answered and was promptly shushed.

"I know Daniel," volunteered the flutist who had saved the oboe.

"Good. Would you phone him, Wanda? As for the rest of us, I doubt that we'll do much in the next half hour. Let's call it a night."

Joan sat staring at George's empty seat, watching Wanda pack up for him and feeling what she knew was a childish guilt at seeing her wish come true. The boor had certainly been muzzled. Much as she disliked the man, she couldn't wish sudden collapse on anyone. No use dwelling on it; she might as well take care of John's viola, which he'd left on his chair, and see what else she should do to close up, since Yoichi was gone too.

"Are you all right?" Sam Wade swiveled to look at her. "You took quite a fall a while back."

"Yes, I'm fine. Just a little startled." In the back of her mind she realized why. The scene she had just witnessed reminded her all too vividly of her young husband's sudden heart attack. Mustn't think of that right now.

"You're Sam Wade, aren't you?" she made herself ask. "I'm told I went to school with your wife."

"College?"

"No, elementary school. Nancy Van Allen says we were all three in the same class."

"Let's see if Evelyn remembers." He looked around vaguely and then spotted the woman whose elegance had struck Joan the week before. A slight jerk of his head brought her to them, at her own high-heeled pace.

"Evelyn, this is—but I forgot to ask your name." His rueful smile melted her.

"Joan Zimmerman—at least that's who I was back in Miss Duffy's sixth grade, I hate to think how many years ago. Nancy tells me you were there, too."

"How interesting. What brings you to Oliver?" The queen greeting the commoner.

"We needed a change and my son wanted to look over the college for next year." Pretty lame, but Evelyn didn't seem to notice.

"Poor boy, he'll have to live in a dormitory. He can't move into a fraternity until his sophomore year, you know."

"I don't think he'll do that." I'm not about to tell this one he might have to live at home, or why, Joan thought.

"Sam's a Mu Tau Kappa man. It's the best on campus. Your son really should get to know those young men."

"I'll mention it to Andrew."

Evelyn turned her back ever so subtly.

"Sam, dear, what happened to George Petris? I was helping Glenda put the refreshment supplies in her car when they brought him out and drove off. He looked terrible."

"I don't know. He was fine one minute and then he couldn't play at all."

"He never could play as well as you. I still don't understand why you're willing to sit second to him. You know, Joan, Sam is a superb musician. The orchestra is lucky to have him. It's sad that he'll probably have even less time for it next year than he does now."

Joan didn't let her have the satisfaction of explaining.

"I'm sorry to hear that. Music is a joy to me. I'd hate to crowd it out of my life. But speaking of time, I should let you go. I still have a job to do here. Thank you, Sam, for picking me up. See you next week."

She left them and began collecting folders, irritated at herself for letting the woman bother her, but not altogether dissatisfied with what she'd done about it. She noticed that almost everyone had left. Alex came to ask if she needed help.

"Thanks, I think I'll be fine. What do you suggest I do about John's viola?"

"Yoichi left his violin, too. I imagine they'll both come back here. If you're finished before they come, would you be willing to take the instruments and leave them a note? The janitor stays until ten. They'll be able to get in until then. You might check with them in the morning if they haven't called you."

"Sure. I'll see you next week, then."

Alex trundled off. Joan wished she'd remembered to ask whether the janitor was paid to clean up after some of the messier players. She found Styrofoam cups, some still containing dregs of punch and an occasional cigarette butt, under a number of seats. Nancy, coming for her ride home, helped her toss the mess into the trash. They decided that the shavings around the oboes' seats were certainly the janitor's job, but Joan picked up the little bottle of reeds she had kicked earlier. She found the lid on the floor and screwed it on tightly so that it wouldn't leak onto the music in the librarian's box.

Just as they were leaving, John arrived. He couldn't tell them much. "Yoichi sat in the back seat with him. I drove."

"It was good of you to go."

"I hope so. I'm afraid he might have been better off if we'd found a way to call an ambulance after all. By the time we got there, he was having a terrible time breathing. Yoichi said his uncle died just like that. He took George right into the emergency room. I only hope they didn't make him wait."

"Why should he have to wait?"

"He shouldn't, of course. It's not like Saturday night. Although, if enough doctors take Wednesday afternoon off, the place is sometimes pretty busy on Wednesday night. I broke a foot once on a Wednesday and I recommend choosing another day."

"They're fairly conservative around here," said Nancy. "There's someone on duty, but they'd much rather wait to treat you until your own physician meets you at the hospital."

"I certainly hope he's all right. Are we ready to go?"

Nancy's self-absorbed chatter let Joan retreat into her own thoughts on the way home. In the house, she dumped the music box in a corner, slid her viola and Yoichi's violin under a table, and flopped into a big chair.

For the first time in months, she unloaded on Andrew.

"It was so...cold. They did all the right things, but nobody seemed to care. Nobody acted as if he mattered. Just their precious music and their own social climbing. I don't know if I want to go back to that bunch, Andrew."

"Are they all that bad?"

"I don't know. I suppose not. It just made me feel sick inside."

"You're thinking about Dad, aren't you?" He hugged her. "He'd tell them where to get off."

She smiled. Andrew still idolized his father as a dragon slayer, at war with pomposity and afraid of no one.

It was true, Joan thought. Year after year, in one parish after another, Ken had stood up to trustees and committees with the moral courage that had sent him marching to Selma in 1965, young and armed only with his unshakable belief in a just cause. She had never tried to stop him, whether it was his job or his life that he put in danger. His death, when it came, had given her no warning after all.

Joan ducked quarrels. The family joke had been "Dad insists on his way, but Mom gets hers." But that had been easy, with Ken to run interference for her. Now tears threatened. She blew her nose loudly.

"I thought I was past all that a long time ago. I'm sorry, Andrew. I didn't mean to do that to you."

"Any time, Mom."

"You're probably right. John and Yoichi were just great. After all, most people who get sick do recover. I'm probably the only one who doesn't expect George to be back and twice as nasty next week."

FIVE

YOICHI SHOWED UP on her doorstep while she was eating breakfast. Joan opened the door wide.

"Come in and have a cup of coffee. I don't have to leave for half an hour."

"Thank you. If it isn't any trouble, I would like that." He didn't smile or look at her.

"No trouble at all. Here you are." She set a steaming mug before him and pushed the sweet rolls in his direction. "Help yourself to a napkin. I gather you got my note."

He sat very still for a moment. "Note? No, I didn't receive any note."

"I left one at the school. All it said was that I had your violin." She pulled it out from under the table. He took it and ducked his head at her.

"I hoped you would know where it was. I came to ask and to thank you. I left you with all the work." That stillness again. He slid the double zipper tabs on the canvas case cover back and forth absently.

"I was glad to do something. How is George, Yoichi?"

His face answered her before his voice could. "George died in the emergency room last night."

"Oh, Yoichi, I am so very sorry." Memories threatened her composure again. Hang on, she thought. Don't go all soggy.

"So am I. They tried to make him breathe again, but they couldn't."

"Was his son there?" Someone—Wanda, the flutist—had gone to call him.

"Daniel came too late."

"What happened, do they know?"

"No, they don't know. And I don't understand how it could happen here."

"What do you mean, here?"

"My Uncle Katsuo died in the same way, in Japan. There they recognized immediately what caused his death. It was *fugu sashimi*."

"Foogoo...?"

"It is a very special fish. It is served raw, prepared in beautiful designs. But part of the fish is a powerful poison. Only people who know exactly how to clean the fish are licensed to prepare the *sashimi*."

Oh, *fugu*. She'd read about it somewhere.

"I remember now. There's a photograph in one of my cookbooks. And something about a tingle. Don't some people think the tingle comes from the excitement of eating something that could be dangerous?"

"It is real, if any of the poison remains in the fish. But after the tingle, the mouth becomes numb, without feeling, and then the limbs also lose their feeling and control. Finally breathing stops, the heart stops, and the person dies."

"Numb—that's what George said."

"Excuse me, please?" He leaned forward intently.

"When George stopped playing, he said 'num.' I thought it was only part of a word."

"Then I am certain. I told the doctors and one of them took me seriously, I think. He is *nisei*—Japanese-American. But by the time he saw George, many poisons could have caused his symptoms."

"Can't they test for it?"

His forehead wrinkled. "I asked them to. But I am afraid it will not be possible."

"Surely, if he ate the fish, they could find the fish."

"That is why I think they do not believe me. Daniel Petris told them his father hates—hated fish. They ate dinner at a steak house before the rehearsal, he says."

"Is Daniel truthful?" she asked.

"As you say, the doctors will soon know what he ate. But I have seen only two people ill in this way. I don't understand it."

"Yoichi, were you with your uncle when he died?"

"Yes. We had spent the day together fishing. We often caught small *fugu*, but he usually threw them back. That day we caught a big one he thought he could prepare safely. It is a great delicacy—very expensive in a restaurant. He refused to let me take the risk, because I was only fifteen. He was my favorite uncle."

"I know how you must be feeling." She told him how George's sudden collapse had evoked feelings about her husband's fatal attack.

For the first time, Yoichi showed signs of anger. His voice rose in pitch, and his careful pronunciation of L and R failed him.

"You think I remember my uncle's death so strongly that I was imagining this similarity?"

"Not imagining. But don't you think there are other illnesses that would cause such symptoms?" I'm not helping him at all, she thought. Why should I try to argue with him? "We may never know just how George died," she tried.

"That is not what concerns me."

"Then . . ."

"If I am right and Daniel is telling the truth, then George did not just die. He was murdered."

Oh, my, she thought. He's more upset than I realized. "Did you suggest that possibility to the doctors?"

"Yes, I did."

"What did they say?"

"Very little. I don't think they will do anything. I think they believe it is my imagination."

"Yoichi, if you truly believe that somebody may have murdered George Petris you must go to the police. Or..."

"Yes?"

"I wonder. Isn't Sam Wade the prosecutor? Couldn't you ask him to investigate? I don't know if that's the way things are usually done, but since he's in the orchestra—he sat right next to George, for goodness sake—he would surely want to help."

Yoichi stared at her, too startled for Japanese courtesy.

"Of course. I should have thought of him." He remembered his manners, glanced away, and thanked her for the untouched coffee and for keeping his violin. "Please excuse me."

She saw him to the door, wondering how much of all this could have anything to do with reality. Surely no one would send to Japan for poisonous fish to commit a murder, much less hide it in a steak. It all sounded very strange, but Yoichi seemed much more in control of himself, and she was glad to have offered him a way to do something.

George Petris murdered. She'd felt tempted herself a time or two. But, as she had said to someone, he was more a petty annoyance than anything else. Could anyone really have hated him enough to kill him?

SIX

"HEY, LUNDQUIST, get your phone."

Fred Lundquist smoothed his thinning blond hair, flicked a crumb from one gray lapel, and covered the distance from the coffeepot to his desk in three long strides.

"Lieutenant Lundquist."

"Fred, Sam Wade's holding for you. He's come up with a weird one. Do what you can with it—he asked for you." Captain Warren Altschuler, chief of detectives, was a realist.

Lundquist waited for the click and answered again.

"Lundquist."

"Fred, this is Sam Wade. I'd appreciate it if you'd respond to a complaint for me."

"What's up?"

"Probably nothing, but officially I'm asking you to look into a suspected homicide. George Petris died last night in emergency. You know him?"

"The Greek restaurant?"

"No, this one's a professor, but I knew him from the orchestra. He collapsed in the middle of last night's rehearsal. A couple of people took him to emergency and he died almost as soon as they got him there—the hospital says heart. One of the fellows who took him over is convinced he was poisoned with some Japanese fish. Yoichi Nakamura—our manager—very conscientious, but it sounds to me as if he's off the deep end on this one. I have to respond, though. I sat next to Petris, for Christ's sake."

"Yeah, sure, I'll check it out. You want to spell those
names for me?"

Sam spelled them.

Keep the public happy for the politicians. Wade didn't
think there was anything to it, but he didn't mind tying up
your day proving it to a worrywart. Lundquist picked up the
phone again and dialed.

"Mr. Nakamura? Detective Lieutenant Lundquist, Oliver
Police Department. The prosecutor has asked me to investigate your problem. Yes. I'd like to come over to ask you
some questions. Your address...? I'll be there."

He didn't hurry. The whole thing sounded like a hand-
holding job, not an investigation, and it wasn't the first time
he'd had that sort of call recently. At fifty, a Democratic fish
in stagnant Republican waters, Fred Lundquist knew he'd
never make captain, much less chief. He'd long since lost any
illusions about the merit system. His outstanding record in
his years of big-city experience had little to do with the real-
ities of starting over in a place like Oliver. Party aside, being
anything other than an Oliver native counted against him. If
Wade really suspected a homicide, particularly one that a
good detective could get credit for cracking, he'd call on a
Deckard, not a Lundquist. In the near-campus traffic, he
took his time and meditated on the advantages of taking an
early retirement.

He could afford it. The divorce had left him remarkably
unencumbered. No child support, not even alimony. She had
the house.... He'd probably never be able to swing a house
again. If she'd stuck it out, if they'd had kids...if. He'd
thought moving back to a smaller town would help, but even
here she couldn't take being a cop's wife. Or could she?
Maybe she just couldn't take Fred Lundquist. He wasn't all
that fond of himself some days.

A lot of guys had small businesses set up, more in preparation for retirement than anything else. You could see some of them becoming more and more involved in their moonlighting—and less and less effective on the job. Burned out as he was feeling, he didn't think he could hold up his head if he let that happen. Not that he had anything to worry about. The closest thing to moonlighting he had going was the occasional sourdough he baked for Catherine's Catering. In his present mood, slapping the loaves around appealed to him in a therapeutic sort of way—but a future of nothing but baking? He shuddered.

He turned into the narrow street and swerved to avoid four Muslim girls, heads covered and long skirts swaying gracefully as they walked to class, oblivious to sidewalks and oncoming traffic. Ten years ago, he thought, a group like that would have turned heads. Now they were commonplace. Foreign oil was flooding even this small college town with new students.

Nakamura was waiting for him on the front porch of the rambling house. They passed half a dozen mailboxes by the front door and climbed two flights to an apartment carved out of an attic. At five-eleven, Lundquist could stand erect only in the center of the single room, furnished even more sparsely than his own place. Nakamura slipped out of his shoes so smoothly that Lundquist almost missed it. For a moment he considered following suit, but he repressed the impulse. Nakamura seemed not to notice. From a corner he brought a large cushion covered in rough cotton.

"Please forgive me. I almost never have visitors. If you are uncomfortable, I will be happy to borrow a chair from my neighbor. Will you have some tea with me?"

"Thank you. This is just fine." Lundquist planted both feet on the floor and leaned forward, ignoring the peculiar angle of his knees. "Suppose you tell me what happened."

"It was during the orchestra rehearsal last night," Naka-mura said, kneeling on the floor, his back straight. "The first half was just a rehearsal. No problem. George—Mr. Pe-tris—was playing very well. He usually did. I spoke to him during the break at eight-thirty and he was fine then, too. But when we started again, he couldn't play and almost dropped his instrument. A viola player drove him to the hospital and I went along to help. He died only a few moments after we arrived."

"Did a doctor see him?"

"Yes. Dr. Ito was examining him when he died."

Somewhere, a teakettle burbled and whistled.

"Excuse me, please." Nakamura rose and disappeared behind a screen.

"Did he give you an opinion about the cause of death?" Lundquist called.

"Not me." Nakamura came back carrying a round tray with a plain brown teapot and two cups without handles. Kneeling, he set the tray on the floor in front of Lundquist. "He told Daniel Petris that it was his heart."

"And you think?"

A long pause. Nakamura kept his eyes on his hands as he poured the tea.

"I don't know what to think," he said.

Lundquist inhaled the green tea, wishing it were coffee. Give me strength, he thought. Now I have to drag it out of him.

"Thank you," he said aloud. "Mr. Nakamura, you called the prosecutor's office."

"Yes."

"Why?"

The pause was even longer this time. Nakamura stared into his teacup.

"I was afraid someone had murdered him." His voice was almost inaudible.

Lundquist too spoke softly.

"What made you suspect that, Mr. Nakamura?"

Maybe it was the tea. Maybe it was the difference between "think" and "suspect." For whatever reasons, the young man stopped hesitating.

"Dr. Ito didn't see him in the orchestra. By the time he saw him, I'm sure it was his heart. But I heard a fine oboe player suddenly lose his lip and then saw him lose control over his fingers, and my assistant heard him say the word 'numb.' Then he could no longer speak at all. We had to help him to the car. He never cried out or complained of pain. He didn't hold his chest or stomach. In the car, he was scarcely breathing. By the time we arrived at the hospital, he couldn't move at all."

He paused. "I don't know how to explain it. I am not a doctor. I can only tell you that the death of George Petris was nothing like the death of my friend's mother. She died of a heart attack, and I remember it clearly. But everything that happened to George happened to my uncle, who ate a poisonous Japanese fish. It is called *fugu* in Japanese. I looked it up in my dictionary for you. You call it a puffer fish."

Something vaguely familiar nudged the back of Lundquist's mind. Where had he read about puffer fish recently?

"What did Dr. Ito say—did you tell him about your uncle?"

"He said it was possible."

"Even if Mr. Petris did die from eating this puffer fish, why would that make you suspect murder?"

"No place in Oliver serves Japanese food. His son says he ate steak last night and only fresh vegetables. If he died from this poison—or even from one of the others like it—I don't

think the poison could have been in his food unless someone put it there.''

"Do you know if he had any enemies?''

No answer. Nakamura poured more tea.

"Mr. Nakamura, help me. I can talk to the people you
mentioned, but I might as well go home if they won't tell me
what they know. You called us, remember?''

"I don't know anything. But I think that very few people
liked George Petris. He was not . . . a courteous man.''

"That's all? People don't kill people for their manners.
We'd have daily slaughter on the roads if they did.'' He heard
his own words. All too close to the truth.

"I don't think anyone would want to kill a man for the
things I have seen. But I wonder if a person who is so insen-
sitive in small matters is not also unkind in larger things. I
don't know if anyone loved George. I will not be surprised
to learn that someone hated him.''

"Was he married?''

"I don't know. No one mentioned his wife.''

"How did the son react—Daniel, did you say?''

"Yes. He said almost nothing. He didn't want to look at
his father. I asked all the questions. The doctor said they
would keep George's body for an autopsy because he died so
suddenly. Daniel said, 'All right.' Then he left.''

If it was Daniel, they were looking for a slow poison.
Lundquist's legs were beginning to cramp. He tried a new
position.

"What time did the rehearsal begin?''

"At seven-thirty.''

"And Petris wasn't sick until after eight-thirty?''

"That's right. He even had some refreshments. I talked to
him then.''

"He what?''

"Oh..." The light dawned. "I didn't think of that. The orchestra has a cold drink and some çookies during the rehearsal break.

"How is that set up? Do you serve yourselves? Who provides it?"

"The women of the guild bring it in and serve it to us. Last night Mrs. Wade and Mrs. Wallston were there."

"Do you know their full names?"

"Mrs. Wade is Evelyn—Sam Wade's wife. I think it's Glenda Wallston. I don't know her husband."

"Did you see which of them served George Petris last night?"

"No."

"Who cleans up afterwards?"

"The women who serve." Nakamura returned his cup to the tray. Lundquist followed suit.

"Do you have any reason to suspect one of those women?"

"No..." It was not all convincing. Lundquist waited.

"I have no reason to suspect anyone. I only think of my uncle. He lived only a few minutes after eating that fish on the dock, instead of taking it to someone who could prepare it safely. And a few minutes after the refreshments were served, George became ill. Maybe someone else was there when he picked up his drink."

"A player?"

Nakamura sat silent, not meeting his eyes.

"Can you give me a list of the members of the orchestra?"

"Yes. I had prepared the lists to hand out last night, but I forgot to do it. They were with my violin when I picked it up this morning."

"You went back to the school?"

"No, I went to the home of Joan Spencer, my new assistant. She kept everything for me." He knelt by a small cupboard under the eaves and brought out a neat list of names, addresses, phone numbers, and instruments. "She took over after I left. She says she knew about the fish, too, from a cookbook. Her name is there with the violas. I added the address and phone of the place she works."

"Thank you. You do meet each week at the high school?"

"Yes. I assume we will rehearse next week. I don't know whether we can find another oboe by then."

Lundquist's joints creaked when he stood up.

"Thank you for your help, Mr. Nakamura. I wish I could tell you that I am sure we'll find out what happened, but I'm not. I'm certain the prosecutor will proceed if we discover anything that confirms your suspicion." Listen to me, he thought. I should go into politics myself.

On the way back down the stairs, the cooking smells of a miniature United Nations set his mouth watering. He promised himself lunch at the new Lebanese place before checking back at the station and beginning the work this nebulous investigation would involve. Hospital first, for some hard facts. Then, just in case there was anything to it, he'd better take a look at the school and pay a visit to Daniel Petris. He might talk first to the Spencer woman. She seemed to have picked up the loose ends. The school janitor would have wiped out any physical evidence, unless by some unbelievable luck the drinks had been served in glasses. Even so, they'd be clean by now, especially if one of the two who served had had it in for Petris. No longer convinced that Nakamura was making it all up, he still saw little chance of uncovering much. It was a typical Lundquist assignment, all right.

SEVEN

To Joan's relief, the center had been quiet in the morning. She was grateful to sink into herself for long minutes without any need to hide her feelings. In a few minutes, she knew, the women—mostly—would arrive to open the Senior Craft Shop.

It would be an afternoon of unforced companionship with no program to push, as the knitters and quilters and crocheters plied their needles together while waiting for the few loyal customers who had discovered this inexpensive source of handmade gifts.

An hour later, the shop was in full swing. Customers were indeed scarce, but nobody seemed to mind. As she had suspected, conversation took precedence over cash. A pregnant woman buying baby booties was being instructed by the diminutive top-knotted knitter selling them. "We'll have to keep an eye on Annie," Joan teased. "She's converting the customers."

"Never you mind," said Annie. "I'd rather teach someone how to knit than sell booties any day. You find a color you like, honey, and I'll help you make a sweater and hat, too. That quaker stitch pattern 's older 'n you are. It's mighty sweet on a baby, and not a bit hard."

The young woman smiled shyly, eyes sparkling. "Would you really teach me? I bought some yarn and I've been trying, but I get it all wrong. I'd love to make something for the baby."

"'Course you would. And if you come when I'm not here, there's half a dozen others could show you."

When the mother-to-be left, Joan suddenly recognized her as the cellist who had struggled with her knitting during the orchestra rehearsal. And next through the door was Elmer Rush, pushing his granddaughter in a wheelchair. Joan greeted them warmly.

"I've been wondering when I'd see you here."

"Julie likes to come on craft shop days. She brought her newest potholders, didn't you, punkin?" He leaned down and stroked the girl's short hair.

"Oh, I'm glad. That's what I want to buy today."

Julie beamed pleasure. She held out a package of bright colors. "I make 'em."

"They're very pretty. I like the blue ones best. And the red ones. Do you have two of each?"

Julie looked at Elmer. "Here's a blue one, Julie. Now find another one just like it." To Joan he said, "She's learning colors with these things. That's why each one in this batch is all one color."

"I like them plain. It's a long hard job, isn't it, Elmer? How old is she?"

"She'll be twenty-seven next month. It's really very kind of the ladies here to let her in on their craft sales."

"I don't think they're sticklers for rules."

"A blue one!" Julie said loudly.

"Good girl. Now look for a red one. Good. And another red one."

Julie proudly held out the four potholders to Joan. "I make 'em."

"Thank you, Julie. How much do they cost?"

Julie looked at Elmer again. "Tell her a quarter, Julie." She did. Joan hunted up her purse and sorted out four quarters while Elmer settled Julie at the table. She pocketed the quarters and began almost immediately to stretch red jersey loops over the prongs of her metal loom.

"She's set for a while now," said Elmer. "She'll need help for some of the weaving, but she can do this part alone."

Already the women at the table were talking to her. Elmer turned back to Joan. "I heard on the noon news that George Petris died."

"Yoichi came to pick up his violin and he told me."

"It was so sudden."

"According to Yoichi, they barely made it to the hospital. He stopped breathing and they couldn't revive him."

"Maybe it's just as well." He looked over at Julie.

"Do you really mean that, Elmer?"

"Some days I think I do. If they'd just brought her back a little sooner. Most people either drown or are fine. But Julie..."

"How did it happen?"

"Oh, the pool hired its usual crew—good enough kids, a little whistle happy. Then this hotshot. Thought he was God's gift to women. Scrawny crew-cut kid with shoulders and a tan. He was supposed to be guarding the kiddy pool at the club where Bob—my daughter's husband—used to like to play golf. Martha would go out on the course with him and she'd have the babysitter take Julie to the pool. That day she got caught on the bottom of the pool and not a soul was paying attention."

"What about the guard and the sitter?"

"They were drinking and necking on the lifeguard's bench. Seems she'd been packing vodka in Julie's little beach bag all summer. When she'd show up, he'd volunteer for the kiddy pool. The other guards thought it was pretty boring, and they knew he had a girl, so no one checked up on him."

"Couldn't anyone see them?"

"The little pool was around the corner. That's why they needed an extra guard."

"What finally happened?"

"My wife and I drove in from Palo Alto to surprise Martha and Bob. When we found them gone, we knew where to look and I figured Julie would be at the pool. She was sweet as she is now, and sharp as a tack."

Julie, opening and closing her mouth in concentration as she struggled with the obstreperous loops, looked up suddenly, smiled at Elmer, and went back to her task.

"Couldn't they do anything for her?"

"Oh, yes. When she was in a coma for so long, one physical therapist taught us exercises to keep her muscle tone and flexibility. The woman wouldn't let us quit. Said if we did, Julie'd spend the rest of her life in bed, all twisted. She has a lot compared to that and she improves a little all the time. But it's very slow, even now."

"Will she ever walk?"

"She walks, but it's slow. The wheelchair is handy, that's all. Kind of a big stroller."

"Elmer, what happened to the lifeguard and the girl?"

"He was under eighteen. Had his hand slapped as a juvenile. They charged him with criminal negligence or whatever they call it for juveniles—I think only because of the alcohol. Lost his job, of course, and went back home on some kind of probation. The girl was eighteen. She paid a fine and served a few days."

"That's all?"

"That's all. I wonder how they live with themselves."

"Do they know?"

"They knew then. Maybe they've managed to forget." His lips tightened and the fingers of his right hand tapped a steady rhythm on his thigh. "I only wish we could."

"Maybe George *was* lucky." Maybe Ken was, too, she suddenly thought. But she instantly rejected the idea. Maybe we're all lucky not to have lived in Hiroshima, or during the Spanish Inquisition. While I'm thinking lucky, why don't I think them back alive and well, and Julie bright and active, as she would have been?

"Maybe," Elmer answered her spoken words. "But you know, I love her and I'm glad she's here, even like this. Selfish of me, isn't it?" His faded blue eyes glistened.

"She's lucky to have you, Elmer. Any girl would be." She gave him a quick hug. Not quick enough.

"Look out, look out," said Annie. "That man'll charm the socks off you and leave you checking to see if you still have ten toes."

Joan blushed. Elmer grinned at her. "No privacy around here. Peddle your knitting, Annie, and give a feller a chance."

It was a long time since anyone but Andrew had teased her. It felt good.

She didn't notice the door opening again until Annie nudged her with a knitting needle.

"There you go, Joanie. This one's more your type."

"Go on," Joan said, laughing, but a moment later she had to admire Annie's taste in Vikings. The tall man looking down at her and calling her by name had blue eyes that were anything but faded, and something about his mouth reminded her a little of Ken.

LUNDQUIST, ENTERING, saw a radiant woman whose warmth reached out to those around her. He had no trouble picking her out; except for the girl in the wheelchair, she was the only person in the room under sixty.

"Mrs. Spencer? Detective Lieutenant Lundquist, Oliver Police. Is there a place we could talk for a few minutes?"

"Yes, of course. Come into the office." She exchanged glances with the man next to her and patted the girl's shoulder.

He felt the eyes of all the old ladies bore into his back as he followed her to the tiny room with a desk and two chairs. She beckoned him to one that looked sturdy enough for his frame and sat down in a canvas contraption he would have been less willing to test.

"How can I help you, Lieutenant?" Wisps of dark hair had strayed from a wooden clasp to curl around her ears. Her voice and smiling eyes more than compensated for a nose with a slight but unmistakable similarity to a ski jump.

"I'm checking into the death of George Petris."

"Yoichi did go to the prosecutor, then?" she asked.

"Yes. How did you know?"

"I'm afraid I suggested it."

He waited.

"He was so upset. And he was convinced that George had died the way his uncle died—did he tell you all this?"

He nodded.

"It didn't sound very likely, but I thought maybe Sam would know what to do. I'm glad he didn't dismiss him without doing anything at all."

"No, he didn't." He dumped it in my lap, instead. "At this stage of things, I don't know what we're dealing with. I may need to talk to you again, but right now I have only a couple of questions."

"All right."

"You're Nakamura's assistant? He says you were probably one of the last people at the rehearsal."

"Yes, that's right. I was the last person there, except for Nancy Van Allen, who rode home with me, and John Hocking, who came to pick up his viola after driving George to the hospital."

"And the janitor?"

"Hadn't arrived yet."

"I'm especially interested in the refreshments that were served during the intermission. Were there any leftovers?"

"There might have been. But surely... We all had them. There was nothing fishy about them. I mean..."

"Not literally. Sure. But the preliminary medical report is not inconsistent with poisoning of some kind."

"Oh. You'd have to ask Evelyn Wade about leftovers. Or Glenda somebody. I don't know all the names yet."

"What about cups?"

"Styrofoam. They all went into the trash."

"Exactly what was served?"

"Chocolate chip cookies and something wet and horrible. Kool-Aid, maybe. It was fairly bitter both times I had it at rehearsal. I think you could put anything in it and nobody would notice."

"Do you know why anybody might want George Petris dead?"

She hesitated. "I met him only a week ago. I found him very unpleasant and I heard gossip about him that might suggest several people. He was a me-first kind of person. Somebody might have resented coming last. Even I..."

He raised his eyebrows. "Even you...?"

"Only a few minutes before he fell, I was wishing terrible things for him. It's silly, but I can't help feeling that it's all my fault." There was no smile in her eyes now.

"Did anyone like him?"

"I'm told that some women found him irresistible. And, you know, Elmer Rush and he were getting along very well last night. He's the man with the retarded grandchild over there at the crafts table. He sat behind George."

"Old friends?"

"No, Elmer is new in town. I imagine they met last week."

"You mentioned gossip."

"Nancy was telling me a rather involved story. I'd rather you asked her. I'd never get it right, even if it's true."

She looked uncomfortable. He didn't push it.

"I wonder if he didn't just get sick," she said. "People do, you know."

"It's certainly possible." I'm going through the motions to keep old Sam looking good, that's all. "By the way, Mr. Nakamura mentioned that you had a book with some information about that fish of his."

"Yes, a cookbook. Would you like me to hunt it up for you? It's still in the moving boxes."

"I'm not sure how much use it will be, but I'd appreciate it."

"That's all right. If you aren't in a hurry, though, I'll wait until Saturday to tackle those boxes."

"No hurry. It's a long shot. I'll come by your place Saturday."

She saw him to the door. He considered stopping to talk to the old man but decided he'd keep. Several faces turned blankly from the television set tuned to one of the soaps as he passed their upholstered corner. To a bridge foursome deep in a postmortem he didn't exist, but the old ladies at the crafts table, who had heard him announce himself, weren't missing a thing. Under their scrutiny he felt like a teenager on his first date.

She caught the expression on his face. "They are rather intimidating, aren't they?" She grinned. "They were giving me a hard time just before you came in. It's like having a whole crew of big sisters."

"Joanie, we're just looking out for your interests," said a plump woman behind the cash box.

"And Elmer's," another put in.

"You're terrible." She was laughing now. Not an embarrassed laugh, but a comfortable one among friends. He enjoyed watching her.

"Saturday, then," he said, deadpan. Abandoning her to them without mercy, he ducked out the door.

EIGHT

THE SHOWER MUST BE ICY by now. Joan called up the stairs, knowing full well he couldn't hear her.

"Andrew, supper in five minutes."

The water stopped. ESP, maybe. She heard a muffled acknowledgment to her second call.

He appeared, shaking his wet head, puppy-like. Still barefoot, but dressed in a soft blue shirt, clean jeans, and a denim vest, he clearly had plans for the evening.

"You look reasonably spiffy."

"Clean clear through. What's for supper?" He pulled up his chair.

"Pork chops, baked potatoes, salad, and apple crisp."

"Smells great. Okay if I pass on the dessert?"

"Sure. Have it for breakfast. Why?"

"Got a date. Might need the space. You don't need the car tonight, do you?" He speared a pork chop.

"You can have it. Where are you going?"

"I'm not sure yet. I just met this girl today. I've seen her around school—she's a senior—and this afternoon she was hanging out over at the Student Union, on campus. I think her dad's a professor. Chem or bio, I'm not sure. Say, Mom, people were really talking about Mr. Petris today. You should have heard all the garbage they were saying."

"What kind of garbage?"

"Well, you know. You do know, don't you? I mean, what happened to him?"

"I know he died. I heard that this morning."

"So did everyone else. I guess it was on the radio or something. And nobody liked him. The students at the Union really hated his guts. Some girl said he committed suicide and they shouted her down—said he didn't have enough sense. Someone else said it was a student he flunked last year, getting revenge. I told them he just got sick last night and you saw it."

"That's true, Andrew, but it doesn't really tell you much. The police didn't mention suicide, but they're looking into the possibility that he was murdered. Yoichi came by this morning and told me he thought George was poisoned with a Japanese fish."

"Mom, that's crazy."

"He was very persuasive. But I think you're right."

"Wait'll they hear that."

"Not from you, I hope."

"It'll get around without me, don't worry. Gotta go. Thanks for supper. See you late—I hope." He leered at her.

"I don't promise to wait up."

"Good. New chick—no telling what time." Twirling an imaginary mustache, he flashed her an expensively straight set of teeth and took the stairs two at a time, presumably to put on his shoes. From the look of him tonight, she thought he might even tie them.

She was still clearing the dishes when Nancy phoned to propose a movie. Joan jumped at the chance. She didn't want to spend this particular evening at home alone. When she got into Nancy's car, however, she found she wouldn't escape so easily.

"Joan, I couldn't believe it when I heard it on the radio!" Nancy greeted her, starting up with only one eye on the road. "I called Yoichi and he said it was all true."

"What was?"

"The radio said George died of unknown causes, but Yoichi said he thought it was murder, and that you told him to call the police."

"Not exactly. He felt terrible and I suggested that Sam might look into it for him."

"But the police talked to him. And he said he mentioned you. Did they come to you, too?"

"Well, yes."

"You see? And they'll probably talk to Daniel. They always check on the family first. I wouldn't blame that boy if he did kill his father. In fact, it wouldn't be hard to blame anyone for doing George in."

"Nancy!"

"You didn't know him. I told you how he took over Daniel's girlfriend, Lisa Wallston, and then dumped her flat. Did you realize that Lisa's mother served the punch last night?"

"She did what?" Joan asked weakly, having heard it clearly the first time.

"She was handing out the punch. She and Evelyn. Don't you remember? When Alex asked who knew Daniel—to call him—someone had the nerve to suggest Glenda Wallston. Talk about tactless."

"Do you think she poisoned George's punch?"

"Heavens, I don't know. But she'd probably know how. She's a nurse, you know."

"No, I—"

"Yes. She works at the hospital—in OB, I think—but surely anyone over there could find out enough about poison to kill a man. And if there ever was a person who had reason to, Glenda's the one. Lisa isn't twenty-one yet, but the rumors flying around town have shot her reputation. I've heard she was sleeping with George and Daniel at the same time, that she was pregnant and had an abortion, that she didn't have an abortion and gave up the baby for adoption because her mother wouldn't let her bring it home. Even that she's become a lesbian. You name it, somebody's said it about Lisa."

"You think gossip would make Glenda kill George?"

"Gossip—and ruining her daughter's life. Of course, it might not be Glenda. There's Daniel. Poor Daniel. His father gave him enough grief before all that."

"He did?" More and more, she was regretting having mentioned Nancy and her gossip to Lieutenant Lundquist.

"George was such a snob. Wouldn't you know he'd have a son whose ambition is to work with his hands. Daniel is a marvel with wood, but you'd never catch George recognizing anything but abstract academic ability. I think he looked down on engineers as mere technicians. Daniel can't even have a shop at home. He has to sneak off to Isaac, the violin maker. I've seen him at the shop when I've done ads for it, and it looks to me as if he's quietly apprenticed himself to Isaac. It's the only place I've ever seen him look happy. You'd think a man would be proud to have a future Stradivarius for a son, but not George. I'll bet he never knew what Daniel was up to, or he would have managed to stop it somehow. Well, he can't stop it now."

"Look, Nancy, someone's pulling out of that space. Is it big enough?" To Joan's relief, Nancy shifted her attention to the trick of parking a large car in a short parallel spot between two small ones. The movie that had seemed a welcome diversion failed to hold Joan's attention. When they left the theater, she couldn't have described the plot, but she was grateful that Nancy chose to dissect it on the way home. An occasional "uh-huh" was all that was required of her.

The light in Andrew's window surprised her.

"Nancy, I'd ask you in, but Andrew's home. I didn't expect him so early. I'd better see if he's all right."

If Nancy saw through the deception, she put a good face on it. Upstairs, Joan called to Andrew, heard him answer, and fell asleep in less time than she would have thought possible.

It was morning before she learned why he had come home so soon. He leaned against the refrigerator and watched her wash up after breakfast.

"I thought I had a date, but it sure wasn't much. We took a walk and she let me buy her an egg roll at Liu's Place. Then she asked me to give her dad a ride home from work."

"Night shift?" She tried to remember what he'd said about the girl.

"No, he's a biology professor. We picked him up at his lab. Actually, it was pretty interesting. He showed us around and talked about what he was doing. Maybe that's why Jennifer wanted me to go there. She's a funny girl."

"Should I ask?"

"Not weird, Mom, just hard to figure out. I mean, going to her dad's lab to get rid of a date is a little extreme. All she had to do was say she wanted to go home."

"Maybe her dad needed a ride."

"Maybe, but this isn't the first time."

"I thought you just met her."

"I did, but she told me she takes guys there all the time. I think she likes to show him off. She took Daniel Petris there on a date, too. She was talking about him some. She didn't think he'd be all that broken up about his dad."

"No one seems to be." She drained the sink.

"Jennifer sure wasn't. She plays oboe. I mean, she's serious about it. She says that when the symphony's youth concerto competitions came around, Petris always judged woodwinds. He didn't criticize her technique—I guess she's so good you couldn't—but he marked her way low on her tone and said she was unmusical, whatever that means. The other two judges told her they liked her, but she's lost two years in a row, even though there was only one of him and two of them. She was afraid she wouldn't get into music school if she couldn't win again this year. She's really relieved."

Joan took a deep breath. "I think if I hear one more person isn't sorry he died, I'll...I don't know what. Let's change the subject, okay? Tell me about the lab."

"Sure. You're not squeamish about frogs, are you, Mom?"

"Frogs? No I think you're safe."

"Well, Mr. Werner's doing an experiment on how their olfactory bulb works—that's the part of their brain in charge of smelling. He has tubes hooked up to jars full of smells, and he puffs air on what looks like the frog's nostrils—it's really the olfactory epithelium. Then he measures the frog's reaction."

"And the frog just sits there and lets him do that?"

"The frog doesn't have any choice. Before he starts the experiment—this is why I asked how you felt about frogs—he destroys its brain and its spinal cord. It can't move. It can't feel anything, either. It's like brain death. It's really a dead frog."

"Then how can it be smelling?"

"It isn't, exactly. Not the way a live frog does. Its olfactory bulb is separate from the rest of its brain—that's why he chose frogs—and that bulb is still hooked up to the frog's face, where the airs puffs hit. Mr. Werner is studying a certain kind of nerve cell that way. He uses a nerve poison called TTX to block out the impulses from the other nerve cells and leave him with just the kind he wants to study. It's really interesting."

"I didn't know you were interested in that sort of thing."

"Neither did I, until I started telling you about it. That's funny."

"You didn't like biology that much when you took it, did you?"

"It was so dead. What I like is that he doesn't know how it's going to come out. And he says it could help us understand how nervous systems process information. That could be really important."

She couldn't remember this long a speech from Andrew in months. His eyes were alight, and he was running his hands through his hair as he talked, an old habit of his father's.

"Does he use student assistants?"

"In the lab? I don't know. I bet he doesn't hire them, because he was talking about all kinds of places he cuts corners to save money. Oliver doesn't exactly have a big research budget." He paused and said slowly, "I wonder if he'd let me work for him for free."

"Maybe it wasn't a wasted date after all."

"Maybe. And maybe if I worked in the lab, Jennifer would go out with me on a real one sometime. He probably stakes her out in the Union as bait to trap him a stable of lab assistants."

"You have a conniving mind. That doesn't mean *he* does."

"He connived enough to get himself written up in the paper. Big feature story. Jennifer framed the article and hung it on the wall. I think it embarrassed him, though."

"What's he like as a person?"

"Not bad. You could tell he was excited about what he was doing, but he didn't push it down your throat. He has a sense of humor, too. He showed us a couple of puffs on the frog he was finishing up, and when he packed up for the night and put the dead frog in the freezer, he said he hated to waste good frog's legs but he didn't want to do us in. That TTX is really powerful stuff. Maybe someone fed Petris a used frog's leg or two."

"Andrew!"

"Sorry, Mom. That wasn't funny. And he didn't say it. But you know, someone could have. Done it, I mean. Anyone could walk in there. The building was open when we got there at nine. His lab was unlocked, too. He was down the hall, and Jennifer just marched me upstairs and into the lab to wait for him. The whole town would know about the TTX. It was in that big article about him last year."

"Lots of people have poisons."

"I guess so. See you tonight, Mom. I'll be home for supper and I don't have a date. Jennifer can snare another guy for her dad tonight."

NINE

THURSDAY'S PAPER HAD REPORTED the sudden death of Professor George Petris. His obituary mentioned his novel—starting a minor flurry in both local bookstores (which hadn't sold a copy for months), his temporary deanship half a dozen years before (the scars of which were just beginning to heal), and his membership in the First Methodist Church (which came as a surprise to a number of active Methodists). He was, it said, survived by one son, Daniel, of Oliver, and a daughter, Emily, of San Jose, California. Arrangements were pending at Snarr's Funeral Home.

By the time Friday's paper announced that the police were investigating the matter, most residents of Oliver already thought they knew more than the meager story told. Well acquainted with the crop of wagging tongues, Lundquist cultivated it for the occasional grain of truth among the chaff. He spent Friday morning answering and returning telephone calls from people who thought they could set the police straight.

Most were complaints about the murdered man and generous hints about other people who would be glad to have seen the last of him. He heard a number of versions of the story about Lisa Wallston and her relationships with the Petris men. A woman who sang in the church choir with Glenda accused her of keeping up her membership as a blind to conceal her murderous inclinations. An orchestra member who had heard the poison story was certain Evelyn Wade must have dropped something in Petris's punch to get first chair for Sam. Sure.

Then he heard from Harold Williams. Williams wasn't blaming anyone in particular.

"There was no love lost between us, but I didn't kill him, and if someone did, I don't want him to get away with it. Is it true that he was poisoned?"

"It's possible."

"I've been talking with Yoichi Nakamura. I run Aqua Heaven, the aquarium shop on North Rogers. We don't have any puffer fish, but we do carry a salamander that contains the same poison. Actually, there are quite a few varieties of fish like that, but the Japanese puffer fish and our California salamanders share exactly the same poison. And I know it's deadly."

"Are you suggesting that someone used your salamanders?"

"It could be done."

"Have you sold any recently?"

"Not many. Lisa Wallston came in a week or so ago and replaced her whole aquarium. Something had fouled the water and killed everything. She must have bought a dozen."

"Oh?"

"Of course, it's not very likely someone would do that, not when the straight poison is available."

"The straight poison?"

"Well, sure. Over at the college. That's the stuff Carl Werner is using in his experiments. There was a big thing in the paper about it last spring. That's where I learned that the puffer fish poison and the poison in my salamanders was the same."

Lundquist nodded. He'd remembered all along that he'd read something about puffer fish.

"Mr. Williams, you've been very helpful. I appreciate your call."

"No trouble. Just hope you catch up with whoever did it."

He sat for a moment, chewing his lip. Then he picked up the phone again and quickly confirmed what he'd begun to suspect. As he already knew, the preliminary autopsy results on Petris had showed nothing inconsistent with poisoning, but there had been no fish in the contents of his stomach and no trace of any poison. There were some signs of coronary artery disease. Heart attack was still the best guess. In the absence of Nakamura's insistence, it would have been the only guess. The pathologist knew the poison in the fish. In its pure form the stuff was so lethal—more than a thousand times as toxic as arsenic, about a hundred times as deadly as curare—that the tiny amount needed to kill might very well all be metabolized in the short time before the victim died. Yes, he would try sending to a special lab for the toxicology, but it was a long shot. Gas chromatography and mass spectrometry might have a chance of finding something.

"Don't hold your breath," the pathologist warned. "You may not get the report for a couple of months."

Lundquist leaned back in his swivel chair, anchoring his toes under a desk drawer against its tendency to tilt unexpectedly. He had no more real evidence than before and from the sound of it, he wasn't likely to get any. In his heart of hearts, however, he'd just switched from a case of political babysitting to a homicide investigation. But for the coincidence of Nakamura's uncle, no one would even be doing the babysitting. Petris would simply have died, and from what he'd learned so far, no one would have mourned him.

How did you go back to the mother and tell her the baby had just passed puberty while in your care? And become impossible in the process, Lundquist thought wryly. It was all very well to make Wade look good with an investigation after which he could report to all the good citizens that no murder had existed and they were safe in their beds. He wouldn't welcome a real murder he didn't have the first chance of clearing up.

Lundquist had no desire to face the prosecutor with his suspicion. Or his own supervisor of detectives, for that matter. He knew what they'd say about hunches. He could wait. The murderer (if there was one, he reminded himself) should be feeling safe. Anybody who knew enough to use that stuff must know enough not to expect it to be traced. Or would he? If the whole town knew about Werner's lab, the murderer might not be an expert. He needed to see that article. Bob Peterson at the *Courier* would dig it up for him. Bob owed him for a story or two.

DANIEL PETRIS MET HIM at the door and took him down the hallway of a house that seemed to be insulated with books, past a door through which he glimpsed a desk his former wife would have itched to straighten.

Lundquist saw no flowers, smelled no baked meats, met no relatives.

They sat opposite each other in massive leather chairs before the cold fireplace in the living room, lined with books as the hall and study had been. Not the matched sets of a decorator, but the hodgepodge of a real reader. A slender young man not more than five-seven, Daniel was almost swallowed up in the upholstery. His calloused fingers were bitten to the quick and he nibbled at the sides of a thumb.

"I'm sorry to intrude," Lundquist said formally. "I was hoping you could help me with a few questions about your father."

"Like what?"

"The hospital told me that he had no personal physician. I wondered if that was correct, or if he was simply unable to tell them anything."

"It's probably true. The only time I remember hearing him mention a doctor, he called them all quacks. He never got sick and he had very little patience with people who did."

"So you wouldn't know whether he had a history of heart problems?"

"I never heard about any. He was big on aerobic exercise. Most mornings he'd either swim or run."

"Did he seem his normal self that evening, before the rehearsal? I understand you ate together."

"Yes. Look, I don't understand why you're here. Do the police always come when someone dies?"

"Not always. But we do when we're not sure what happened."

"Wasn't it his heart?"

"It looks that way. The doctor hasn't signed the death certificate yet, though. In cases of sudden death, it's good procedure to rule out other possibilities."

"That's what they told me when they said there would be an autopsy. Isn't that enough?"

"Sometimes."

"Is that all you want to know from me?" Daniel started on the other thumb.

"Not quite. I suppose I'm looking for some idea of the kind of man your father was."

"Oh, a great man. Just ask him," Daniel shot back and then caught himself. "Oh, God, how could I say that?"

"You didn't get along too well, is that it?"

"What are you doing? Aren't you supposed to read me my rights or something?" He stood up, clenching his bitten thumbs.

"No, you're not a suspect. At the moment nobody is. We're not even sure there's anything to suspect anybody of. People do die suddenly."

"And now you want to see how sorry I am."

"And now I want to learn anything I can that will help me find out who might have deprived you of a father."

Daniel sat down slowly. In the depths of the chair, he seemed smaller again. "I didn't kill him. But if someone else did, he didn't deprive me of a father. That happened a long time ago."

Lundquist leaned forward. "Do you want to tell me about it, son?" he asked.

"There's nothing to tell. It wasn't something that happened. It was what didn't happen. I didn't turn out to be the literary genius my father expected any son of his to be, that's all. He never knew me at all. I learned to keep out of his way and let him think what he wanted to think."

"And your mother?"

"That's really ancient history."

"Is she living?"

"Oh, she's alive, all right. She went back home, where she grew up. Took my sister with her. But I had to stay here."

"Why was that?"

"I think she was afraid I'd turn out like him. She didn't discuss it. She just left."

"How old were you?"

"When she left? Fifteen. Just finishing my first year of high school."

"Were you like your father at that age?"

"Dad would never talk much about his teens. Neither would she—she knew him then, though. I know what he thought of *me* at that age. I wasn't a real guy, because I didn't have lots of girls hanging around all the time. I wasn't a real brain, because I didn't read all the books he did. And he knew I'd never swim to Catalina Island. Can you believe it? He even did that."

"Do you still hear from your mother?"

"When she thinks of it."

"Now?"

"We talked on the phone. I told her I'd be all right. She didn't offer to come."

Lundquist heard the unshed tears. He changed the subject.

"Will you stay on here?"

"Where would I go?" Daniel's surprise appeared genuine. "You mean the house? I guess so. I mean, I think it's paid for. I don't really know. I haven't even started looking for papers and things. Dad's lawyer called. I'm supposed to talk with him on Monday. I'll stay in town, if that's what you're worried about. In spite of what my father thought, I'm learning a lot here. And I have a job. I can support myself."

"You're free to go anywhere," Lundquist assured him. "If you have any reason to leave town, though, I'd appreciate it if you'd leave word, in case we need to reach you." He paused. "There is one other thing you might be able to tell me."

Daniel waited.

"I take it your parents were divorced."

A nod.

"What kind of social life did your father have?"

"You mean women?"

"That's what I'm asking."

"He wasn't gay, if that's what you're after." Daniel bristled.

"Simmer down, son. It's been what—six or seven years since your mother left? And you said something earlier that made me think your father was interested in lots of girls when he was younger."

"He didn't change." There was no mistaking the bitterness in the young man's voice. "That's why my mother got out." He looked Lundquist in the eye. "Are you just fishing, or do you know something?"

"No, I don't know anything. But people do talk, don't they?"

"And some bigmouth told you my father stole my girl." His voice was dead now and he stared at the floor.

"Something like that."

"Well, it's true. And then he dumped her for the next good-looking woman who came along. I don't know how many he's had since then. If you think I killed him for that, I can't stop you. But I didn't." Slumped in the big chair, he didn't move.

"Did he have any enemies that you know of?"

"I think he collected them. But I never heard of anyone who hated him that much."

"Do you know if he left a will?"

"No. I guess the lawyer will tell me on Monday."

Lundquist took the names and addresses of his mother, sister, and lawyer, thanked him, and left. The kid was hurting, no question about that. Rejected by both parents—and the business about the girl—no wonder. Grief? Maybe. But for what? Guilt? Possibly. Daniel had plenty of reason to hate his father, and they had eaten together that night. He could write up those facts into a pretty damning set of circumstances, but how could he write up his gut feeling about this boy? One hunch deserves another, he decided, and reported back to the station determined not to write anything.

On his desk was a photocopy of the *Courier* story about Professor Werner and his experiments. Good. It would have to wait, though. He was due in court in half an hour to testify on a burglary case so old that he'd need at least that long to knock the cobwebs off his memory. He slid the story into the Petris file. With luck, he might be able to see the professor before he left the laboratory. Come to think of it, that probably wouldn't be too hard. Some of those publish-or-perish guys worked all hours.

He did put in a quick call to the prosecutor, telling him the preliminary investigation was inconclusive, but he'd keep him posted if anything turned up.

"Maybe when we get the results of those tests . . ."

"Sure, Fred, you let me know. I'll tell Nakamura we're working on it."

All of us, Lundquist thought.

"You do that, Sam."

TEN

STANDING AJAR, the laboratory door was covered with cartoons. Frank and Ernest predominated, in white lab coats and frazzled hair. Lundquist knocked without reading them—a test of willpower.

"She's here, Daddy," a girl's voice called, and the door flew open.

"Oh, I was expecting someone else," said a slender blond girl of about sixteen in T-shirt, shorts, and sneakers. "Did you want my father?"

"I'm looking for Professor Werner."

"That's me." Somewhat stooped, casually shaven, Werner wore no white coat. His work pants and bulging pockets suggested an electrician, missing only the tool belt. "What can I do for you?" he asked.

The girl draped herself around a chair and assumed a look of boredom. She wouldn't miss a word.

"Detective Lieutenant Lundquist, Oliver Police. I'd appreciate a few minutes of your time."

"Come in. Jennifer, get your things together."

She unwrapped herself from the chair in slow motion and began searching the scratched desks, tables, and chairs that gave the laboratory the appearance of a garage sale. Electronic gadgets covered many tables and wires dangled from others on shelves.

Werner led Lundquist past a screened cubicle and a little jungle of plastic and glass tubing to a dingy corner with two chairs, one a sturdy kitchen castoff, the other a secretarial model with wheels.

"Sit down, please, and tell me what's up."

"That's just it. I'm not sure anything is. I've heard something about the research you're doing and need to understand it a little better. It may tie in to an investigation."

"What do you want to know?"

"I hear it has something to do with Japanese fish."

"You must have the wrong man. I use frogs."

"Didn't the newspaper article last year mention puffer fish?"

"Oh, that. Probably. But it's pretty remote."

"Suppose you tell me what you do."

"Well, there are some local circuits in the nervous system that get very little attention. The little we know about them is pretty interesting, but they're hard to study. That's where the puffer fish would come in."

"How's that?"

"It's one of the sources of a substance that blocks the transmission of nerve impulses. The stuff is called tetrodotoxin—TTX for short. It gives me a crack at the signals I want to record."

"How can it help you, if it blocks the impulses?"

"That's just it. The microcircuits I'm looking for activate other cells by graded electrical signals, not by impulses. So you see, blocking the impulses of the long cells unclutters things and leaves me with just what I want."

"I'll take your word for it. You feed the TTX to the frog?"

"No, I use it on the olfactory bulb. The microcircuits have been studied in the eye with TTX. Mudpuppy retina, usually. I'm following up on that work in another sensory system. The principle ought to be the same. I compare the electrical responses to odor with and without the TTX. We know quite a lot about the frog's sense of smell and it's fairly easy to get well-controlled stimuli. Here, have a whiff."

He reached up, unhooked a bottle from the tangle of tubing, and removed the stopper.

Lundquist didn't need to sniff. The powerful odor of rotting flesh reached him quickly.

"Daddy!"

"Sorry, Jennifer. That was putrescine. Here's amyl acetate."

A sharp, penetrating chemical smell was a clear contrast.

"If I could afford it, I'd have a tank of compressed air here, but I make do with an electric aquarium pump. Hang on while I turn on the exhaust to get rid of the stink. A charcoal filter in the tubing does it for the frog."

Breathing comfortably again, Lundquist decided it was time to cut the lecture short.

"I gather the TTX is poisonous."

"Sure is. Blocking those nerve impulses may be good for my experimental purposes, but it's no way to go on living."

"Do you prepare it yourself from the puffer fish?"

"No, it's commercially available now."

"Where do you get it?"

"Swann's Biological Supply, in Chicago."

"Can you show me what it looks like?"

"Sure." Crossing the room, Werner reached for a wire key ring hanging from a nail on a wooden cabinet. Dangling from the ring was a Hills Brothers coffee can. "An old student got tired of my losing my keys," he said over his shoulder. Unlocking the cabinet, he took out a slip of paper and bent to a padlock on a small refrigerator.

High heels clicked on the smooth lab floor.

"Jennifer, are you ready?"

Startled, Lundquist recognized Evelyn Wade in an off-the-shoulder job and fragile-looking sandals that showed her slender feet and ankles to best advantage. When he stood to greet her, he saw Sam behind her in an ordinary suit, looking rumpled by comparison.

"I'll be right there, Mrs. Wade. I just have to find my history book. It was right here a minute ago." Jennifer put her book bag down and disappeared into a back room.

"Hurry, please. We're running late as it is. I don't like to leave the children alone, but I had to pick Mr. Wade up at work tonight. His Mercedes is in the shop. Carl, how are you?" The big police lieutenant was invisible to her.

"Surviving." Werner smiled warmly at her, a small bottle in his hand.

"You driven men. Just like Sam. He was working until seven tonight, and he'll hardly have time to bathe and change for the Bryans' dinner. Frank Bryan has decided to endorse Sam for the nomination, you know. It's just a matter of timing."

Sam nodded quietly at Lundquist. "Fred."

"Sam."

"Making any progress?"

"Too soon to tell. Professor Werner is helping me on some background."

"Thanks. I'm afraid I'm in for a long evening. I appreciate it."

"Sure."

Jennifer emerged and they left.

There were worse things than being divorced, Fred reflected. Sam didn't give the impression of an unhappy man, though. He looked at Evelyn the way most men look at women they haven't married yet. She didn't appeal to Fred. He'd like at least to be in charge of himself, he thought, if not of the whole family.

The door opened again and a curly head poked around it.

"Hi, Mr. Werner. Oh, I'm sorry. You're busy."

"It's all right, Andrew, but Jennifer just left on a baby-sitting job."

"I was really hoping to see you." He came in. "Ever since Jennifer brought me to the lab last night, I've been wondering if I could help you out sometime and learn more about what you're doing. You wouldn't have to pay me."

Werner's slow smile broke through. "I like the price. Sure, Andrew, I'd be glad to have you. When can you start?"

"Any time. Now, if you want."

"Fine. You could start by unpacking that box. I think everything in it belongs in that cabinet. You'll see how it's organized. Oh, and put this combination on the top shelf." He handed him the combination and the keys. "Hang the keys on that nail when you're done, would you?"

He showed Lundquist the small brown bottle, clearly labeled TTX—POISON.

"Here's the tetrodotoxin. It comes as a powder. I dissolve it only as I need it."

"How much would it take to kill a man?"

"About what you could put on a pinhead, maybe a little more."

Lundquist watched the boy stocking the supply cabinet.

"How many people have access to this laboratory?"

"We're pretty open. I've had very little pilferage—mostly the ballpoint pen variety. The M.D.s have more drug problems, and if you're looking for local sources of poison, I think you'd do better at Oliver Hardware or the Garden Center. That's why I lock the TTX, though. I'd hate to have someone come looking for a high and wind up dead."

"Is the laboratory door locked when no one is working here?"

"I lock up when I go home at night. Not when I'm in and out."

"Who might come in?"

"Any of my departmental colleagues. Jennifer shows up after school or in the evening, sometimes with a friend, like Andrew here. Students, of course. And anybody looking for one of us." He returned the TTX to the safe. "Don't you think it's about time you told me what you're after?"

"You've been very patient, Dr. Werner. If you could just answer one more question first."

"What is it?"

"To your knowledge, has anyone on this list ever visited the laboratory?" He handed him the orchestra personnel list prepared by Yoichi Nakamura.

Werner perched on the edge of a table and studied the list.

"I don't know a lot of these folks. Some may be students. The Wades you just saw here—Jennifer babysits for them on a fairly regular basis. Harold Williams brought the air pump in person and helped me fix it up. That's all I can recognize, but now I know why you're here. It's about George Petris, isn't it? Jennifer was spouting some nonsense about poison."

"Afraid so. Only it's a little more specific than that, if there's anything to it at all."

"What's that supposed to mean?"

"There's a possibility that it was the puffer fish poison. We have to check. This is a list of people who were with Petris the night he died."

Werner sat with his head bowed.

"It's possible," he said finally. "I don't keep close tabs on the TTX. I'd never miss the little it would take to kill a man. Anyone could have taken some. George was a difficult man, but I'll have a hard time forgiving myself if my carelessness led to his death."

"Let's not borrow trouble. So far we have no medical confirmation."

Werner couldn't look at him.

"That still won't mean it didn't happen. I'll change the lock tomorrow and keep the lab locked from now on when I so much as go across the hall." His shoulders stooped even more.

"I think that's wise. And if you think of anyone else who had access to the poison, I'd appreciate a call."

"I suppose Daniel did." The words came slowly, unwillingly.

"His son?"

"Yes, a couple of times recently he's stopped by with Jennifer after an egg roll. She eats those things like candy."

A strange sound came from behind the cabinet door.

"You all right, Andrew?" Werner asked.

"Uh, sure, I'm fine." Slow in coming, the reply was oddly muffled.

"One last question," Lundquist said. "Do you know a young woman named Lisa Wallston, or her family?"

"Never heard of them."

"Thank you. You've been very helpful."

On the way home, he mulled it over. The lab had been wide open. Any disgruntled student or faculty member—he didn't doubt that there had been both—would have had easy access to the TTX. Williams and Wade were hardly a surprise. In a town the size of Oliver the greater surprise would have been if no one from an orchestra of fifty or sixty people had been among Werner's acquaintances. Williams had, after all, told him about Werner. Sam must have read the article, too, though without the particular interest it would have had for an aquarium expert.

Then there was Daniel. He'd have to keep an open mind about Daniel. And about Werner. Most forthcoming with information that he must have known was leading to questions about the poison. Jennifer he could surely dismiss. What possible reason could she have to do in an English professor? On the other hand, if the stories he'd been hearing about Petris were true, and Daniel had confirmed them at least in part, then even Jennifer could have been entangled in his life. She had dated his son, if you could call egg rolls dates. And Werner might not be so unworldly as all that. He, too, could be concerned about his daughter, once she became even remotely involved with the Petris men. She seemed young for Daniel.

Lundquist trudged upstairs to his sterile rooms, remembering only after releasing his tired feet from their leather prisons that he had promised Catherine sourdough bread for a large party she was catering Saturday night. He retrieved the starter from its covered dish at the back of the refrigerator, divided it into two bowls, and added flour, water, and a spoonful of sugar to activate the culture. Gluten flour in one and rye in the other. If she wanted variety, he'd give it to her. Covering the lumpy messes, he cleared his mind.

Five minutes later, he slept.

ELEVEN

SATURDAY BEGAN peacefully enough. Having luxuriated in bed until half past nine, Joan woke to bright sunshine streaming through the window. She pulled on jeans and a sweatshirt, made a pot of coffee, and threw a batch of popovers into the oven. If that didn't lure Andrew out of bed, nothing would.

Her own mouth watering at the delicious odor beginning to waft out of the kitchen, Joan parked her coffee mug on the fraying rug and attacked the dusty boxes of books. Their little house, long rented to students, was in many ways spartan, but it did feature built-in bookshelves in abundance.

Leaving a spot near the kitchen for cookbooks, she filled the shelves at one end of the old sofa with the art books Aunt Margit always sent for birthdays and Christmas. Klee and Miro flanked Lautrec and Leonardo. She sat back on her heels and debated that. Maybe Lautrec should be filed under T. Another day.

Shakespeare, the boxed set of the Greeks she'd always meant to read, well-thumbed volumes of Frost and Mörike, Sandburg's Lincoln books and the *Rutabaga Stories*, and Conan Doyle hobnobbed with Schweitzer's *Quest for the Historical Jesus* at the other end. She kicked herself for not having organized the books in her leisurely, unemployed days. Filled with new resolve, she closed the lid firmly on a box of childhood favorites. Where were the cookbooks?

She had just found them when Andrew came down the stairs barefoot, tying his robe and twitching his nose.

"Tell me, am I dreaming, or did I die and go to heaven?"

"Cute. Set the table, would you, Andrew? I'm all dusty and breakfast is about ready."

The doorbell sent him scuttling upstairs.

It was Lieutenant Lundquist in a checked flannel shirt with the sleeves rolled up, looking much less official than he had on his visit to the center.

"Come in, won't you?" Joan called to him through the screen. "Don't mind the boxes. There must be an empty chair around here somewhere." Bent double, she waved in the general direction of one.

The travel alarm she used as a timer shrilled as he shut the door.

"Oh, no! It's ten-thirty. That's the popovers and I haven't even washed my hands."

"May I take them out for you?" he offered. "When popovers are ready, they can't wait."

A cook? She wouldn't have guessed it. Come on, Sherlock, she told herself. Fine detective you'd make. There's flour all down the sides of his pants.

"Thanks, you sure could. Won't you have some with us?"

"I'll never say no."

She watched him out of the corner of her eye while scrubbing her hands and setting three places. He flipped the popovers into the waiting basket without tearing even one.

They were on their seconds when Andrew joined them, fully dressed. Hair combed, too, she noticed.

"This is my son Andrew. Andrew, this is Lieutenant Lundquist. He's trying to find out what happened to George Petris."

"Hello," said Andrew around a steaming bite. "Didn't I see you in Mr. Werner's lab last night?"

"That's right," Lundquist answered. "You came to volunteer. How was it?"

"Boring at first. I just put away supplies. But then he let me photograph some of the signals he was picking up and he explained what he thinks they mean."

"I didn't know you'd met, Lieutenant," Joan said.

"My name is Fred," Lundquist told her. "I'd feel better if you'd use it."

"All right, Fred. I'm Joan." He had nice eyes, she thought. Butter leaked down her chin to rob her of any last remnants of dignity and she discovered she didn't care.

"Have some of Annie Morrison's strawberry preserves," she said. "Remember the little old lady at the center who gave you the gimlet eye?"

"I remember a whole row of them. Did they rib you when I left?" He had the grace to sound ashamed, but a twinkle gave him away.

"You did that on purpose!"

Andrew sat mystified. She let him wonder. Comfortable now, she asked Fred how he had learned about baking.

"This kind I saw at home. But my dad was a baker, years ago. I used to watch him. For a long time, I knew I wanted to be a baker like my father. Then I got hooked on police work and now baking's just a hobby."

"You're doing it today, aren't you?" she asked.

No Watson, he looked at his pants and nodded. "I'm making some sourdough for a friend's catering service."

"That sounds like more than a hobby."

"It's just to help her out." Her. Wouldn't you know it?

"Excuse me, please. I think I'll go find that book." She wiped her fingers on the seat of her pants.

"Don't mind us," said Andrew. "Want the last one?" He offered Lundquist the basket.

"Thanks, you keep it. I'm one ahead of you. Besides, that bread's been rising for hours in this heat. I'll get what I came for and take off."

He was halfway to the living room before Andrew spoke. "My name is Fred" had clearly not been aimed at him, but "Lieutenant Lundquist" was too formal for his taste. Andrew compromised.

"Uh, Mr. Lundquist, can I ask you what you've found out about Mr. Petris? The students have some wild ideas."

"What have you heard?" The big man stopped.

"Oh, just talk." Andrew backed off. "Nothing, really."

"You tell anybody who thinks he knows something to call the station. They know how to reach me even when I'm off duty."

On cue, the telephone rang. Andrew picked it up.

"Yes, he's here." Handing over the receiver, he eavesdropped openly.

"Lundquist." He listened, the nice eyes suddenly cold, and looked at his watch. "Give me the address." He pulled a notebook from his back pocket. "One twenty-five North Merrifield. Right. I got that. I'm on my way."

He looked at their faces.

"You might as well know. Daniel Petris says he's found a dead woman. Was Wanda Borowski in the orchestra?"

Joan handed him the Time-Life *Cooking of Japan*—she'd finally found it—as if it contained eggshells.

"A Wanda sat next to George," she said. "A flutist. She packed up his oboe."

He nodded.

"You're sure she's dead?" She couldn't help asking, but in the pit of her stomach she knew.

"Sounds like it." He watched her closely. "He says her throat was cut."

Joan conquered her rising gorge. "If I can help . . ."

He thanked her for everything and left, not hurrying, but wasting no motion.

THE OFFER TO help had been automatic. The phone call some ten minutes later was not.

"Joan, this is Fred Lundquist. I have an awkward kind of favor to ask."

"Yes?"

"I'm at the Borowskis' and we're short-handed. Her kids may come home any minute, but we haven't been able to reach their father. I want them out of all this."

"Was she really...?"

"Yes. She's dead, and it's messy. If the neighbors were a little younger, I'd turn to them, but they're on the trembly side. Look, it's all right. I can send them to the station."

"No, don't." Andrew had been awed by the rescue squad that failed to save his father, but she remembered how tightly his hand had clung to hers, even while he tried to comfort her. "I'll come."

TWELVE

SHE MADE IT IN five minutes. A small crowd had already gathered, attracted by the ambulance and the police cars, their lights flashing and radios clearly audible half a block away.

In this part of town, mostly rentals, there were no bossy neighbors plunging in to take over. Most of the onlookers stood in clumps across the street, talking among themselves, but the kids had no such restraint. Joan feared for Wanda's small but immaculate lawn. She carefully followed the curving path past a pair of limestone cubes balanced on their corners, up to the shaded front porch, where she gave her name to a uniformed man. Feeling like a goldfish in a bowl, she sat on the porch swing, her toes touching the floor, and avoided curious eyes by staring up at the spider plant and strawberry begonia that hung in pots from the porch roof. Not macramé, but some kind of crocheted holders supported them.

Lundquist didn't keep her waiting long. He led her into the living room—what her grandmother would have called the parlor. The contrast with the mess she had left at home overwhelmed her. The room smelled of furniture polish and scented candles. Fragile knickknacks and African violets crowded together on small tables, and Joan marveled at starched doilies. One overstuffed chair even wore an antimacassar. She had stepped into another world. Yet Wanda had been a young woman. She had found time to play the flute, competently enough to hold first chair. No sloppiness anywhere. Joan wondered about the children. Were they allowed to live in this house?

"They haven't dusted in here," Fred was saying. "Can I trust you not to touch anything?"

Best-dusted room I've seen in years, she thought. But he meant the police, didn't he? Their kind of dusting would turn this fussy perfection into a nightmare for the woman who had created it. Joan reminded herself that Wanda would never know. She nodded mutely.

"If you don't mind listening," he said, "I think I'll bring Daniel in here to talk."

She wondered why he trusted her. It didn't seem very professional of him. Or did he?

"Are you sure you want me to hear it?" she asked.

"Yes. You might catch something I don't. This could tie in to his father and the orchestra."

"Then doesn't that make us all suspect?" There. She'd said it aloud.

"Not you." He smiled. "Wanda spoke to the two old ladies next door when she sent her children off to the park at ten-thirty this morning. They're sure of the time. They missed the beginning of their favorite television program."

"On Saturday morning?" Yogi Bear, maybe?

"You know, I wondered that, too. Seems they fall asleep before 'Masterpiece Theatre' on Sunday night, but the station runs a repeat at ten-thirty Saturday."

The light dawned. At ten-thirty, he had been taking popovers out of her oven.

"Sit tight," he said. "I'll be right back."

She sat on the spotless sofa listening to the sounds of the house. Murmuring voices, mostly, and heavy feet. An automatic washer spinning. Then Fred and the others calling back and forth.

Torn between fascination and horror, she wished for ear-lids.

"No prints, Fred. Faucets are wiped clean. He wasn't so careful about the sink, though. Traces of blood here. Probably hers."

"Weapon?" That was Fred. He'd be calm in a hurricane.

"I checked the toilet tank and the laundry hamper. Sheets, towels, kids' clothes. A penny and a couple of nickels. That's it in here."

"No razor?"

"There's an electric shaver. And some Nair."

"Come on back in the bedroom, then. And keep your big feet out of the blood."

Joan shuddered. Although she hadn't seen that gory bedroom, her all too vivid imagination was sparing her nothing.

A dapper little man with a mustache appeared from somewhere behind her, his shining shoes in sharp contrast to the scuffed medical bag he carried. Moments later, two uniformed attendants maneuvered an empty stretcher in the front door and through the living room. The murmuring began again, punctuated by occasional shouts and grunts, and then the stretcher, covered, came back through the bric-a-brac. Joan stood quietly, out of some notion of respect, she supposed, although certainly no one was paying attention to anything she did. She sat down with a feeling of relief. At least the children would be spared that.

Fred returned finally with a slender young man in whose dark features she could see something of George Petris. None of the aggressive impatience she remembered, though. Fred introduced them without mentioning Joan's relationship to the orchestra. Daniel sat stiffly, his hands in his lap.

"I'm sorry you're having such a rough time," Joan said.

He looked as if that was the last thing he'd expected to hear.

"I'm all right."

She plodded on. "It seems to me you've had more than your share of sudden death."

He didn't answer, but began biting a thumbnail.

Fred broke the silence. "Would you mind telling me again what happened?"

"From when?"

"From when you first heard of her."

A smile threatened the corners of Daniel's mouth.

"I was twelve. She was on my paper route."

"How well did you know her?"

"I didn't. She was a customer."

"Good tipper?"

"No, but she never made me wait for the money."

"Do you know her family?"

"I used to see her outside with a baby. Sometimes her husband would be sitting on the porch with a beer when I delivered. We never talked."

"I take it you haven't seen her recently."

"No. I quit the papers after a couple of years."

"Why did you come here this morning?"

"She called me—I think on Thursday—and said she had my father's oboe and I should come for it."

"But you waited until today."

"I was busy. I can't play the thing, anyway."

"Go on."

"So today I called her to see if I could pick it up."

"Did you answer the phone?"

"I guess so." He was suddenly cautious. "I mean, she doesn't have a sister or anything, does she?"

Joan held her breath.

"Relax," Fred said. "I'm not setting traps. Far as I know, she lived here with her husband and three little girls. They're young enough I don't think you could confuse their voices."

"Okay, then, she answered. And she said sure, come on over. So I did. You know what I found." Backing away from the specifics, he gnawed at the corner of a little fingernail.

"What time was that call?"

"I don't know," Daniel said. "Maybe ten, ten-thirty. I didn't want to call early. I mean, it's Saturday, and some people sleep in."

"And you left home right away?"

"Yes."

"That's about a ten-minute drive?"

"I walked. It took maybe half an hour. I don't know." His arms were bare to the elbow. No watch. "It's a couple of miles and I wasn't hurrying."

"Exactly what happened when you got here?"

"I rang the bell, but nobody came. So I rang it again. Still nothing. I figured she couldn't hear the bell. The door was open and I knew she was expecting me, so I called and walked in."

"What made you go into the bedroom?"

"I didn't know it was the bedroom, honest!" A trace of panic had crept into his voice. "I didn't see her here or in the kitchen, so I started down the hall. That was the first door. When I stuck my head in, I saw her lying there in all that blood, just the way you found her."

"Then what?"

"Then I called the cops. I asked for you because you were the only one I knew."

"Think carefully. What did you move?"

"I didn't move anything. I didn't even touch anything. I just backed out and called you."

"On what?"

"Oh...yeah. I touched the phone. That one." He pointed to a little telephone table with a seat, of a sort Joan hadn't seen for at least twenty years. Another doily. "I don't think I moved it any."

"Anything in her room? In the bathroom?"

"I didn't even *go* in those rooms!" The panic was unmistakable now.

"But you felt comfortable walking into her house."

"I'd just talked to her. I told you. She was expecting me."

"To pick up your father's oboe."

"Right."

Very quietly. "Then where's the oboe?"

Daniel's jaw dropped. He sagged back on the sofa. "My God," he said. "I forgot all about it."

Lundquist waited.

"You didn't find it?" Daniel asked. "You aren't putting me on?"

"No, we didn't find it."

Daniel shook his head stupidly and then suddenly came to life.

"That proves it!"

"What's that?" Fred asked.

"That I didn't kill her. Oh, I know you suspect me. I didn't have to answer any of these questions, but I know I didn't do it. Don't you see, that proves it. If I killed her, then I'd have the oboe. But I didn't, and I don't."

"Can you think of anyone who might have killed her? Maybe someone who knew your dad, too?"

"Look, I didn't even know they knew each other. She called me up, that's all."

Abruptly, Lundquist stood up.

"Thank you very much."

Daniel looked at him. "That's it?"

"That's it. If you think of anything you'd like to add, you know how to reach me. I'll ask Sergeant Pruitt to take you over to the station to make a formal statement."

He escorted Daniel to the door. Through the window that faced onto the porch, Joan thought she saw a mobile TV unit. Yes, there was the cameraman zeroing in on Daniel. Then Sergeant Pruitt, a bulky man, blocked the camera's view, and they drove off.

She dreaded running that electronic gauntlet when her turn came. She supposed she could leave by the back door—no, then the children would have to come through the house. It might not be so bad, though, if only they didn't have to see their mother's room. Maybe even less frightening than being forbidden to enter their own house entirely.

I hope I can get some of their things for them, she thought. A sudden silence told her that the washer had finished spinning. Maybe she ought to put the laundry in the dryer.

"Well," said Fred beside her, "what did you think?"

"About Daniel? I thought he was used to being suspected of doing something wrong."

He looked at her with the raised eyebrows of respect. She dared a question.

"He sounded genuinely surprised about the oboe, as if he'd forgotten all about it. Is it really missing?"

"We haven't found it. You'd think she'd have it ready, if she knew he was coming. Of course, we haven't found the murder weapon, either, unless it's an ordinary household knife. We're going through every drawer in the house. It's not on Daniel. He asked us to search him and we did."

"And he did call you."

"Well, he couldn't be sure someone hadn't seen him. Discovering the body is an old one. But he did volunteer to answer questions after we read him his rights."

"Not to change the subject, but does everything really have to stay as it is until you solve this?"

"What do you have in mind?"

"Does the family have to get out and leave everything behind? I was thinking that would be awfully hard on them."

"We'll probably seal her room for a few days. I imagine they'll want to be somewhere else until it's cleaned up. We can't do that yet."

"What about clothes and things?"

"They can take what they need. Why?"

"I thought while I'm waiting, maybe I could finish the laundry in case they'll need it. I wouldn't mind."

"What do you mean, finish?"

"I heard the washer shut off when Daniel left. I could put the things in the dryer, if that's okay."

"I'll see if they're done in there yet."

In a few moments he beckoned to her.

"You go right ahead."

After the living room, an orderly kitchen was only to be expected. Something was simmering in a Crock Pot and the dishes in the drainer were covered with a clean towel. An ironing board stood ready, the iron plugged in but not turned on. Dampened rolls in a wicker basket took Joan back to her young married days, before new fabrics—and new attitudes—had changed everything. Well, she'd volunteered; she might as well iron the stuff before it mildewed. Inspecting the contents of the basket briefly, she set the iron on Cotton to heat.

When she opened the lid of the washer, she thought for a moment it was empty. Centrifugal force had flattened the two bulky items against the tub's perforations, embossing little round bumps on their terry cloth surfaces, which she saw when she peeled them off the sides and tossed them into the dryer.

A sudden thought stopped her hand before it touched the knob.

"Fred," she called.

He came with that rapid but unhurried walk she'd seen earlier.

"Look at these. They're wet."

"You expected dry?"

"Fred, I'm serious."

"You'd better tell me." A certain I'm-being-patient-with-this-nonsense tone.

"Fred, this tells us she was still alive about forty minutes ago."

The respect was missing from his raised eyebrows this time.

"Sure," she insisted. "I used to have almost the twin of this machine. Set like this, it takes about forty minutes from start to finish. I heard it when I came in and I told you just now when it went off. Maybe Daniel heard it, too, without hearing it, if you know what I mean. Remember, he said he thought she couldn't hear the doorbell?"

Now he was nodding. He reached into the dryer and shook out a large white bath towel and a blue terrycloth robe with a hood.

"Forty minutes, you say?"

"Mine would take that long. A little less, maybe, if she set it to wash six minutes instead of twelve. You can't tell that. Most of it is the filling and spinning time, though. This one is set on regular, extra high, with a cold wash and cold rinse—the things are cold, aren't they? That usually takes longer than a warm rinse, because water comes in from only one faucet. It's easy enough to check. Just start it. It won't matter whether there's anything in it or not."

"We'll do that. I think, on the whole, you'd better not dry these. I'll keep them. We might need a statement from you about hearing the washer."

He bore the wet things off. Joan sighed. She hitched up her jeans and wiped her forehead. Testing the iron's sizzle with two wet fingers, she unwrapped the first blue cotton bundle and set herself to a chore she hadn't faced at home in months.

Ironing wasn't her idea of fun, but it beat sitting in that painfully neat parlor doing nothing while the police carried out their routine. She welcomed the physical task that left her mind free even as she resented the man who would expect his wife to iron cotton work shirts. No, that wasn't fair. Wanda probably chose them herself. They went with the doilies.

BY THE TIME the uniformed officer came to tell her that Mr. Borowski had come home, she knew something didn't make sense. Thinking about it was like trying to get a good look at one of the little floaters in her eye. When she'd aim at it, it would slide off in the opposite direction, only to swim back annoyingly into her peripheral vision where she couldn't focus clearly.

THIRTEEN

STANISLAUS BOROWSKI kept repeating himself.

He stood in the middle of the living room, his arms outstretched and his calloused hands squeezing the air in front of him. Sweat stained his familiar blue cotton shirt.

"She was fine when I left home," he was saying. "How's a guy supposed to know a thing like this is gonna happen? They call me for some overtime. She's fine, the kids are fine, I go. A man's gotta work, you know? Why'd anybody do a thing like this? How'm I supposed to know? My God, they didn't even take the cash off the dresser. Why'd anybody want to do a thing like this?"

"We all want to know, Mr. Borowski," Lundquist said. "We want to get the person who did it."

"How's that gonna help me, huh? Where's that leave me? How's that gonna take care of the kids? My God, she was fine this morning."

From the kitchen doorway, Joan recognized his outraged disbelief and overtones of guilt. Clothed in pious words, or expressed as openly as this, it was a part of grief she knew all too well. She had reacted to Ken's death with stunned silence and tears, but the monologue inside her head would have shocked many of her friends.

She waited for a cue from Fred. It came.

"Mr. Borowski, this is Mrs. Spencer. She knew your wife and is willing to take the children home with her today, while you get your bearings. Would that help?"

He seemed to notice her for the first time. He dropped his hands.

"Thanks, lady, but no, thanks. I'll call my sister." He wheeled around to face Fred. "Where are they, anyhow?"

"Your neighbors say they went to the park a couple of hours ago. We have a man looking."

"I gotta find 'em. You do anything you want to about that damn killer. I gotta find my girls." He charged out the front door, ignoring the crowd.

Fred motioned to a plainclothesman. "Stick with him, Joe, and phone in when you know the kids are safe. We'll talk to him later."

Churning inside, Joan found her purse and left.

HOURS LATER, Lundquist unlocked his own door. The smell hit him first, and the phone started ringing before he made it to the kitchen. He knew what was coming, but it was worse than he had imagined. Both ways.

Tucking the receiver between a shoulder and an ear, he began scraping dough off the tabletop and floor. "Hello."

"Fred, where on earth have you been?" Catherine's voice combined whining and demanding into one shrill tone. "Do you have any idea what time it is?"

"Pushing seven?" He peeled the once-wet towels off the stickiness overflowing his two-foot wooden proofing bowls and resisted the temptation to throw the scrapings back in. Sure, the bread would be sterile after an hour in a hot oven, but no one would tolerate finding even a sterile hair in a sandwich.

"I came by to pick up the bread two hours ago and I've called every fifteen minutes since. What do you think you're doing?"

"Well, Catherine, I'll tell you. I think I'm doing my job. We had a little emergency today."

"I'm coming now."

"No, wait." He caught her before she hung up. "Don't. I didn't bake it."

"You what?" Her dismay deafened him.

"I didn't even get it into the pans. I'm sorry. I should have warned you sooner."

Risen and then fallen back on itself, the bread would be dry at best. Edible, maybe, if he skipped the second rising and baked the loaves immediately after shaping them.

Her voice yammered on as if one batch of sourdough were the be-all and end-all. He half-listened while punching down what hadn't landed on the floor. The dough didn't fight back. It lay in the bowls inertly, without elasticity. There was no point in letting her go on.

"Catherine, I really am sorry. There's nothing I can do with this stuff. The best I can offer is to stop by Brackett's for you. Their cottage cheese dill bread is good, and their pumpernickel."

"Forget it. I'll manage."

He pulled the receiver away from his ear just in time. Even at arm's length he could hear her slam down the phone. He suspected her of smashing it onto a table before hanging up. It wasn't the first time. The next step in the dance, he knew, was for him to arrive on her doorstep with flowers and apologies. Poised to rush off to her party, she would accept with a devastating graciousness that stung worse than the anger she was dishing out now. Not tonight. He wasn't up to being devastated.

He dumped the dough into the wet garbage. Let Milligan's pigs party tomorrow.

When the phone rang again, he didn't bother to hide his fatigue. "Yeah?"

"Fred, it's Joan. Am I interrupting your supper?"

"No, I just walked in. Problem?" He leaned against the wall, afraid to sit down.

"I'm all right. I've been thinking about Wanda and I may have figured out a connection. Would you like to come over? We haven't eaten yet either. There's plenty."

"I'm on my way."

SHE FED HIM FIRST. One look at his face had told her that much. Andrew, too, seemed to recognize Fred's weariness. He kept up a line of patter that required little response, avoiding what was on all their minds.

Over coffee in the living room, Joan finally brought it up.

"Did they find the children, Fred?"

"Oh, sure. They were on their way home. Borowski broke it to them and took them to their aunt's. They're pretty tough."

"He was taking it hard. You don't suspect him, do you?"

"We did, of course. There was no break-in. No sign of an intruder. Nothing was stolen, not even her grandmother's silver from Poland. She wasn't beaten or raped. She probably let the killer in. The door was open and the screen was unhooked."

Joan thought with a sinking feeling of her own wide-open house. Fred went on.

"The neighbors say she was careful, but she seems to have trusted the killer enough to walk into the bedroom while he was there. There's no sign of force. Sure, we suspected him. According to the neighbors, their home life wasn't all that peaceful. Actually, they said she did most of the yelling. If he'd been killed, I'd have to be looking at her."

"I wondered if she was hard to live with. I was thinking more of the kids, though."

"It doesn't matter. Stan Borowski spent the morning fixing a broken water main across from the post office. He was on a six-man crew from seven-thirty until we found him.

He's clear, short of putting out a contract on his wife, and that I don't see.''

"No. Fred, the oboe is the obvious connection, isn't it?''

"Which we don't have.''

"Which the murderer probably took. Even if it was Daniel. When Andrew carried the paper, he knew every shortcut and garbage can on his route. Daniel could have hidden the oboe somewhere. The case isn't all that big. If Wanda called him as he said she did, he'd have to come back. For all he'd know, she might have told someone else he was coming, and then not showing up would be something he'd have to explain away.''

"And the weapon might be with the oboe,'' he said. "Could be.''

"It might have been with it all along.''

"Come again?''

"Fred, have you ever seen a reed knife?''

"A reed knife?''

"It looks a little bit like a straight razor, but it doesn't fold up. At least the ones I've seen don't. You know, those double reeds on oboes and bassoons cost a small fortune, and they're so unreliable that most players cut their own. It's the only way to get them the way they want them. They almost all shape them, even if they buy them ready-made. A real snob like George wouldn't dream of that, though.''

"I never got past a number two Rico sax reed in the marching band.''

"Sax and clarinet reeds are cheaper. Not so many people bother. But good players work them over, too, and when they get one they like, they save it for performances.''

"You think Petris had a reed knife with his oboe?''

"I know he had one. I saw him using it.''

"And this knife would be strong enough—you didn't see her, did you?''

"They look plenty strong to me. You could check Sam's or Elmer's."

"Is the whole orchestra armed to the teeth?"

"Hardly. The other bassoonist probably has one. The clarinets might. Why would they want to kill Wanda?"

"Why would anyone? This isn't narrowing it down. If the knife was in the oboe case and she had it out for Daniel, anyone could have used it. For that matter, a sharp pocket-knife could probably have done the job."

"I keep coming back to that oboe," she said. "Maybe somebody wanted it. Maybe that's why they were both killed."

"Who would want an oboe?"

"I don't know, but it's gone. Of course, it might not have been the oboe at all. The murderer could have taken it so we wouldn't notice that the knife was missing. Maybe George was killed for some other reason and Wanda was too close to him. If she saw something important and remembered it, that would make her too dangerous. Maybe she was just in the wrong place at the wrong time."

"Can you draw me a map? Where was everybody when Petris collapsed?"

She tried. It was all out of proportion, but it did place the violins on the conductor's left, with the firsts on the outside and the seconds next to them. On the far right, she put the cellos and beside them, the violas. In the inner circle of the fan-shaped orchestra, she drew the first stand of each of the strings, except, of course, the basses, who stood at the back. In the second row were two cellos, John Hocking, Joan, Sam Wade, George Petris, Wanda Borowski, another flute, and four violins. Behind herself, Joan remembered a space not quite big enough to protect her ears from the trumpets. Behind Sam sat the demoted lady bassoonist; behind George, Elmer Rush; and to his right, the clarinets. Across the back row were the basses, the tuba, Nancy and the other trombones, the horns, and, on the far side, the tympani.

Fred led her again through the story of George's collapse and the end of the rehearsal. Nothing new.

"Do you remember where any of these people were when the refreshments were being served?"

"I've gone over it a dozen times in my mind. About all I can tell you are some who didn't have any."

"That might be a start."

"John didn't leave his seat. He's dieting. His daughter was doing homework. The horns were practicing and so was one of the trumpets. I could find out which one, but I'd guess it was the first. Sam stayed put, too, thank goodness. I would have been the first casualty if he hadn't been there to catch me when I tripped on my own big feet. A lot of people went outside to beat the heat, but I don't know how many of them stopped at the table. The concertmaster was out, I know. He took his sweet time coming back. Not much help, is it?"

"Was Petris one of the ones who went out?"

"I don't know. Not for long, if he did. He did have a drink. I think Nancy said Glenda Wallston served him."

"Oh, she did, did she?"

"You've heard that story?"

"Not from you," he said.

"I told you there was gossip."

"There sure is," Andrew said. "I heard about Lisa Wallston from Jennifer."

"I'll look into it." Fred didn't tell them what Daniel had already confirmed.

"Fred, I don't believe half the things I've heard about George," Joan said. "You'd think death would make people kinder, but it seems to do just the opposite." She tried to sip from her empty coffee cup and put it down absently. "It's obscene to go digging into his life like that."

"This isn't just death, Joan. This is murder. If you're right, then those three children are motherless because someone wanted to kill George Petris. We don't know who that someone is or what he might do next, or why. It doesn't even matter what was true about Petris. What matters is what someone out there believes. What would be obscene would be to hold back anything now that might help prevent still another murder."

"You don't think . . ." Her voice trailed off.

"I do think. I think you're right about why Wanda Borowski was killed. I spent the afternoon talking with people about her. Family, friends, neighbors, even her priest. Nothing. If there's no connection to Petris, I'm lost, and the only one I can see besides Daniel and the oboe itself is the orchestra. I think any one of you could be in danger, especially the people who sat near enough to Petris to see whatever she might have seen."

He consulted her drawing. "I'll warn Sam. He's the next closest. And those two bassoon players behind them. Don't take any chances yourself, Joan. I can't tell you to watch out for strangers. It's probably not a stranger. Just—don't trust anyone too far, you hear?"

Andrew cleared his throat noisily.

"In that case, I better tell you," he said. "You remember, Mom, Jennifer was afraid she'd never get into music school if Mr. Petris judged the concerto competition this year."

"Mmm."

"While I was working in the lab, Mr. Werner said Jennifer went out with Daniel Petris for an egg roll. I nearly choked when I heard that. And then later one of the other professors came in and started talking about how Petris screwed up the biology requirements when he was dean. You could tell Mr. Werner didn't want to talk about it, but the other guy wouldn't shut up. He said he'd thought they were safe with Werner on the curriculum committee to stand up to Petris, but then Petris made monkeys out of all of them. Mr. Werner didn't like that. He's pretty quiet, but he got all red in the face and said he fought the S.O.B.—that's what he called him—he fought him every way he could, but you couldn't win against a dean like that. If Jennifer knew how he felt, maybe she helped Daniel get the poison.''

There went the fingers through his hair again, just like his father's. Suddenly it was hitting too close.

"Andrew, I don't think you should go back there.''

"To the lab? Come on, Mom, you don't mean that. I'm maybe right in the middle of a murder and you want me to leave now and miss everything? I notice you took off like an ambulance chaser when you got that phone call today. Why should you have all the fun?''

"Andrew!''

"Admit it, Mom. You left this big mess—which, by the way, *I* picked up—just so you could play detective.''

She bristled.

"I wasn't playing anything. I even did the ironing over there.'' He knew how she felt about ironing.

"There. Not here.''

Joan sat speechless. Serpents' teeth couldn't spread butter compared to this child, she thought. Pay the bills, do the laundry, that's me.

"Everyone thinks you're so good to people,'' Andrew continued relentlessly. "They don't know you're just nosy. Why do you expect me to be any different?''

That last sentence and the grin that went with it cut through the guilt she'd been hearing him pile on her. Suddenly she saw the funny side of it all. He had her dead to rights, but it no longer threatened her. She turned to Lundquist, her eyes dancing.

"What do you think, Fred? Is a mouth like that safe out in public?"

"He does all right," Fred said, dodging the squabble. "If you're asking whether it's safe to go back to the lab, I don't know why not. In fact, I could use an insider. What you told us tonight may turn out to be important, Andrew. But don't confide in anyone but me. The less you talk, the safer you'll be. Listen all you like, but stay away from keyholes. Leave the fancy stuff to the professionals."

Andrew nodded soberly.

"And, Joan, if you remember anything more about the night Petris died, don't put off letting me know. You may know something you don't realize is important and it could be worth your life."

They were both quiet after he left. Andrew cleared the table without being asked and spread out his pre-calculus. Standing at the kitchen sink, Joan saw her own face reflected in the dark glass. The window was a perfect one-way mirror at night; anyone going by would be able to see her clearly.

For the first time since moving back to Oliver, she snapped the shutters tight.

FOURTEEN

THE SUNDAY *Courier* screamed bloody murder. A fuzzy snapshot of Wanda Borowski and her children smiled beside a photograph of the crowd gawking at that covered stretcher and the natty little man identified as Dr. James Henshaw, county coroner.

Most of the information on the case was attributed to "Lieutenant Fred Lundquist, veteran of the Oliver police force and formerly high point man on the special Indianapolis detective squad that solved the so-called Hoosier Hysteria murders that marred little Clear Creek's one and only championship in the Indiana High School Athletic Association basketball tourney."

Lundquist groaned. Bob Peterson never had made the mental switch from the sports page to page one. It might have been worse, though. There were no glaring inaccuracies.

"According to Dr. Henshaw, Wanda Borowski died within moments of the fatal blow," he read. "Neither the weapon nor a suicide note was found. Borowski, 5–2 and 105 pounds, showed no signs of having resisted her attacker. Discovered lying in a pool of congealing blood on the bedroom floor, her body was fully clothed. She had not been abused sexually."

The paper told no more than he wanted revealed at this point. Bob had kept his promise not to get in the way. Enterprising as usual, he had noticed that this was the symphony's second sudden death in a week. Without knowing who had discovered the body, he had proposed a feature about orchestral murders, maybe with a Phantom of the Opera angle.

Fred had been plain: "I can't stop you. Go ahead, print the name of every last fiddler. Drag in the tuba and the tympani. Hamstring the investigation. Those people can't help but be alert when I come around, but they might think of Sam Wade as just another player if you don't screw things up. Think your cute story is worth it?"

Apparently not. Mention of the orchestra was buried in the tame little obituary on page two, surrounded by Wanda's church and volunteer activities. Bob had made the most of the children's fresh-scrubbed innocence, their father's grief, and their mother's quiet lifestyle and spotless housekeeping. He featured the shocked reaction of the two old neighbor ladies who worried about what the world was coming to "if a woman can have her throat slashed in her own home in broad daylight for no good reason."

Fred wondered what reason they would consider sufficient.

Licking a last crumb of doughnut glaze from his fingers, he folded the paper napkin he used for a breakfast plate, rinsed out his coffee mug, and checked his watch. At ten o'clock he shouldn't rouse too many people out of bed, even on a Sunday. He consulted the personnel list Nakamura had given him and started on his rounds.

Elmer Rush was already out.

"I'm sorry. Was he expecting you?" The slender woman with freckles and faded red hair already looked tired. A dustcloth hung from her pocket.

"I took a chance. Do you expect him back soon?"

"I couldn't say. What are you selling?"

When he identified himself, some of the lines in her face relaxed.

"Come in, won't you? I really expect him back any time, but I don't like to say much to just anybody. I'm Martha Lambert, his daughter. He's not himself today and I didn't want him bothered by another door-to-door salesman. We seem to get a steady stream of them."

She led him into a room furnished mostly with well-polished antiques of the simplest, straightest lines. Rag rugs warmed the old floor and plain muslin curtains gave the windows a clean, fresh look. The sofa, on the other hand, had been through the wars. She followed his glance and smiled ruefully.

"I've given up worrying, what with three kids and a dog. Besides, who has money these days for furniture? Tell me, officer, what do you want with my dad?" Her face changed suddenly and she clutched the dustcloth as if for support. "Has something happened?"

"No, it's just routine. I understand he plays in the Oliver Civic Symphony."

"That's right."

"I'm checking facts in a couple of cases involving members of the orchestra. I'm sorry if he's ill."

"He's all right. Sit down, please."

Avoiding the dog hair, he chose a Shaker chair. She paced, absently pulling the cloth through her fingers.

"He's not sick, but it's a bad day. He gets these fierce moods sometimes when he'd not fit to live with. I was glad he decided to take a walk. He took Julie in her chair so he could really move along. It'll do them both good, I hope." She crossed the room.

"Julie's your daughter?" She nodded. "I saw them together the other day at the Senior Citizens' Center," he said.

"I didn't realize you'd met."

"We haven't. I was talking to someone who works there and his name was mentioned. He seems devoted to Julie."

"He's been trying to make it up to us, ever since it happened."

"Pardon me?"

"Julie almost drowned once because of a couple of kids we trusted her with cared more about cheap thrills than about her. Dad came along in time to save her life—he about killed the lifeguard—but she's been retarded ever since. It was easier when my husband was alive, but I swear, I think it shortened his life. Now I don't know what I'd do without Dad. Only sometimes..." She crossed the room again, and stared out the window.

"Sometimes?"

"Sometimes he scares me. He scared me a lot when I was little. Then when I left home, I forgot, and when I saw him on visits he was generally on his good behavior. Now...now it's the way I remember it. He's all sweetness and love one minute, and the next, you think he'll slap you down if you look at him crooked. I've seen him go into rages at strangers. When I was in school my friends wouldn't spend the night with me. I know my mother never crossed him." Her voice shrank. "I leave him with Julie so much. What if he hurts her?"

Lundquist pulled out a card and wrote swiftly on the back.

"This is the crisis number of the women's shelter nearest us. It's answered day and night. And I'll respond if you call me. Has he ever touched you?"

"Hit me? No." Very small now. "He spanked me sometimes when I was a little girl."

"Julie?"

"I don't think so, but how could I be sure she'd tell me?" The tears spilled. She brushed at them, smudging her cheeks.

"I think you'd guess," he said. "Does she act afraid of him? Have you ever seen bruises or scrapes, or even a red spot?"

"No."

He unfolded a clean handkerchief and held it out. She wiped her eyes and blew her nose loudly.

"Thank you," she said. "You've helped me a lot."

His big hand patted her shoulder clumsily. I'm no good at this sort of thing, he thought.

"I'll be back," he said. "I really do want to ask your father a couple of questions."

"You won't say anything to him?"

"Don't worry."

She was still standing in the doorway when he drove away. He glimpsed his own white handkerchief, waving.

JOAN, TOO, began Sunday morning with the *Courier*. She learned nothing from Peterson's story. For once, she knew more than the paper. Turning to Wanda's obituary, she read that funeral arrangements were still pending. She wondered how long it took for the police to collect all the evidence a body could give them.

Another name leaped at her from the obituaries: Walter Bergdorfer. She remembered at once the irascible old man who had shouted at her and all the other neighborhood children for hopping the chain he'd strung across his lawn to discourage them from beating a path in the grass as they cut the corner. She had never felt guilt, but only mild triumph at clearing the hurdle.

The paper gave Mr. Bergdorfer's age as seventy-three. Joan realized with a start that she was now within spitting distance of being as old as the decrepit grouch she remembered had been.

The phone interrupted her count of her gray hairs. At the sound of Nancy's voice, Joan girded herself for a long session of "Isn't it awful?" and was relieved when Nancy paid mere lip service to the murder and invited her instead to represent the orchestra at the hospital. Charlotte Hodden, the little cellist, had produced a baby boy on Saturday.

"Didn't you see it in the birth announcements? Someone ought to go. She's a sweet little thing, very faithful. I bet she's back at rehearsal within two weeks."

"Nancy, I'm glad you noticed. I didn't even know her name yet. Do you want to take flowers?"

"That's why I called you. The orchestra usually buys them, but you know Yoichi isn't going to brave an OB ward. Actually, Evelyn suggested you. She wants to go, but she says she's too busy to pick up flowers. Didn't I tell you?"

Joan refrained from pointing out that Nancy herself might know her way to a florist.

"All right. How much do I spend?" I may as well check prices on funeral bouquets while I'm at it, she thought.

"I think around ten—ask Yoichi. The Rose Basket's good and they donate to the orchestra. Just don't let them fob blue carnations off on you. I can't stand them."

"Trust me." Or do it yourself. "When are visiting hours?"

They settled on two o'clock.

Yoichi welcomed her call. "I am a little stiff and sore today," he said. "I fell off my bicycle yesterday."

"No broken bones, I hope."

"No, only some scratches. Do you know how to get blood out of a white sweater? I am afraid I have ruined the one my mother gave me when I went home to Japan this summer. She made it herself."

"Cold water. Let it soak a long time. Then wash it the way you usually do. Bleach helps, but you mustn't use it on wool."

She had answered automatically, but her thoughts raced ahead after she hung up. Yoichi worried about bloodstained clothing the day after Wanda's throat was cut? Yoichi? He had been on the scene when George died, in a good position to be sure that no one revived him in time. But why would he have told her about the poison at all? Surely it would have been safer to let everyone go on believing in a sudden illness.

Joan poured herself another cup of coffee and tried to read the rest of the paper. Her mind refused to follow the words on the page.

Maybe Yoichi had planned to say nothing. Then Wanda had seen something and the emergency room doctor had turned out to be Japanese, a man who might have guessed the truth about Japanese puffer fish poison on his own. Far better to blow the whistle and sound innocent.

But why Yoichi?

Why anybody? Fred's question came back to her. It wasn't hard to imagine that anyone might hate George Petris, but she found it impossible to think that the soft-spoken young man she knew would commit cold-blooded murder. And not once, but twice.

Don't be silly, she told herself. If he did it, you don't know him at all. All you know is the act he's been putting on for your benefit. It would explain why he unburdened himself to you when he'd scarcely met you. And you thought it was your good listening ear. He's certainly thorough, if he even scratched himself to explain away any blood he picked up.

Feeling foolish but sure that he wouldn't laugh, she called Fred to relay her latest brainstorm. No answer. She'd try again after the hospital.

FIFTEEN

WITH THE GLOWING, slightly overstuffed look of new mothers everywhere, Charlotte Hodden seemed a little flustered by her visitors. Small wonder, Joan thought. Evelyn Wade was playing gracious lady to the hilt. (Joan had felt Nancy's nudge when Evelyn had deftly relieved her of the chrysanthemums on their way down the long hospital corridor.)

She herself was inclined to the opinion that half the reason for having a baby in the hospital was to escape all social obligations for at least a few days. Now, fifteen minutes after their arrival, she was sure they had become such an obligation. She tried a couple of graceful exit lines, but neither Nancy (who, indeed, might not know better) or Evelyn (who should) showed signs of budging from the two comfortable guest chairs in the semi-private room. Joan was sitting on the edge of the second bed, which was temporarily empty. She stood up and made another attempt.

"Is there anything we could do for you while you're getting your strength back?" Maybe that would remind them.

"Oh, I couldn't ask you . . ."

"Anything, dear," Evelyn gushed. "I remember how long it took me after ours were born. Of course, it's even harder with the second—there's never a moment to rest—though the delivery itself isn't so bad."

"What do you need?" Joan asked, hoping to nip any more maternal reminiscing in the bud.

"It's my cello."

That stopped them.

"You don't expect to practice here!" Evelyn sounded shocked. Not unless obstetrics has taken a giant leap, Joan thought, wincing as she pictured the edge-of-the-chair posture favored by many cellists.

Charlotte giggled. "Wouldn't that set them on their ears?"

"What, then?" Nancy asked.

"Well, you know, the baby wasn't really due for another week or two. He kind of took me by surprise. And my cello needs some work. I had it all fixed with Mr. Isaac that I'd take it to him next week, so it would be ready by the time I could start playing again. I suppose I could have left it with him on the way over here Friday, but that was the last thing on our minds, especially Ed's. It was all I could do to convince him I wouldn't drop the baby in the shower. Anyhow, the cello's at home and I just know Ed's not going to want to mess with it."

Joan expected Evelyn to deliver them from the pregnant silence that followed, but an unruly mum suddenly needed to be coaxed into a more artistic place. Oh, well.

"I haven't found Isaac's shop yet," she said. "Where is it?"

"Just across the street from the old depot—only that's a tavern now," Nancy answered. "Of course, I never go to him. He's strictly strings. You'd be the natural, Joan."

Mmm. "I do need a couple of strings. How can I pick up the cello?"

"You're sure? Please don't go to a lot of trouble on my account," Charlotte said, looking relieved.

"I'm sure."

"Ed's home today, probably watching the ball game. I'll warn him to expect you to call." She beamed. "This is such a help. Thank you a lot. Mr. Isaac is going to work on the fingerboard and cut me a new bridge so I can play above third position on the inside strings. I just hope I can still manage lessons, what with the baby and all. I didn't expect to be so tired."

"I don't wonder you're tired," said a voice behind Joan. A nurse had entered the room on soundless soles, without the warning starched skirts once gave. Her brisk cheerfulness belied the dark circles under her own eyes. She pulled the hermetically sealed venetian blinds to darken the room slightly.

"You didn't get much sleep in thirty hours of labor," she said. "I can guarantee you won't get much after you go home, either. You've had a big visit now. Try to rest some before the babies are out again."

"Glenda! How nice to see you here," said Evelyn, turning from the flowers.

"Hello, Evelyn. Don't look so surprised; I work here, you know. And it really is time to leave."

"Oh, Glenda, please show them the baby!" Charlotte begged. "I almost feel as if he was yours, the way you stuck with me. She was so great," she said to the women now being herded out the door.

"I will."

Glenda kept her promise, stopping at the nursery window to point out a baby with a minuscule chin and a mop of black hair.

"Did you really stay with her thirty hours?" Nancy asked.

"No, of course not. I only work from seven to three. But I was here when she first came in, and then things were so quiet yesterday that I could almost special her. She was alone and scared. That Ed Hodden is no prize. He dropped her here and went off to do his worrying in a bar, from the looks of him when he finally showed up. We talked a lot until her labor picked up. She's a sweet girl."

A quick look at her name tag confirmed Joan's suspicion that this was Glenda Wallston, the symphony guild member whose daughter had been entangled with the Petris men. It was easy to understand her lack of sympathy for the sins of the fathers.

"I'm glad the orchestra sent flowers," Glenda went on. "Ed sure didn't. Are we doing something about Wanda, too?"

"I've checked with the undertaker," Joan said. "When the plans are settled, we'll do whatever is appropriate. We don't have the word on a memorial for George Petris yet, either, but I assume we will." Nor had anyone brought up the question. It seemed as good a time as any.

Glenda didn't turn a hair. "I suppose. Should I know you?"

Nancy introduced them. "Glenda's a member of the symphony guild, Joan. But of course, you saw her at rehearsal. She and Evelyn did the refreshments last Wednesday, remember?"

For once, Joan did remember. "That's right. You told me she served George. We've all been trying to remember, Glenda. Did George drink anything, or did he just eat cookies? I'm sure you've heard there's some question about his death."

"I wouldn't know. I was filling cups and Evelyn was handing them out. A lot of people just picked them up. I doubt if he ate anything, though."

"That's right," Evelyn said. "Sam always waits until after he's played. Most of the wind players do. We usually keep something out for them."

"Did you give him a cup, Evelyn?" Nancy asked.

"I don't remember. All that fuss, now really. I'm sure the man died of a heart attack, the way the doctor said. Your punch isn't that bad, Glenda."

No one laughed. Glenda looked pointedly at her watch.

"Sorry I can't stay to chat, but some of us have to make a living."

She stepped behind the nurse's desk and flipped open a chart.

Evelyn sailed out of the ward with her chin high. Joan and Nancy trailed in her wake.

"I don't see what got her so hot and bothered," Evelyn said as they stood waiting for the elevators, which seemed to be running in convoys.

"Is there a Mr. Wallston?" Joan asked.

"Not around here," Nancy answered. "He flew the coop years ago. Left Glenda with nothing—no money, no house, no car, no job. Just Lisa, who was about five. Fortunately, Glenda finished her training before she met the bum. She's managed, but it hasn't been any picnic."

"Did I say it had?" Evelyn asked huffily.

No, of course not, Joan thought. All you did was loll around in your Ultrasuede suit and your alligator shoes, looking as if you'd never washed a dish, much less a bedpan. Then you cracked jokes about her punch. You're lucky she didn't punch you.

Aloud, she said, "I think she was just tired. I know the feeling."

Nancy dropped Evelyn off first.

"Can you believe her?" she asked. "I know I have it easy compared to Glenda, but I don't think Evelyn has the faintest idea of what work is all about. You'd never catch her doing what you did over at Wanda's."

Joan's head swiveled in astonishment.

"Oh, I heard about that," Nancy said. "Things get around in Oliver. Actually, one of the fingerprint guys lives down the street from us. He didn't think his wife would have gone over there in the first place, much less done the laundry. And I can tell you for a fact that Evelyn wouldn't stoop to such a thing. I don't think she could iron a shirt if she had to. I'll bet it's been years since she even changed a bed."

"She did look elegant today."

"I would, too, if I spent the time and money she does shopping and at the beauty parlor. She was complaining that it took her all day yesterday to find those shoes. I didn't think there were that many shoes to choose from in Oliver. She shopped all morning on foot and then went back in the afternoon to try on everything over again. I feel for the clerks."

"At least she bought some."

"True. I'd hate to keep her in clothes, but I suppose it does help the local economy. Wonder if Sam makes her shop in town."

"Very politic of him."

Nancy looked blank for the briefest of moments. "He's a good politician, all right. But that Evelyn."

"Mmm." Saved by the driveway. "Thanks for the ride, Nancy. I'll see you Wednesday. I hope to goodness I find some time between now and then to practice. This has been a wicked week." In more ways than one.

"Don't forget the cello!" Nancy called, and was gone.

SIXTEEN

CHECKING THE PHONE BOOK, Joan found that Isaac's Violin Studio kept a Saturday rather than a Sunday sabbath. Might as well get it over with.

Ed Hodden answered the doorbell barefoot and barechested, a can of beer in one hand and the cello dangling precariously from the other by the frayed strap of its canvas case. Joan hugged it to her side like a drunken friend and was glad she had when the strap broke while she was wrestling with the door to the studio.

Squeezed between a pizza parlor and a pawnshop, the violin shop was distinctly grubby, at least on the outside. Joan looked across the street at the depot-turned-tavern and remembered vaguely going there with her father to meet someone's train.

It seemed like a strange neighborhood for a music shop. Maybe the rent was low. She found it hard to imagine that Oliver could support someone who dealt only in strings, unless he included guitars.

A little bell jingled as she pulled the stubborn door shut. No clerk stood behind the small counter, but a voice called out, "Be right with you." Joan held the cello carefully by the neck, resting it on its endpin. Violins of all sizes hung from nails on the walls around her, supported by miniature nooses. With a body no more than six or seven inches long, the smallest looked like one of the plastic toy fiddles once sold in dime stores. It might be an eighth size or maybe even a sixteenth. What kind of tone could such a tiny box possibly produce?

She was fascinated by a full-sized violin missing most of its top and back. It looked like bare bones. At first she thought it must be in for repair, but then she could see that it was beautifully finished as it was. Fully strung, it even had a chin rest.

"Whatever for?" she wondered aloud.

"For your world tour. Very useful for practicing in hotel rooms. No one complains when you play out your jet lag at three in the morning. No one else hears."

Short, bent, and with the remains of a crop of wiry curls fringing his ears with gray, the man coming through the door from the back of the shop had to be Mr. Isaac.

"Do you sell a lot of those?" Joan asked.

"Not too many people around here make world tours," he admitted. "On the other hand, once they start thinking about the possibilities, quite a few take a look at a good heavy practice mute. It really cuts down the sound. Wouldn't you like one for your cello? Very reasonable, and when the children are sleeping you can practice in peace, without waking them."

"You flatter me," she said. "It's years since I had a child who went to bed before I did. Besides, this is Charlotte Hodden's cello, not mine. She's the one who's going to need a practice mute."

"I remember. I'm going to raise the fingerboard to two and a half inches and cut a bridge with some curve to it while she's having a baby. I don't know how she could play, as flat as it is now."

"That's it, but the baby didn't wait for you, so she asked me to bring the cello over." She handed it to him, pointing out the broken strap.

"Boy or girl?" he asked, reaching around the cello's curve for a handhold.

"A boy. Lots of hair."

"And how is she doing?"

"Fine. She's tired."

"You tell her not to worry. The cello will be ready before she is."

"I'll tell her. And I need some strings myself."

"Let me put this in a safe place first. What strings do you want?"

"A viola A and G."

"Come on back in the shop. Watch your feet."

She followed him into a room crowded with cases and larger instruments. Several cellos and a bass lay on their sides. Violins and violas in varying states of repair hung from their scrolls in a rack that was a cross between a shadow box and the pipe rack Andrew had once proudly presented his non-smoking father. Compartments under the stripped-down violins held pegs, end buttons, chin rests, bridges, tail pieces, snarls of strings, tuners, and other less easily identifiable bits, presumably to keep them together while the instruments were in the shop. Three shoulder rests under the same violin made Joan wonder how well the system worked.

Bows in need of rehairing hung from nails on another wall, some from the frog and others from the tip, each labeled with a little white sticker on the frog. Hanks of horsehair, both white and black, dangled above one workbench, and blank bridges of all sizes were threaded like fish on a stringer over another. A mended violin top lay on the first bench, cushioned by a scrap of carpet. Half a dozen clamps held its newly glued bass bar in place, and square wooden cleats reinforced a long crack.

Joan recognized vises, clamps, and files. She wasn't so sure about some awl-shaped tools in several sizes. In an odd assortment of small jars and bottles, mostly baby food jars, she could see fluids, from clear to amber to dark brown. Varnish, she supposed. Maybe glue? A familiar white bottle of Elmer's lay on its side in the clutter, but she knew violins predated Elmer's. Dust motes danced in the sunshine above the workbenches.

"Would you mind taking the case with you?" Isaac asked. "I'm very short of space."

"Yes, I can see that."

He unzipped the canvas, tagged the cello, and gave her the case and a receipt for the instrument.

"Don't bend that case too far—the bow's still in there. Now, tell me, what kind of strings did you have in mind?"

"I could really use some advice," she said. "I want a good sound, mostly for orchestral playing, but I can't afford Eudoxas now and my viola chews up gut A strings, even if they're wrapped."

"It shouldn't do that. Bring it in. Maybe there's a rough spot I could file down. In the meantime, why don't you try a Jargar A? It's chrome steel on steel, and I think the tone is better than the Eudoxa steel A. For the G, you could move down to the domestic Gold Label. That's still silver on gut, but you'll save more than three dollars on a single string."

She took his suggestions gratefully and watched him sort out her new G string from the bunches of little identifying tags sticking out of the transparent storage tubes on the wall like so many long-stemmed flowers. He presented it for her inspection and gave her a flexible plastic tube to protect it. The Jargar A came coiled in a white envelope—not such a good sign, but she'd try it.

"You know," she said, as he wrote up the sale, "I'm really surprised to find you here."

"Why is that?"

"Oliver is such a small town. I can't help wondering how you stay in business."

"I keep busy enough," he said. "It's true that I'd go under if I had to depend on Oliver alone. We have customers all over the country through our catalog."

"I wouldn't have thought there were this many instruments to repair here. Do you do that by mail, too?"

"A lot of them do come from out of town. We contract with a dozen school systems to do all their string repair work. Those kids are hard on school instruments. The teachers do a lot of the little routine jobs, but they can't handle a crack like the one over there." He gestured to the mended violin top Joan had noticed earlier.

"And sometimes I sell one of my own instruments," he said. "I'm almost finished with a viola now. People know I'm here. I don't need a factory for what I do and I like Oliver, especially with the college here."

"It's a labor of love, isn't it?" She looked at a half-carved block of curly maple on the second workbench. It was already recognizable as a cello back. "Do you do it all by hand?"

"Almost. We have a drill, and a bench grinder. Unfortunately, my band saw broke down. That was useful. But that cello over there is all handmade. I have a very promising young man working with me. That's his, and it's going to be a beauty."

"Would that be Daniel Petris?"

"That's right. You know Daniel?"

"We've met."

"Very steady hand with a knife, Daniel has. He made me the best knife I ever had. Wonderful blade." He held it up as she would hold a pencil. She admired the grain and varnish of the handle and then watched with a sickening feeling as he demonstrated the wicked-looking angled blade on a scrap of the curly maple.

"Don't you ever cut yourself?" she made herself ask.

"This kind of work you have to do very precisely."

"But it's sharp enough?"

"It could cut you to the bone if you slipped." He looked at her quizzically. "Are you planning to take up violin making?"

"Oh, no. I was just wondering."

She continued to wonder all the way home.

SEVENTEEN

THE OLIVER CIVIC SYMPHONY was turning out to be a churchgoing lot, unless maybe they played golf. The bright blue, almost October weather would tempt anyone.

Fred's elbow on the car's windowsill caught a perfect blend of sun and cool morning breeze. From time to time he passed a jogger; otherwise the streets were quiet. The hills of nearby Brown County, he knew, would already be swarming with tourists eager for a first glimpse of spectacular fall color. He looked down Prospect Avenue. An old maple that had survived a stroke of lightning a few years back was brilliant all down the injured side. Deep purple mixed with yellow and green on the sweet gums. Sassafras mittens were turning golden, and dogwood leaves and berries a bright red. A giant sycamore was shedding leaves the size of dinner plates.

It's all in your press agent, he thought.

No one had been home at the last three homes. Now it looked as if he might be wasting his time at the Wades', too; only a spanking new powder blue Cadillac faced him from the double garage. Then he remembered hearing Evelyn say in Werner's lab that Sam's Mercedes was in the shop. He might be home after all.

Sam, wearing Levis and an Izod shirt, opened the door.

"Something come up?" he asked.

"No, just routine. I'm looking for background information on Wanda Borowski. You're a witness in this one, Sam."

"Come on in."

He entered through a slate foyer. An antique umbrella stand stood ready at his left. Ahead, a sizable fig tree basked in the golden glow of the sun beaming down through a skylight.

There was nothing understated about the elegance of the living room. Fred's feet sank into deeply padded carpet. The Cadillac's pale blue appeared here in velvet chairs and satin draperies. Clutter was conspicuously absent. In a crystal vase, one perfect red rose was unfolding its first petals. He was sure the decorator would have approved.

"Have a seat," Sam said. "Coffee?"

"No, thanks." Fred outlined quickly his thinking about the relationship between Saturday's obvious murder and the nebulous question of George Petris.

"It wouldn't hold up in court, I know," he said. "Even so, I'm convinced that there's more than coincidence here. I'm worried, especially for those of you in the orchestra who were close to Petris. We don't need another Borowski."

"You're going house to house warning people?" Sam sounded faintly amused.

"Something like that. Go ahead, laugh. I'm not laughing, though, and I'd appreciate your help."

"I'll do what I can. Fire away." Sam draped an arm over a velvet cushion and leaned back elegantly.

"Let's stick with Borowski for a minute. What do you know about her?"

"Hardly anything. She was kind of quiet, didn't talk much about anything but the music. She played very well."

"Was she close to anyone in the orchestra? Did she have any enemies?"

"I don't know. I really didn't get to know her."

"How about Petris? I hear he was quite a womanizer."

"She wasn't his type."

"What was his type?"

"Not mousy. That's it, she was mousy."

"How come she had his oboe?"

"She caught it when he fell. I grabbed him and she grabbed it. When we saw how bad he was, she told him she'd take care of it, and he kind of nodded. That was that."

"You know it's missing."

Sam nodded. "I read it in the police report."

"Sam, would an oboe be worth much on the open market? Was there anything special about this one? It seems like an unlikely think to walk off with."

"It's a good instrument, a Lorée, pretty much the twin of mine, although no two are ever quite the same. They depreciate. It might bring fifteen hundred or thereabouts, if you could find the right buyer. You couldn't fence it. The serial number would have a trail a mile wide. Nothing else was stolen?"

"No," Fred said. "It's a funny business."

"I suppose she didn't have much worth taking. I had the impression that she lived fairly simply."

"There was some cash lying around, and antique silver right there in the buffet."

"That's funny, all right." Sam's forehead wrinkled. "You think she surprised a sneak thief before he could take off with the goods, and he killed her and ran with the first thing handy?"

"No. She spent the whole morning at home. The kids and the neighbors agree about that. There's another possibility, though. We still haven't recovered the weapon, and if this was a spur of the moment thing, I wonder if it wasn't the reed knife. Petris did have one, didn't he?"

"Oh, sure."

"I can't remember what they look like. Is yours handy?"

Sam patted his pockets and handed Fred a black-handled knife, its blade covered by a brown leatherette case with a metal rim.

Fred whistled softly when he removed the case. Three inches long and almost an inch wide, the blade tapered from a back an eighth of an inch across to an edge as sharp as any razor's. He found the gap where the blade entered the plastic handle too dark to see how solidly it was seated.

"I'd think one of these would have no trouble doing the job," he said, testing the edge cautiously with his thumb. "The handle would give us decent prints, too, if we got lucky enough to find it. Okay to show this to Henshaw?"

Sam shrugged. "I won't need it till Wednesday."

"Wednesday?" Fred sheathed the blade and pocketed the knife.

"Orchestra night. Far as I know, we're rehearsing."

"I'll want to be there."

"Don't you think you're carrying this orchestra bit a little far? Sure you aren't just interested in that Mrs. Spencer?"

"Where did you get that idea?"

"Catherine Turner catered the dinner Friday. It was one of those stand-up deals. Don't ever go into politics, Fred. There comes a time when your arm drops off from shaking hands, your teeth are dying of exposure, and you can hear your stomach rumbling during what passes for dinner. I finally sneaked out to the kitchen and intercepted a tray of hot things straight from the oven. I almost didn't get away. Catherine and I go way back, and she had a few choice things to say about you and Mrs. Spencer."

"There's nothing to say." Fred tried to keep his voice light. Inside, he fumed. Who did Catherine think she was, staking out a claim on him like that, and to the county attorney?

"That's not the way she heard it. Her Aunt Trudie says you made a date with the lady."

"I don't even know her Aunt Trudie."

"Maybe not, but she knew you when you came into the Senior Citizens' Center. Better watch your step. Catherine was spittin' nails."

That explained the uproar about the sourdough on Saturday. Fred had no intention of becoming Catherine's exclusive property and even less of discussing the matter.

"Speaking of food, Sam, I've been wondering how many wind players eat before they play."

"I always have supper."

"I was thinking of the refreshments at the orchestra break."

"You're really taking this poisoning business seriously, aren't you?"

Fred didn't answer.

"All right, all right. Me, I stick to water. Anything else gunks up the instrument."

"That's what my old band director always tried to tell us at football games. You can imagine how well we listened. How about Petris and Borowski?"

"They both kept away from crumbs, too, but I think he usually had whatever they were offering to drink. I'm not sure about her. It didn't seem to affect his playing any."

"Good, was he?"

"We were lucky to have him as a player." A large "but" hung there, unspoken.

"And otherwise?"

"I got along with him all right. I'm sure you've heard by now that he'd never win a popularity contest."

"Any of the other folks who knew about reed knives likely to have it in for him—or for Borowski?"

"I still think you're barking up the wrong tree." Sam stood up. "Tell you what, Fred. Go talk it over with the little Mrs. Spencer. You wouldn't want to make a liar out of Aunt Trudie, would you?"

Fred accepted the pleasantry as the dismissal it was. At the door, he turned back for one last question.

"Almost forgot, Sam. Where were you between ten o'clock and noon yesterday?"

The politician's smile held.

"In and out of the office. Maxine keeps a log."

"Thanks. See you Wednesday, if not before."

He decided to give Elmer Rush another try before stopping for a late lunch. As he pulled up in front of the house, he saw the wheelchair halfway down the block and went on foot to meet it.

RUSH REMEMBERED HIM from his visit to the Senior Citizens' Center. Frowning, he introduced Julie in a friendly enough tone.

"Mr. Lundquist is a policeman, Julie," he told her.

Her smile made Fred wish he could add a dozen of his excess years to her mental ones. He held out his hand.

"Hello, Julie. How are you?"

"Fine." She beamed at him and took his hand as a small child would.

"I met Julie's mother," he said over her head. "She explained about her. Sounds like a freak accident."

"Accident, my foot!" Rush exploded. "It was criminal. Someone had been fooling with the safety grill over the pool's filter. Julie must have dislodged it, and the suction of the pump held her underwater. By the time I finally got the so-called lifeguard to turn it off, the bruise on her back was the shape of the drain."

Julie was beginning to look back and forth at their troubled faces. Her own mouth turned down.

"But now you're just fine, aren't you, punkin?" her grandfather said quickly, giving the wheelchair a twirl. She giggled, sounding like any little girl on a merry-go-round.

"What can I do for you, Lieutenant?" Rush asked, maintaining the light tone he had just used with Julie.

"It's about Mrs. Borowski."

"Mrs. who?"

"She played flute in the symphony."

"I don't know her."

"Maybe you read about her or heard it on the news. She was murdered yesterday."

"I saw the story, but I didn't read it. Those things depress me." He gripped the chair and marched it toward the house. Fred's long strides kept up easily.

"I don't want to upset you, but I do hope you can help me with a couple of things. Would you rather wait until Julie's home?"

"If you must."

They left Julie with her mother and continued walking. As soon as they were out of earshot, Rush turned on Fred.

"What business did you have bothering my daughter?"

"I was looking for you."

"You were dredging up old horror stories. There's no call for that." Grim-faced, he marched on, his back straight and his every step a slap at the pavement.

"No, there wouldn't be. I mentioned to Mrs. Lambert that I had seen you at the Senior Citizens' Center with Julie. She told me less than you did about what happened to her."

"You called it a freak accident."

"Mr. Rush, I've seen a lot of drownings. It's a rare thing that someone survives after being under long enough to have problems from it, and it was even less common some years back. I'm sorry it happened to Julie. She's a beautiful young woman."

"What did you want with me?" He wasn't yielding an inch.

"As I said, I'm investigating the death of Wanda Borowski. She was the flute player who sat almost immediately in front of you in the symphony rehearsal last Wednesday— the one who packed up the oboe when George Petris became ill."

"Oh, her." Rush scratched the top of his ear. "I don't know what I could tell you about her."

"What about him? I didn't want to alarm your daughter, but there is some question about his death, too. We're considering the possibility that Mrs. Borowski might have been killed because she was in a position to notice something before he died."

"That's pretty far-fetched."

"I hope so. If not, I'm afraid you might be in some danger yourself."

"Oh." They took a few steps in silence. "I can't think of anything. I really think you'd do better to talk to people who knew him longer."

"I understand that you and he had become fairly friendly by last Wednesday."

"All I did was set out to make a little peace. I see no point in playing in a group like that if there's constant backbiting."

"Backbiting?"

"I don't know what that man's problem was, but I learned a long time ago that the best way to win someone over is to ask his advice. I've been winding reeds since before he was born, so I let him teach me how to do it. Never fails." His eyes suddenly twinkled.

Fred ran through the details of the rehearsal and the break. Rush had gone out for some cool air, but he hadn't bothered with the punch and cookies nor taken particular notice of those who had.

"I drank that stuff the week before and wished I hadn't. This old dog learns fast." He grinned. His anger seemed to have disappeared completely. Fred was beginning to understand what Martha Lambert had meant about her father's moods. They turned the corner at the end of the block.

"Did you notice anything unusual about the oboe itself?"

"No, I was paying more attention to the man. Then I was packing up."

"Just for the record, can you remember where you were yesterday morning, say between ten and noon?"

"Home. Martha took the other kids out shopping. I stayed with Julie."

"Would she remember that, if I asked her?"

"There's no point in bothering Julie. She'd remember anything I told her to—for a little while, anyway. One day's the same as another to Julie."

More questioning yielded nothing useful. Fred finally had to content himself with warning the old man again.

"Don't worry, Lieutenant." The fire was back in the faded blue eyes. "When I got the golden handshake at sixty-five, I didn't think I'd ever be needed again, but Martha and Julie need me now. I'm not going to let anything more happen to that child. *Nobody* is going to take me away from my family."

I hope not, Fred thought.

EIGHTEEN

REACHING FOR THE PHONE to call Fred, Joan jumped when it rang. For a moment she thought he had read her mind, but it was only Yoichi, asking apologetically whether she would be willing to copy some bowings on string parts he had just received from Alex.

"They came in the mail yesterday and she doesn't want to use any rehearsal time," he explained. "She has marked the first stands' parts; we won't have to work for the score."

Joan thought personally that violin sectionals would save more time in rehearsal than anything she and Yoichi could put on paper, but she felt too much like the new kid on the block to suggest such a thing. Other people's behavior during rehearsal suggested that Alex had been wasting their time for years.

"Can you bring them over?"

"It will take some time. The bicycle is not working properly. I think something is wrong with the gears."

"Do you think that's why you fell?"

"I don't know. I am not very mechanical. I will take it to be repaired tomorrow."

There went any chance of practicing today. Her own laundry awaited her, and the dozen small chores she now put off until weekends. Still, a thousand a year was worth some minor inconvenience. She wrote down his address and promised to arrive before suppertime.

She reached Fred on her second try and told him as succinctly as she could about Daniel's prowess with sharp knives and about Yoichi's fall and bloody sweater.

"How does he look?" Fred asked.

"I don't know. I'll see him soon. I'm leaving to pick up some music from him."

"Not alone, you're not. I'll meet you in ten minutes. I want to see for myself."

If Yoichi was startled when they arrived together, he managed not to show it. He thanked Joan for her advice. The sweater, he said, was like new. Dividing up the parts, he gave Joan the seconds and violas to mark, and kept the firsts and cellos for himself.

Joan saw with a sinking heart that the music was Rezniček's overture to *Donna Diana*, whose soaring theme once heralded the grueling radio adventures of Sergeant Preston of the Yukon.

For her, however, it evoked instantly a nightmarish summer high school music camp at which she had been the sole violist, faced with a long series of arpeggios filled with accidentals that demanded rapid string crossings and forays into half and second positions, all at a tempo beyond what she could manage. It wasn't a solo—the oboe had the melody—but only the viola part supplied that tricky underpinning, and only Joan had registered to play viola that session.

She had spent most of her practice time on the dreaded passage, bringing it to a shaky adequacy at the last minute. Briefly, the weight of the world had been lifted from her shoulders by the arrival of a "ringer" from a nearby music school for the dress rehearsal and final concert. It had crashed down on her again when, the first time through the overture, the music student had told her quietly, "You're on your own. I'm going to have to fake this one. I'd never get it right with only one rehearsal." All these years later, just seeing the music could still start her adrenaline flowing. Maybe the new kid could suggest a viola sectional, she thought. At least I won't be alone this time.

Yoichi was responding to Fred's friendly questions about his accident. No, he hadn't been hurt badly enough to need a doctor. He had been riding to the grocery, he said, but he'd postponed his shopping and returned home instead to clean up.

"What time did all this happen?" The question was still friendly, but Joan wondered how Yoichi could possibly miss its purpose.

"Eleven o'clock. I heard the chimes on the college square before I fell." He smiled, a little stiffly because of the crusted-over place on his left cheek, but his eyes didn't meet the big detective's.

"Were you leaving from home?"

"Yes, I was studying here in the morning."

"Alone?"

"Yes. I can't prove it. What time did she die?"

No flies on him, Joan thought.

"We're working on that," Fred answered, still friendly. "Thank you for your help."

In one fluid motion Yoichi knelt to retrieve a violin part that had slipped to the floor. He reminded Joan to use a soft pencil and to mark the bowings lightly.

"Alex may change her mind, or the concertmaster. I hope she consulted him this time. I think he sometimes makes changes only to show that he is concertmaster. Not always good ones." He smiled, but Joan was sure he meant it.

On the way back, Fred was quiet. Pulling up in front of Joan's house, he said, "I wish I could believe him. His face is scraped about right for a fall."

"But?"

"Did you see him pick that music off the floor? You told me he was stiff and sore."

"He's probably more accustomed to kneeling than we are. Besides, how do you know it didn't hurt?"

"I can't put my finger on it. I always have the feeling that he's holding something back."

She avoided his eyes.

"You, too?" he asked. She laughed.

"No, that was an experiment. The sweater business made me wonder and I don't really know him at all. But I do know not to worry that he doesn't look me in the eye. That's not Japanese. Yoichi has been here for some time, you can tell, but under stress I suspect he'll always come across as shifty-eyed if you don't know better."

"Could be. Humor me, though—don't spend any time alone with him. I'll be there Wednesday night, by the way. I'm talking with individual members today, but I think I'd better see a rehearsal."

" 'See' is right. It's much too early to listen. We're still awfully ragged."

After he left, she flicked through the music. The fearsome stretch jumped out at her. She could imagine the cutting remarks from the oboe section—but no, not this week. Still, a knot twisted somewhere in the middle when she thought of the speed at which Alex would probably take those unending broken chords. She set the marked viola part on her stand, and tossed the others and the seconds into the box of orchestra folders. The bowings could wait.

When Andrew arrived home, she was woodshedding away and not inclined to stop. She'd already put in so many fingerings that she knew she'd have to label another copy Viola 1 and keep this one for herself. Maybe John Hocking wouldn't mind playing from it and she wouldn't have to remember what she'd worked out. She was pleased to find that she knew the key changes solidly, at least in her ears. Unfortunately, memory hadn't carried over to her fingers at all. If Alex would show a little mercy on the tempo, though, she thought she might manage something more than pure faking by Wednesday.

"What's for supper?" Andrew asked, tossing his books on the sofa.

"I don't know. Surprise me." She dug into another six-note pattern, first repeating it over and over, and then connecting it to those before and after it. It was the changes that threw her, and the lack of let-up.

"You're really messing up," Andrew said.

Joan repressed a snarl.

"Andrew, can you say 'rubber baby buggy bumpers'?"

"Rubber baby buggy bumpers. Why?"

"Now say it ten times, fast."

"Come on, Mom."

"Go ahead, try."

He survived three before degenerating into "bubby bunkers" and retreating into the kitchen, where she could hear him slamming doors and muttering to himself. Half an hour later, she was willing to call a truce with the overture. She wiped the excess rosin off the strings and laid the viola in its case. Andrew appeared in the doorway.

"Which omelet do you want, Mom, the one with onion or the plain cheese?"

It wasn't a joke. He had managed two perfectly browned omelets, light and moist in the middle. The coffee was hot, the toast crisp, and the salad fresh.

"Who taught you to make an omelet?" Joan asked, after the first forkful of the cheese. "This is wonderful."

"It is, isn't it?" he said between bites. "I think I have a natural gift. I should cook more often."

"That could be arranged. What else can you do?"

"Depends on what's in the refrigerator. Ham, turkey, mushrooms—combinations. Almost did a turkey-cheese-onion tonight, but we were out of turkey."

"All omelets?"

"You don't like omelets?" His face was innocence itself.

"Love 'em," she said firmly. "I'll probably die young, full of cholesterol, but with a smile on my face."

SHE WAS TELLING Margaret Duffy about it while they pitched in to fold mimeographed newsletters after the Senior Citizens' Center board meeting on Monday morning.

"He keeps surprising me. I'm enjoying him and I don't think I'm cramping his style too much."

"You probably give him the kind of freedom your folks gave you. I'll tell you, the Zimmermans set this town on its ear with their notions about bringing up children."

"Notions? My parents?"

"I'll never forget the night they took on the PTA over the issue of corporal punishment. There was some disagreement about what teachers should be allowed to do to other people's children, but your parents went out on a limb all by themselves when they said in public that they didn't spank their own."

"They never mentioned it at home," Joan said.

"Probably not, but the teachers' lounge buzzed for a week about how you'd turn out."

"And then we left town before they could find out. I wonder what they'd think if they knew I was a Zimmerman."

"Well, it did come up when you applied for this job."

"It didn't!" She stopped folding in surprise. "And they hired me."

"Alvin Hannauer didn't hurt. He was tickled to have your father on the dig that year. Experienced anthropologists didn't drop in every day, you know, especially not with a grant in hand to study Rattlesnake Mound. Mostly he had to manage with students who wanted him to pay them while he tried to teach them not to destroy all the evidence every time they discovered an artifact."

Joan chuckled. "He sounds just like Dad."

"They had a lot in common," Margaret said. "Anyway, when the board was dragging its feet about you—you didn't have the qualifications on paper, and even worse, you were a stranger—Alvin said he'd heard about you in letters for years and we'd be lucky to get you."

Touched to know that her usually uncommunicative father had written anything about her at all, much less letters with such an effect, Joan was grateful to the man who had spoken up for her.

"I'll have to thank him. I didn't think anybody but you would know about me."

"Well, of course, I didn't, not really," Margaret said. "Not the way I know the people I watch grow up around here. I taught two generations of quite a few families—three of some."

Of course. Margaret would know Oliver inside out.

"You probably taught a lot of the people in the orchestra, didn't you?" Joan asked, reaching for a stack of mailing labels.

"Well, yes, over the years. Most of them left town. It's amazing how little the ones who stayed have changed, though. Nancy Krebs never listened in class and she's still too wound up in her own affairs to hear what anyone else has to say. Makes for boring conversation."

Trust Margaret Duffy to put her finger on it.

"Nancy says Evelyn Wade was in our class, too, but I don't remember her."

"You and Evelyn didn't see much of each other. She was a bossy little thing—spoiled rotten, I thought. But that sounds like a whiny child and she never whined. Still, when she set out after something, she was accustomed to getting it and she always made it show. She was big on show—used to draw little circles over all the i's in her schoolwork but couldn't be bothered about spelling. You were just the opposite. Pigtails and shoelaces always coming undone. I expect she would have looked down on you, if you'd noticed her. But you went around with your nose in a book and missed half the snubs that came your way."

"I remember enough." Joan resisted the temptation to check her back hair. "Did you teach Wanda Borowski or George Petris?"

"I taught Daniel and Emily Petris. The parents came from somewhere on the West Coast. Emily followed her mother back there when that marriage broke up. Daniel floated around Oliver like a lost soul for a year or two, but he seems to have pulled himself together recently."

"Probably because of Mr. Isaac." Joan described her visit to the violin studio and Isaac's obvious pride in the beautiful cello back Daniel was carving. She caught herself before mentioning anything about knives, even to Margaret, although it seemed a laughable precaution. Instead, she asked about Wanda.

"Yes, I remember Wanda," Margaret said. "She came to me fresh from St. Paul's. I often wondered whether she'd become a nun herself."

"Why?"

"I don't know. I suppose it was because she was so meticulous in everything she did. She was quiet, never boisterous, seemed almost afraid of boys. Five years in all-girl classes might account for that, but it didn't have that effect on most of the girls. But I was wrong."

"Maybe you weren't that far off. Her house felt like a convent to me. Old-fashioned, painfully clean. I remember wondering if the children were ever allowed to mess things up. And she planned ahead. At eleven in the morning, she had supper going in a slow cooker, and I think she must have sprinkled those shirts the night before or at the crack of dawn, they were so evenly damp. It felt like the old nursery rhyme: 'This is the day we iron our shirts.'"

"Old habits die hard, Joan. There was a time I thought the world would come to an end if I washed on Saturday instead of Monday, but what else could a schoolteacher do? Of course, back then it took all day—you couldn't just toss a few things into the automatic when you wanted them. But I still organize my life that way. Only now it's Saturday that feels like the only right day, even as long as I've been retired."

Joan was sitting very still, her fingers idle.

"Joan, are you all right?"

She came to life slowly.

"I'm sorry, Margaret, did you say something? I wasn't tuned in. I think...I think I've just figured something out."

NINETEEN

A CUP OF Monday morning coffee at his elbow, Fred hunched over his desk in the windowless squadroom sifting through a fat stack of reports on the Borowski murder and his own skimpy notes on the Petris case.

The poisoned cup, he was convinced, had been burned with the rest of the trash. The only angle he could see on George Petris was the possibility that the killer considered Wanda Borowski a threat, and he knew he was swimming upstream on that. He hadn't been pulled off the case, but he could feel the stifled snickers when his back was turned.

I'm paranoid, he told himself, and turned to the reports. Still no weapon. All the Borowski kitchen knives were clean as the proverbial whistle. Whoever coined that expression had spent precious little time with wind instruments, he thought. They all smelled of spit sooner or later. Clean or not, though, George's oboe hadn't been turned up by an exhaustive search of the Borowskis' neighborhood.

Isaac had sworn that none of his knives had left the violin studio, which was locked on Saturday. It mattered very little, after all. Daniel might have made a knife of his own—he'd shown his talent in that direction. Or, like anyone else arriving at Wanda's house when she had the oboe waiting for him, he might have used his father's missing reed knife. Fred picked up the phone to check with the pathologist about the knife Sam had lent him Sunday.

"Just saw it," Dr. Henshaw answered, much too cheerfully for a Monday morning. "Sure, it would make a clean cut like that. Too bad the end of the blade is rounded off, though. Give me a nice wedge-shaped end, now, and I might be able to match it to a mark that would pin it down."

"You found a mark?" This was news.

"No, but if I had."

If we had some ham, we could have ham and eggs, Fred thought gloomily, if we had some eggs.

"Okay if I send it back with the kitchen knives?" Henshaw asked.

"As long as it's here Wednesday."

"No problem."

Fred turned back to the reports. Although he had kept the time of Wanda's death out of the paper, there was little mystery about it. The old ladies had seen her alive and apparently well at ten-thirty, and Fred himself had recorded the call from Daniel Petris at eleven. It stretched credulity to picture Daniel first making that call and then murdering the lady. Besides, Henshaw had put the time of death at not later than eleven, and they had run the washing machine through its cycle. Working back from the time Joan heard it stop, Fred estimated that Wanda must have started that last load no earlier than ten minutes to eleven. Sometime in those ten minutes, then, someone had walked into her house unobserved, killed her without rousing the neighbors, and left without leaving so much as a footprint in the blood that splattered the bedroom floor and puddled around her body.

So it was going to come down to the tedium of ten-minute alibis. He gave a copy of the orchestra personnel list to Kyle Pruitt and explained what he wanted.

"Hate to do this to you, son."

"You really think one of them in the orchestra cut her?" The young sergeant's eagerness reminded him of his own at the same age. With a round face, red hair, and a toothy grin, Pruitt looked a little too much like a plump version of the "What, me worry?" kid to be taken seriously in plain clothes. A former high school linebacker, he now resembled a budding sumo wrestler more than a lean, hard cop, and he knew it.

"I don't know, but it's time to start weeding out the ones who couldn't have." Fred borrowed the paper back and made little checks by the names of Elmer Rush and Yoichi Nakamura. "I've already talked to these two."

"You sure you want me to talk to Wade?" asked Kyle, always leery of the bureaucrats.

"Just check with his secretary. They were working Saturday."

"And the ladies?" Kyle's big forefinger indicated the members of the symphony guild.

"Mrs. Wallston and Mrs. Wade were at the rehearsal when Petris died. I think you can skip the others for now. And, Kyle..." He paused.

"Sir?"

"Anybody can't tell you where he was, you just say thanks anyway and leave. The polite cop, that's you. All I want this time out are the easy answers."

"Take their word for it?"

"Get all the confirmation you can. Just don't pick a fight to do it."

Kyle blushed as only a redhead can. It hadn't been an idle reminder. That eagerness had landed him in hot water more than once. He left, looking somewhat subdued. Fred hoped the mood would last.

He was a little curious to know how long it would take for the word to get around that the police were connecting Borowski and Petris. Not that Kyle Pruitt would be saying any such thing. He was to approach the members of the orchestra as people who knew the victim of a brutal murder and to ask whether they had seen her the morning she was killed. Routine questions about possible enemies or reasons someone might have had for killing her would lead up to a last-minute turn and a casual "By the way, where were you Saturday between ten and twelve?" If Kyle managed the approach skillfully enough, he might not have to ask the question at all. All things considered, however, Fred gave the Oliver grapevine an hour at most.

FORTY MINUTES LATER, the desk sergeant buzzed him with the news that a young woman wanted to make a statement about the Borowski murder.

"Who is she?"

"Name of Lisa Wallston."

"Send her in. No, I'll come for her."

Fred threaded his way through the maze of desks and corridors to the front. Daniel Petris had called her good-looking. He hadn't said she was a knockout. Slender, blond, with summer's tan still warm on her skin, Lisa filled her trim slacks and simple cotton blouse in all the right places. The longest, darkest lashes he'd ever seen on a face untouched by cosmetics fringed her surprising brown eyes. She turned them on him full force, with no trace of a smile.

"Detective Lundquist?"

"Miss Wallston." They shook hands.

"I've come to tell you about Daniel."

He led her back to an empty office, aware as she surely must be of the heads turning in their direction. She gave no sign of noticing. He supposed she must be used to it. Nevertheless, he pulled the door half shut. He swiveled his chair toward hers, leaned back, and hooked his toes under the desk drawer.

"So, tell me about Daniel. You do mean Daniel Petris?"

"The whole town knows I mean Daniel Petris. Where have you been?" Her accent was soft Hoosier, but her voice had a hard edge he wasn't altogether sure he believed.

He waited. She glared at him.

"They say you're asking where people were yesterday morning, when that woman was killed."

"That's right."

"Daniel was with me. I don't know what he said—he maybe didn't want to drag me into this—but we spent the night in my apartment. I'm surprised the busybodies haven't already told you." She challenged him to make something of it.

"When did he leave?" Fred asked, not rising to the bait.

"Noon, maybe. I'm not exactly sure." She tucked a long strand of straight blond hair back behind her right ear.

"You mean you're not sure when she was killed."

"No, that's not what I mean at all." She bristled.

"You haven't talked to him."

"Not since Saturday." Now she was beginning to hedge.

"Miss Wallston, I might as well tell you. We know Daniel was at the Borowskis' house by eleven Saturday morning." He tilted his chair upright and leaned toward her. "Why did you come?"

All the starch had gone out of her. Suddenly she shrugged and smiled, dazzlingly.

"I guess I thought he was worth it. I couldn't let him get messed up in something like this." The smile faded. "Daniel didn't kill that woman, I know he didn't."

"Maybe not, but you didn't help him any—or yourself, for that matter."

"So it was dumb. I've done worse things. He didn't deserve them either. Only this time I was trying to help."

"Why did you think Daniel might be involved? His name hasn't been mentioned."

"But I thought..." Lisa stopped in some confusion. The hair escaped from behind her ear. She pushed it back.

"You thought?" Fred prompted.

"I thought you thought the person who killed George killed this Mrs. Borowski, too."

The grapevine wins again. "And you thought Daniel killed his father, is that it?"

"N-no." She backpedaled rapidly. "I don't know what I thought. I just know Daniel is twice the man his father ever was. George talked a wonderful line, but he never lived up to an obligation in his life. He flunked fatherhood, made a mess out of his marriage, and wrecked my life. I'm not sorry he's dead and I won't pretend to be."

"I understand your mother was serving refreshments at the rehearsal the night he died."

"Was she?" She stopped short. "You don't think for a minute my mother would kill a man! Why, she's a nurse," she said, as if that made all the difference.

"Do you know where she was Saturday morning?"

"She was working. I was home. That part was true." She pushed the hair back again, her fingers following the curve of her ear. "Daniel didn't spend the night. I haven't seen him or his crummy father for months."

"Any neighbors around? Anybody see you?"

"No."

"Phone calls?"

"No."

Fred added her to his list of unconfirmed alibis. True, she hadn't been anywhere near Petris during the rehearsal, but her mother had. And although it would be easy to check whether her mother had been on duty Saturday, Lisa herself might have been anywhere. Together, they had opportunity—and undeniable motive, if the second murder was in some way to cover the first. From what he'd seen at Werner's lab, access to the poison wouldn't have been a problem for anyone who knew what to look for. For that matter, hadn't the aquarium man said something about salamanders and Lisa? Hers had all died. Maybe her mother had helped them along.

All along, he'd been wondering why Glenda Wallston would be willing to be in the same room as the man who had ruined her daughter's life. In his early rash of phone calls, one of Lisa's busybodies had suggested that Glenda was struggling with her Christian duty to forgive and avoid judging George Petris. A little hard to forgive a man you haven't judged, he thought, but he knew he was splitting hairs. Real forgiveness would be asking a good deal. And whether or not Glenda herself would have killed Wanda, who had done her no wrong, he had no trouble seeing Lisa impetuously rush in to protect her mother from suspicion. Glenda might not even have known about the second murder.

As Wanda's killer, Lisa would know Daniel to be innocent but not know that he had followed her to the Borowski house so closely as to disprove her lie on his behalf. Fred decided to let her stew in her own juice for a while, whatever her reason for lying. He walked her back to the door, ignoring as she did the looks that came their way.

At the blind corner that was the scene of countless spilled cups of coffee, they collided with three men who were as oblivious to Lisa as she was to them. Kyle Pruitt recovered first, but not even he gave her more than an automatic apology. Captain Warren Altschuler, chief of detectives, didn't bother.

"My office, Lundquist," he said over his shoulder. "Come in, Sam."

TWENTY

FRED FOLLOWED SAM WADE into the captain's office. The door closed in Kyle Pruitt's face, but not on his mouth, Fred was sure. The whole squadroom would know what was up before he did.

He was wrong.

"Just what do you think you're doing, sending Pruitt to grill my secretary?" Sam exploded. "I got there this morning and found myself murder suspect number one, with the whole staff drinking it in."

"What's this all about, Fred?" Altschuler asked, somewhat more mildly. "I told Sam this was the first I'd heard he was under suspicion of any kind."

Fred looked down at the stocky, pug-nosed captain, his homely face the antithesis of Sam's polished good looks.

"He's not. Just what did Pruitt say?"

"It wasn't what he said, it was what he did. He had Maxine going through her log for Saturday morning, accounting for every ten minutes of Sam's time. What was he even doing in that office?"

Fred sighed. Kyle himself had known better. I should have listened to him, he thought.

"Making a mountain out of a molehill, it sounds like. We've narrowed the Borowski murder down to a ten-minute period. I sent him out with a list of orchestra personnel to thin out the possibles. We even rehearsed what he'd say to the players before asking them about times, but I guess he knew better than to try to snow Maxine. Besides, he knew Sam already told us what he could about Petris and Borowski. He was just there to confirm it." He gritted his teeth. "I'm sorry if he made it into a major scene. Kyle gets a little carried away sometimes. I'll talk to him."

The apology cost him something, even though every word was true.

He intercepted an exchange of glances between the chief and the prosecutor. At Sam's almost imperceptible nod, Altschuler let fly.

"Let's get something straight and let's get it straight right now. We are seriously undermanned and we all know that the Petris thing is a crock. I left you on Borowski because you'd already spent time on the kid who called it in. Maybe the husband killed her, maybe the kid killed her, I don't know. What I do know is that you're grasping at straws to make connections with this crazy idea about the orchestra. Forget it. Stick to Borowski. I want some solid facts and I want them soon. Is that clear?"

It was clear, all right. So clear that something inside Fred snapped and the resentment he'd been swallowing for years poured over him. He was the dumb Democrat Swede to be passed over for promotions. Lundquist the has-been, hanging onto press clippings as if they meant something. Good enough for crocks, not crooks. Ready for the golden handshake Elmer Rush had resented.

"Oh, sure." He didn't bother to disguise the bitterness he felt. "It's clear. You want me to blow it, so you can say I don't have what it takes anymore. But as long as I'm on the force, I'm going to give it my damnedest, no matter what you think.

"You both asked me to check out Nakamura's fish story. And now that I've got some evidence it's not so crazy after all, you say forget it. If I forget Petris, I might as well forget Borowski. As far as I'm concerned, everybody in the room when Petris collapsed is a suspect in both cases. Not the only ones, by a long shot, but the best ones I have right now."

He'd been looking from one man to the other. Now he turned to Altschuler.

"Why you want me to avoid clearing Sam I can't imagine," he said. "I always thought you two were on the same side of the fence. But what do I know? You want me to leave him on the list or you want to get the hell out of my way and let me work?"

He towered over Altschuler, who stood up to the onslaught without flinching, but the chief's answering glare flickered briefly, and Fred saw Sam's eyes rolling wearily toward the ceiling. Humor him, the eyes said. Or maybe it was, Oh God, there goes the hothead again. Altschuler's mouth was moving.

" . . . blown out of all proportion. I have great respect for your abilities, Fred, you know that. But sending Pruitt on a routine check is like going after flies with an elephant swatter. If you really think all this legwork is necessary, take Ketcham. He'll cover twice the ground in half the time."

Older and subtler, Ketcham would have been Fred's choice in the first place.

"All right," he said, his heart still pounding. "Do I have to clear every move he makes with the prosecuting attorney's office?"

Sam reached out a conciliatory hand. "I'll tell Maxine to relax. You have my full support."

And I'll want yours on election day, that's the rest of the speech. Fred fought down his anger and returned the obligatory handshake.

At his desk a few minutes later, a dozen retorts he might have made crowded into his mind, followed immediately by some of the things he actually had said. The early retirement that had looked so tempting only a week or so before suddenly loomed as disciplinary action—another thing altogether. Dumb Swede, he told himself. Now look what you've done. Sam's "full support," he suspected, would hold up only until some fat cat political contributor squawked at being questioned.

He called Kyle Pruitt over, told him bluntly that he'd been replaced, and asked how far he'd made it down the list before hitting the prosecutor's office.

Pruitt's face was bright pink. "I'm real sorry about that," he said. "That Maxine tore into me so loud, the whole office heard her."

"It happens. What did you learn?"

"I found these two," Kyle said, pointing to the first two viola players, who according to Joan's lopsided map sat immediately in front of the oboes. "They both give violin lessons to little kids all Saturday morning. No breaks. Parents sit in. I got the names of the kids who were there from ten-thirty until eleven-thirty."

"Good. If we're lucky, there will be more like them. What else?"

"Then I ran into Maxine."

"Did she tell you anything?"

"Oh, sure. Wade's clear. She logs the people in that office within an inch of their lives. They say over there she knows more than God. That's what got her so mad. She wanted me to take her word for it, but I made her show me the log. Wade came over here at ten-fifteen Saturday and she logged him back in at ten-fifty-eight. According to our desk, he left here at half past ten."

"And his car was in the shop Saturday," Fred said. "Not that he might not have walked anyway." They both knew that Sam Wade preached physical fitness. Kyle had been the recipient of more than one sermon on the subject. Even Sam's brisk pace, however, wouldn't have allowed him to kill

Wanda Borowski at ten-fifty, mop up the blood, and arrive back in his office eight minutes later.

"Thanks, Kyle."

Fred sat for long minutes, drained but not relieved by his outburst. Being right didn't ease the almost physical pain of knowing how low he really ranked. A heaviness lodged itself under his breastbone, and the back of his throat tightened. For all his defiant words, he wanted nothing more than to curl up and quit.

Ketcham was out. Fred left him a note and took the personnel list, chiefly as an excuse to escape the building. Ethel Cykler, the second bassoonist, would complete the ring of players who had surrounded George Petris. Her address, 9799 North Alcorn Road, meant she lived several miles out of town. Rural residents were still complaining about the new post office regulation that had done away with rural route box numbers, but the police were discovering that street addresses greatly simplified the job of finding them at home. Come to think of it, he thought, maybe that's what they're complaining about.

Hillsides of yellow and green tipped with the flames of oaks and sugar maples and dotted with the deeper reds of sumac and dogwood lifted his spirits as he drove. When he caught himself whistling as if he'd just received a promotion instead of a dressing down, he resolved not to hurry back.

Joan's message lay unread on his cluttered desk.

TWENTY-ONE

ETHEL CYKLER, wearing only a red tank suit and hoop earrings, was pushing an old people-powered mower around the patchy grass in front of her ramshackle farmhouse. Stately maples and stumps of substantial elms testified to better days. Potatoes and onions lay drying in a garden bordered by rhubarb and asparagus fern. Guinea hens shrieked warning when Fred turned into the driveway.

He saw her look up, but she completed her circle around the yard, toes dug into the grass and stringy arm muscles straining. He waited in the car, shutting off the engine so that she'd know he wasn't merely using her drive as a convenient turnaround on the narrow gravel road. He hadn't seen a dog yet, but he wasn't taking any chances.

"Mrs. Cykler?" he called.

"Mother's dead. I'm Ethel," she answered, finally walking over to the car. He got out.

"Detective Lieutenant Lundquist, Oliver police. I'd appreciate a few minutes of your time."

"I've been looking for a reason to rest my feet," she said. "You'll do. Want some water?"

"Please."

They sat in hickory split chairs on the shady porch sipping well water as if it were mint juleps, she apparently unself-conscious in her bathing suit and calloused bare feet. Her skin was deeply tanned, her hair a mass of sweat-dampened gray curls plastered to her head. Skinny and hard, she had a face full of lines, whether from age or sun and wind he couldn't tell. Tough old bird, he thought, wonder-

ing whether he could come within a dozen years of guessing
how old.

"Think you'll know me next time?" she asked sharply.

"Sorry." He felt his face go hot. "Habit, I guess," he said,
knowing that it wasn't. A cop's habit sized people up
quickly, rather than staring at them until they felt it.

She finished her water and began drumming her fingers on
her knee, but he didn't want to get to his reason for coming.
Maybe this was his reason, just the sitting on this porch,
watching the leaves turn. He wrenched his thoughts back to
that bloody room, back to the sturdy little girls who had
comforted their father.

"Miss Cykler," he began.

"Ethel."

He nodded. "How well did you know Wanda Borowski?"

"Depends on what you mean by well. We saw each other
every Wednesday night most weeks out of the past ten years.
Played chamber music a few times. I can't say as I really
knew her, but we were acquainted, don't you know. We
weren't friends."

"Is that typical?"

"Of what?"

"Her, you, the orchestra—take your pick."

"Orchestra." She snorted. "I've played in that orchestra
fifteen years this fall. Up to last week I would've called Alex
Campbell a friend. Then Mr. Charming California walked
in and took over. You want to know something? When a
good-looking man comes along, never mind how old, friends
aren't worth chicken feed. I found that out."

He nodded and sipped. It occurred to him that if Elmer
Rush had been poisoned, Ethel would have been a prime
candidate.

"Fifteen years and I'm right back to second bassoon. I almost walked out, but I wouldn't give her the satisfaction. Besides, the old coot can't hang on forever. I'll outlast him, you watch." She was breathing fire now. Interruptions weren't likely to break the flow.

"Were there other changes this year?"

"Some new people, but nobody else got bumped."

Unless you count Borowski and Petris, he thought.

"You'll be needing two principal players now, won't you?" he asked.

"She'll find them."

"You don't think she'll promote the second flute and oboe?"

"I'm done guessing. I wouldn't put it past her to bring in Eskimos. Might as well call it the Drop-In Symphony as the Oliver, for all it means."

"You sit behind the oboes, is that right?"

"If I bother to sit anywhere again." She was having a high old time. He wondered how many people she'd unloaded this on.

"Did you see anything out of the ordinary last Wednesday night?"

"I saw a man sicken to die. Is that what you mean?"

"Starting before that."

"Can't think of a thing."

"Did Wanda Borowski mention anything to you after she packed up the oboe?"

"Not a word."

"Tell me how it was."

Ethel's description of the rehearsal differed from the others he had heard only in the angle from which she had viewed it. She had passed up the punch table to slip outdoors for a quick cigarette during the break.

"I can tell you who all was out there, if you want to know."

"I'll keep that in mind. For the moment, I'm more interested in those of you who sat near Petris and Mrs. Borowski. Tell me, did you by chance see her on Saturday?"

"Didn't see anybody. Too busy."

"Busy?"

"Puttin' up applesauce. Twenty-eight quarts. I about melted, it was so hot."

"All by yourself?"

"Do I look as if I couldn't?" She was not amused. "Been doin' it alone since Mother had her stroke. She used to help some before that."

"Nobody dropped in that day?"

"Folks don't, mostly. I count it a big social occasion when the mail carrier honks. He likes to do that when there's something worth making a trip down to the box for."

"Did he honk Saturday?"

"No, he just waved and went on by."

"And what time was that?"

"About noon. I was sitting out here quartering apples, to get away from the kitchen. What do you want to know all this for? I didn't make a quick run into town and kill her, if that's what you're thinking."

"You've seen the paper, then," he said.

"Yes, and the TV. I saw you were looking into what happened to old George, too. Why do you think I've let you waste my time like this? But I don't see why you're so interested in who sits where."

"You may be right," he said. "It may be pure coincidence that two people who sat next to each other in the orchestra died so close together, but we'd still like to ask you to be extra careful for a while."

"She was murdered in her own bedroom, wasn't she?" Ethel looked him straight in the eye.

"Yes."

"What do you suggest I do, quit sleeping?" She nodded triumphantly. "Just how hard do you expect it would be to get into this house? Back when it was built, the only lock anyone around here ever used was a shotgun—and I don't hold with that. Too easy to use against you. Besides, it seems to me that the people who ought to be careful are the ones who saw George drink that poison, and I wasn't there. For all I know, Wanda was right next to him then, too. Maybe you can get the word out to the murderer that I don't know a thing."

Was she laughing at him? He couldn't tell, but he took it seriously.

"I'll try. In the meantime, you'd be wise to talk that way yourself. Tell it around that you've already given the police everything you know and that they say you had no new evidence."

"I never see anyone to tell. Think I should hang a note out for the mailman?" Again, he saw that triumphant gleam in her eye.

"You might just mention it at orchestra next week."

She hmphed.

By the time he left, she was midway around the yard again. He reflected that a conductor's lot might at times be unhappier than a policeman's. Imagine having to bust Ethel Cykler down to second bassoon.

He made a mental note to check with her mailman and to talk to Bob Peterson at the *Courier* about "protection" for Ethel—and the others, for that matter. He couldn't name names; that might endanger players not mentioned. It would have to be an innocuous little statement in the context that no evidence had turned up to convince the police that Petris had been murdered. No, that was too strong—murder hadn't been mentioned there yet. He'd work it out with Bob.

He mulled over what Ethel had said. Only Wanda's murder was making him think of the circle of people around George Petris as more likely suspects—or potential victims—than anyone else in the orchestra. Long experience had taught him to distrust coincidence, but it *could* have been only coincidence. Captain Altschuler might be right that these were two entirely separate cases, united only by proximity. Ethel's idea that Wanda was standing next to George when he picked up his drink seemed more probable, he thought, and with luck he could even check it.

And then there was the oboe, or rather, there wasn't. The disappearing oboe connected the two deaths without question. But who would kill to get it? Not Daniel—all he'd have to do was ask for it. Might Wanda have noticed something about the oboe, rather than something during the rehearsal? And blurted it out to Daniel, who then silenced her with the reed knife and got rid of the oboe before calling the police? Or maybe she figured out something unrelated to the oboe, something about Daniel and his father, and he used the reed knife and got rid of it and the oboe along with it.

If Daniel had told the simple truth, though, someone else had wanted that oboe badly enough to kill for it. Not for money—not with cash and silver left behind. Sentiment seemed unlikely, too, unless Lisa Wallston was a more talented liar than he thought or the former Mrs. Petris was playing jet-set tricks. Even as he rejected the notion that she had made a flying trip to Oliver, unnoticed by anyone, he pulled over to the side of the road and wrote himself a cryptic message in the little notebook with which he clung to sanity and details: "Chk wife CA." Ketcham could handle that one. He never would have been able to explain it to Pruitt.

A woman—he tried to remember whether they'd asked the neighbors about a woman. On Saturday, he was sure, they'd all referred to the killer as "he." Had that influenced what people had told them?

Coming into town from the north, he was only a few blocks from the Borowski house. On sudden impulse, he turned onto Posey Avenue and again at Grove Street. He found a parking place a block beyond the little house. The once immaculate lawn, now badly trampled, would soon need mowing. The plants hanging over the porch were already drooping for lack of water.

He didn't expect to find as many people home at midday on a Monday as there had been on Saturday, but odds were with the old ladies next door. He twisted their old-fashioned mechanical doorbell and heard its metallic brring.

Miss Luca, the plump one, came to the door. Oh, my, yes, she'd be glad to help in any way she could. It was such an awful thing. She and Miss Hobbs had hardly slept a wink since last Saturday. You never knew when he'd come back, did you?

No, Miss Hobbs wasn't home. She'd gone over to the Senior Citizens' Center for the afternoon, hadn't left but five minutes ago. She was a great bridge player, but Miss Luca had never cared for it, herself. It seemed to change people's whole personalities. Why, he'd never believe what Miss Hobbs had said to her the last time she'd agreed to play. They'd made their bid—a person would think that would be enough. Well, of course, she always bid on the conservative side, just in case. And she was right. If she'd bid the grand slam Miss Hobbs said was in their hands that day and then forgotten to count trump as she had, it would have been simply terrible.

Well, yes, Saturday had been terrible, too, though in a different way, of course. No, she didn't remember seeing

anyone near dear Wanda's house before they went in for
"Masterpiece Theatre," she'd told him that before, hadn't
she? But she was keeping her eyes peeled now for any sus-
picious-looking man, he could be sure.

A woman? Oh, no, surely not. She couldn't bear to think
it. Women didn't do such terrible things. They were too sen-
sitive and gentle. Why, just last year, when their sweet kitty
had died and the mice had begun running through the
kitchen just as bold as you please, she herself had scarcely
been able to see to bait the trap, and when it had snapped,
she'd thrown away mouse, trap, and all, because she was too
softhearted to touch that furry little body.

Well, yes, she supposed there might have been a woman
around when they went in, but for gracious sake, she and
Miss Hobbs were there, too, and they were women.

No, she didn't remember seeing other mothers and children, but of course that didn't mean there hadn't been any.
She kept a good watch on the street, he could be sure, but
hardly for women and children. Well, dear Wanda was an
exception. Such a considerate neighbor and such dear little
children. It was so very unfortunate that that man had come
at the one time in the week when she and Miss Hobbs were
too busy to see what was happening.

TWENTY-TWO

Miss Hobbs was busy again. Standing behind her, Fred could see no point in announcing himself until she finished finessing the queen of hearts. She was on her way to another slam, and very much in control of this one. Would she feel the need to play it out? Apparently not.

"I think the rest are ours," she said quietly, fanning her cards expertly. If he hadn't seen it, Fred wouldn't have believed her gnarled, arthritic hands capable of such dexterity.

"Well, I never," marveled her partner, whose slender fingers were covered with rings.

"Berta, I wish I knew how you did it," said the man to her right.

Miss Hobbs lowered her eyes. Fred spoke before modesty could yield to the desire for a postmortem.

"Miss Hobbs, I wonder if you'd spare me a few minutes."

She turned slowly and leaned on the table to look up at him, her spine and bent neck rigid.

"Yes, of course, Lieutenant," she said. "Muriel, will you excuse me, please? I won't be offended if you want to find another fourth."

The woman with the rings shook her head emphatically. "Not on your life," she said. "Partners like you don't grow on trees, you know. You'll wait, won't you?" she asked the others. They murmured assent and, with what Fred thought remarkable delicacy, took the cards to another table and started a game of gin rummy.

"They know how much trouble it would be to get me up and moved," Miss Hobbs said matter-of-factly, as if she'd read his mind. "Have you found out who killed my neighbor?"

"We're working on it." He took the chair vacated by the lone male bridge player. "We think we've narrowed it down a little, and I'd appreciate your help."

"I only wish I could help. It makes me so *angry*."

He knew just how she felt. But he went on.

"Maybe you can. Think back to Saturday morning. Try to see the street in your mind, as you saw it just before you went into the house. Was anybody, anybody at all, out there besides you and Mrs. Borowski?"

"The children, of course, and Miss Luca." She wasn't being flip, but seemed to be taking his question literally. Good.

"Yes. Anybody else?"

"The paper boy was already gone, no one delivers milk anymore, and the mail didn't come until after..."

"After the police arrived?"

"Yes."

"You're doing fine."

She shut her eyes, and for a moment he thought she'd fallen asleep, as his grandmother used to do, bolt upright. Little movements under the closed lids suggested, though, that she was scanning the street in her mind's eye.

"Down at the end of the block," she said, opening her eyes again, "there were some other children coming towards the park. Bigger children—maybe ten or twelve years old."

"Would you know them again if you saw them?"

"No, they were too far away. I'm not even sure if they were boys or girls. I remember they were pretty rambunctious, and one of them was bouncing a basketball."

No bouncy children had disturbed the perfect order of the Borowski living room. Scratch children.

"How about women?" he asked.

"I don't remember. Usually I don't notice people all that much, but the children reminded me of myself when I could still get around. Would you believe I played basketball? Out by the barn with my brothers, and I loved every minute of it. Something in me snaps to attention when a basketball goes by. There's nothing like that sound on a sidewalk." Her voice sounded dreamy. He didn't want to lose her.

"So you noticed the kids."

"Yes, and I'm afraid that's all I noticed. I don't remember any men or women, but that doesn't mean they weren't there. Now if you asked me about cars, it would be different."

"Cars?"

"It's a little game I play. I'm a car watcher, the way some people are birdwatchers. Miss Luca, with whom I live, was ecstatic one day last week when she saw two hummingbirds and a rufus-sided towhee in the same morning. I wouldn't hurt her feelings for the world, but I think a Porsche, an MG, and an Edsel top that any day, and I saw all three last Friday."

"Were you watching cars Saturday, too?"

"Not intentionally. It's an automatic thing, you know. Of course I know all the regulars in the neighborhood and I don't even notice them, but let a stranger drive by, and my antennae are out."

"And?"

"It was a disappointing morning. All domestic."

A wild thought occurred to Fred.

"You don't keep a tally, do you?"

"On paper? No, but I think you'll find my memory is excellent."

"Yes, ma'am, I'm sure it is." And he was. "Suppose you tell me all the vehicles you remember seeing on the street when you left Mrs. Borowski on her porch."

"A Buick Skylark, red, this year's model, with a CB antenna. Then a red Ford pickup. I'm not sure of the model year, but it was rusted out all around the fenders."

"That's it?" His pencil paused over the little notebook.

"It was quiet then. It picked up later."

"There was quite a crowd, yes."

"No, I mean while we were still watching television. Not even 'Masterpiece Theatre' can make me miss a Corvette. It was vintage 1959, in wonderful condition. Then a light blue Seville not more than a year old. After a while an elderly green Rabbit with a bad cough and a pink Pinto I hadn't seen for months. It used to go by all the time. That's all."

"Did anybody stop and park?"

"No, but they couldn't very well. There's no parking in our block."

"What about drivers, or passengers?" It was too much to ask, he was sure.

"I couldn't see them from inside the house. Besides, I told you, I watch cars, not people. My friends think I'm a little batty. Maybe they're right." From her impish grin, he could tell that her friends' opinions didn't worry her.

"Today I'd give a lot to be a people watcher instead—but it wouldn't bring her back, would it?" Now she was sober.

"No, it wouldn't." And that was the hell of it, he thought. The best you could hope for was to lay blame at the right door and put the killer out of circulation. He had no idea whether this one would kill again, anyway. He was afraid he'd find out all too soon. His own puny warnings would be forgotten as soon as the fuss died down, as it surely would without news of an arrest.

A light touch on his shoulder jolted him out of his thoughts.

"Hello, Fred. Have you come to learn bridge from the expert?" Joan stood beside Miss Hobbs, her warm eyes smiling at him.

"Not me," he said, feeling too low to think of a clever reply. "I only came to ask her another question or two."

Joan looked puzzled.

"About our neighbor, Joan," said Miss Hobbs. "She was killed on Saturday. Such a shame."

"Oh," said Joan, the light dawning. "You're—" and he saw her get stuck.

"The old biddy next door, I imagine," said Bertha Hobbs, the imp shining through her thick spectacles.

"Not quite that bad," Joan said, laughing. "Don't let me interrupt."

"I'm afraid I've told him everything I know. It's mighty little."

"Thank you, Miss Hobbs. You never know what will make a difference." Fred turned to go.

"Fred, can we talk a minute?" Joan asked.

"Oh, sure." Hearing the lack of enthusiasm in his own voice, he wondered how she would interpret it.

She led him to her cubicle.

"You look a little tired."

"I'll survive. It's not one of my better days." He sank down onto the wooden chair, wishing that it leaned back.

"I take it you didn't get my note," Joan said.

"What note?"

"Just to call." She twiddled a pencil on her desk. "I had an inspiration earlier. It's probably silly, but for a while there, I was so sure."

"A little inspiration wouldn't hurt."

"Fred, I don't think we know when Wanda died, after all."

"Oh?"

"All we know is when she was last seen and when somebody started the washer. I don't know why I didn't see it right away—listen to me, now I'm sure all over again—but that somebody wasn't Wanda."

He bit off the sarcastic remark before it reached his lips. "Go on."

"Think about it for a minute. She had her house clean, her ironing sprinkled, her supper cooking, and her kids in the park by ten-thirty in the morning—on a Saturday. You can't tell me that a woman that well organized would wash one towel and one bathrobe in that big machine and leave a laundry hamper full of dirty sheets and towels." Her eyes sparkled as she warmed to her argument. "Even if she had wanted to wash those things separately, which doesn't make sense, she'd never have left the water level at extra high."

It had a certain logic.

"But if she didn't, then—"

"Then maybe the murderer did," Joan finished triumphantly. "To clean up the blood. It would come right out in cold water if it hadn't had time to set, and since we know she was still alive twenty minutes before someone started the washer, it would hardly have set."

"I don't think the lab would even be able to identify human blood, much less type it, after that," he agreed. "But why bother washing it at all?"

"To slow you down, maybe," she suggested. "Especially if the killer knew Daniel was coming or was afraid the children were on their way home. Weren't you looking for someone covered with blood? Isn't that why you wanted to go with me to Yoichi's, because you heard about his sweaters?"

Of course it was. Even Yoichi had spotted it.

"This does change things," Fred said. "One of the reasons I couldn't see Daniel as a serious possibility was that he was completely clean. He even rolled his sleeves down to let us look. Volunteered it himself. Not that they might not have been rolled up all along, of course. I did figure our man would have blood on him somewhere. I suppose those things were hanging in the bathroom—we can ask the husband."

"Covering up with whatever was hanging in the bathroom doesn't sound like planning ahead," Joan said.

"Oh, I don't know," Fred said. He tilted the chair against the wall, finding something like his customary angle for thinking. "I suppose you would count on finding towels in any bathroom. The robe might have been a lucky break. But I think you're right about the washer. A real planner would have dumped in some other stuff, too. Sure doesn't sound much like a woman."

"Fred Lundquist, you should know better than that," Joan said, exasperation in her voice.

"Than what?"

"All women aren't like Wanda, and you know it. I'm too stingy to waste all that water, even if I'm not the perfect housewife, but I can think of lots of women who wouldn't give it a thought. Evelyn, for instance."

Evelyn Wade, of the powder blue carpets and Cadillac. Was it the light blue Seville Bertha Hobbs had spotted? He whipped out the notebook and wrote, "Chk Cad model."

Joan looked horrified. "You're not taking that down!"

"No," he said, not altogether truthfully. "It made me think of something Miss Hobbs told me." Evelyn Wade had been in all the right places at all the right times—serving drinks, picking up a babysitter at Werner's lab, and even driving by Borowskis' Saturday morning, if that was her car. A certain ruthlessness had always made him uncomfortable

around Evelyn, but he balked at translating it into cold-
blooded murder. The question, of course, was whether
Evelyn would have balked.

"Why?" he asked. "Why would she want to kill those
two?"

"I can't imagine," Joan answered, and he realized that he
had spoken aloud. "I know she's a little pushy, but that's
absurd."

A little pushy was not how Fred would have put it.
"Probably," he said. "I'm willing to consider the absurd
right now, though, and anything else that fits the facts."

"Okay, then, try this on for size. If a woman killed
Wanda, then that might have been the woman Daniel talked
to. Maybe that's why the oboe disappeared. When she answered the phone and heard him say he was coming, she
knew she didn't have time to do much of anything but get
away. So she put the robe and towel in the washer to throw
you off the track, tossed the knife in the oboe case, and took
off fast."

That would fit Lisa Wallston, he thought. The last person
she'd want to see, even on the street, would be Daniel Petris. In that case, though, she'd have known her casual lie
was doomed from the start. Surely she could have come up
with something more convincing. Unless... He remembered how easily she had abandoned her story. Could she
have lied so transparently on purpose, to draw attention to
Daniel as a suspect, thus getting back at both Petris men and
at the same time sounding so ignorant of the facts as to make
herself an unlikely suspect?

Joan knew the gossip about Lisa and Daniel's father. Fred
told her about the visit and his idea that Lisa and her mother
might have committed the two murders independently.

She considered it for long moments. At last she said, "I
met Lisa's mother yesterday in the OB ward. She's bitter, all

right. I don't know how you tell whether a person is angry enough to kill. I just don't know."

Neither does anyone else, Fred thought glumly. They sat in silence, she shaking her head ever so slightly and twirling the pencil, and he letting his chin rest on his collarbone.

Another bitter person came to mind. Unsure how Joan would react, Fred kept silent. Finally, he left.

BACK AT THE STATION he found Sergeant Ketcham buried in the Borowski file.

"What do you think, Johnny?" Fred asked.

"Not much," Ketcham answered, scarcely looking up. "Lot of loose ends. I don't see anybody backing up the neighbors." He peered over wire-rimmed reading glasses. "Any chance they're lying?"

That was a new thought. It tasted wrong, though.

"I can't think why. They sure as hell didn't do it themselves. Miss Hobbs has all she can do to get around, and Miss Luca...well, you look for yourself. There's no reason it couldn't have been a woman, though. That reminds me, I'd like you to find out what you can about where the ex-Mrs. Petris spent last week."

"You want me to keep checking the orchestra people?"

"Let's wait until Wednesday night. It'll be a lot easier when they're all in one place."

A nagging ache reminded him that he hadn't eaten since breakfast. His watch said ten to three—it would have to wait. He was due in court at three to testify in a case involving a string of bicycle thefts. In this college town, ten-speed Peugeots and Fujis amounted to big business, legal or otherwise. On the way out the door he remembered his other note.

"Hey, Johnny," he called. "Who in town drives a Seville?"

"Not your style, Lieutenant," Ketcham answered with a grin. "Save your money. Take it from me, the lady's not worth it."

Think of icebergs, Fred told himself, but the relentless warmth rose to his cheeks. He glowered.

"Just joking, Lieutenant," Ketcham said hastily. "That's the top of the line. Rear end like a Rolls. Mrs. Wade has a new one. So does Dr. Henshaw's wife."

Great. Busting Ethel Cykler to second bassoon would be a picnic compared to coming up with iffy circumstantial evidence that linked Sam Wade's wife to a murder. Still nursing his wounds from the morning's explosion in Altschuler's office, Fred retreated to the comparatively safe territory of the courtroom.

TWENTY-THREE

THE BRIDGE PLAYERS were long gone, the last covered dish from the noonday carry-in had been tucked away for its absent-minded owner to retrieve, and only one of the adult day care participants was still waiting to be picked up. Sitting on the sofa, feet propped on a chair, Joan yielded to weariness.

"Where's Henry?" old Mrs. Skomp asked querulously for at least the fifteenth time in as many minutes.

"He's bringing the car around," Joan answered automatically, reaching over to pat the hand on which veins stood out like fat strands of overcooked spaghetti. "He'll be here soon."

She hoped it was true. Henry Skomp was effusively grateful for the respite the centre provided him from the constant care of his mother. He was also usually late when the time came to take her home again.

Hearing the door open, Joan stood to help the frail woman. To her surprise, the man who entered was not Henry Skomp but Elmer Rush.

"Well, hi, there," she said.

Already halfway across the floor, he scowled at her, or was it at Mrs. Skomp? Surely not, Joan thought. He didn't answer, but turning his back on them both, he suddenly began pushing chairs aside, throwing their cushions onto the floor, and slamming cupboard doors in the craft area.

Joan could hear him muttering under his breath. She stayed where she was, wondering whether to speak again. Mrs. Skomp stared into space. She didn't seem to notice.

"Did you forget something?" Joan finally asked inanely.

He whirled on her, not the man she had begun to think of as a friend, but an angry stranger.

"Did I ask you?"

"Hey, Elmer, it's me. Remember?"

Almost as soon as the storm had begun, it subsided.

"Looking for Julie's loom," he muttered, standing still in the middle of the room.

"Henry, come over here," came the voice from the sofa.

"It's not Henry, Mrs. Skomp," Joan said.

"Where's Henry?"

"He'll be here soon. Would you like me to turn on the television while you wait?"

"Don't like television." Mrs. Skomp snapped her pocketbook open and began searching its depths. "I wish he'd hurry up." With trembly fingers, she folded and refolded an unsullied white handkerchief.

"Dammit," Elmer muttered. He picked up a cushion.

"I hope you find it," Joan said, sinking back down. "I'll keep an eye out for it tomorrow. Tonight I seem to have run out of spizz."

"What's she doing here so late?" It felt like an accusation. "You should have closed up half an hour ago."

"We did, actually, but I couldn't walk off and leave Mrs. Skomp all alone, now could I?"

"Where's Henry?" This time it was Elmer who asked. Mrs. Skomp folded the handkerchief again.

"On his way, I hope. This is the third time he's been late like this since I've worked here. He always shows up eventually. It's hard on his mother, though. She manages all right during the day, but she'd been ready to go home since the first person left at four, and here we still are at five-thirty, with nothing to hold her interest."

Elmer exploded.

"Irresponsible, that's what it is! I'd like to teach him a thing or two!"

His color was rising as high as his voice and he jabbed his finger at her. Joan tried to calm him down.

"Elmer, I'm sure there's some good reason for his being late."

"Then he should have called. He's using you and abusing her, that's what he's doing. I won't have it! I'll take her home myself." He started toward the sofa, his face a thundercloud. In the cocoon of her own world, Mrs. Skomp didn't respond.

"Elmer, he wouldn't know where she was." Neither would Mrs. Skomp, but an inner voice told Joan not to say it.

"Give him a taste of his own medicine! He ought to realize that losing your marbles doesn't mean losing your feelings, too!"

Something clicked.

"Elmer, has someone been hurting Julie's feelings?" Joan asked.

He looked startled.

"How did you—?"

"Where's Henry?" asked Mrs. Skomp.

"Here I am, Mother," he said coming in the door with a jaunty step. "Sorry I'm so late. One last customer was in the store and I didn't have the heart to shoo her out when we locked the door. She was buying a gift for her first great-grandchild."

Joan shot a quick look at Elmer. He was still frowning.

Henry's smile was disarming.

"I'm grateful to you both for waiting with her. I don't know what we'd do without this program. It came along just in time to spare her a nursing home. I'd hate that. She's all I have."

"We're glad to have her, Mr. Skomp," Joan said carefully. "But if you really need someone here past five, and I think you do, we should arrange it formally instead of leaving your mother here after hours day after day. It's hard on her and hard on the staff." Meaning me, she thought. "I'd be happy to arrange an extra half hour with one of the regular day care program people. There might even be others who could use the service."

"That would be grand," he said, flashing that smile again. "And of course I'd want to pay for the extra time. It's well worth it to know that she's happy. Please, let me at least drive you home."

That should make Elmer feel better, Joan thought, but when she turned again to look, he was gone.

"Thanks, but I think I'd rather walk tonight," she told Henry Skomp.

The walk home revived her. She could smell the promise of frost in the cool evening air. Counting back, she remembered seeing her first firefly more than three months ago—frost was overdue. But that hadn't been in Oliver. She supposed it didn't count.

Andrew was hard at work, books and papers spread all over the kitchen table. He'd already made himself a sandwich and was holding it in one hand while scribbling notes with the other.

"D'you mind eating in the living room?" he asked. "Three tests tomorrow."

"Sure. What do you want?"

"Nothing." He looked down at the sandwich and said sheepishly, "Well, nothing fancy. I'll just take care of myself, okay?"

"Okay." Far be it from me to get in your way, she thought. What a familiar refrain that was at the center, at least among those who had all their marbles, as Elmer put it.

She thought of the others, the Mrs. Skomps. Which would be worse, to be afraid to visit the children you loved for fear of intruding on their lives, or to be so lost that you couldn't control what you did, or what they did to you?

For all Henry Skomp's sweet words, she wondered how his mother fared at home. Was he as casual about her needs there as he was about letting her wait at the center? Still, she seemed hardly to know where she was much of the time. Wouldn't it be even harder to be overworked and over-worried at that age, as Elmer was?

Joan ate her own sandwich thoughtfully. In the corner, the box of music reminded her mutely of things left undone. Well, it would have to wait. She'd practice Tuesday night, after Andrew's tests. On the other hand, she supposed marking the parts for Yoichi was unlikely to disturb his studying.

She sharpened a number 2 pencil with the butcher knife and set to it, copying the little vees and staple shapes that would tell all the violas to bow up or down at the same time. She was delighted to see that the orchestra had ordered an extra part. It meant a little more copying, but it also meant that she could probably keep one to practice most of the time. Making quick work of the violas, she reached for the second violin parts still in the box.

Then she saw the familiar prescription bottle that had been hidden beneath them and all at once she knew.

She knew how George had died.

She knew why Wanda had been murdered.

She knew who was now in greatest danger.

Choking back the impulse to tell Andrew, she reached with amazingly steady fingers for the telephone.

TWENTY-FOUR

JOAN SCRUBBED at her fingertips, feeling like Lady Macbeth. Now on cardboard, her spots would be compared to those on the prescription bottle labeled with the name of George Petris, but she couldn't wash away her guilt or her fear.

Fred had met her at the police station. She watched him seal and initial the plastic evidence bag. He laid her print card in a drawer marked To Be Classified, pulled up a swivel chair for her, and tilted his own back at an alarming angle.

"We'll test for latents in the morning," he said. "There's not a chance in a thousand we'll find anything usable, but we'll know until we eliminate your prints. I don't know how tricky it is to detect that poison, either." He sounded bored by the prospect of sifting through the new evidence.

An inarticulate sound of misery began in Joan's throat. She was beginning to shake. He leaned forward and touched her hand.

"Joan, are you all right?" he asked, his voice a little more human.

"No, I'm not all right!" she snapped. "I'm scared, and I keep thinking that if I'd seen the reeds Thursday or Friday, Wanda would still be alive. It's all my fault, and next time it could be me."

She heard the wild note in her own voice. I'm not going to be hysterical, she told herself. I'm in control. She shut her eyes, inhaling one long, slow breath and letting it out just as slowly.

"How do you figure that?" Fred asked quietly. She opened her eyes and saw support in his.

"Once we were looking for a way George could have been poisoned, I should have thought of the reeds right away. Oboe players spend half their lives sucking reeds unless they bring water to rehearsal, especially the way Alex rehearses this orchestra. We didn't have an A from the oboe to tune by the second half, but George had a solo after the first few bars of music. He was sitting there sucking on a reed, all ready to play, when Alex stopped us strings to work over the pompoms."

"The what?"

She found a faint grin somewhere. Good, she thought. I must be calming down.

"We keep the beat, pom-pom-pom-pom, pom-pom-pom-pom, and the cellos do a little dum-de-dum-de-duh-um, dum-de-dum-de-dum before the oboe comes with duh-um, de-dum-de-dum-de-duh-ump, dum-dum-duh-um-duh-um." She sang the little tune from the second movement of the Schubert, beating pom-poms against his desk with her hand.

"You'll do Bernstein out of a job." Fred was smiling now.

"Funny man. Anyway, George didn't even make it that far after he sat there with the reed in his mouth while we ran through the pom-poms."

"Nobody could count on that but the conductor."

"No, but it's a long solo and the oboe plays all through the movement. It would have gotten to him sooner or later."

"Anyone would know that?" he asked without enthusiasm.

"Yes. We played through it the week before. The overture has a big oboe solo, too, for that matter."

"What about the first half? Did he play then?"

"Yes. We read through the last movement first. He had a fat part and he sounded fine. We sat out while Alex worked over a bad spot with the violins and then we all took a break.''

''So whether it was the reeds or the Kool-Aid, the poison was administered during the intermission.''

His matter-of-fact tone was helping, but Joan was sure.

''You know it was the reeds. If I'd found them sooner, the killer wouldn't have gone to Wanda's looking for them and ended up killing her, too. It took a while for the word to get around that you thought George was murdered. At first they all thought he was just sick. I thought so, too. No one took Yoichi seriously. And Fred, that's why the oboe disappeared. The murderer had no way of knowing the reeds weren't in the case with the instrument.'' A thought hit her. ''That means at least Nancy didn't do it. She saw me pick up the bottle.''

''Maybe,'' he said. ''Maybe not.'' He held up the bag and peered through it at the bottle. ''We don't know what happened to the reed that was on the oboe when Petris collapsed. If it was packed in the oboe case, then it wouldn't matter when you found these.''

Maybe she hadn't been harboring a murder weapon in her living room after all. She wasn't comforted.

''If you could figure that out now, you'd have figured it out then, too, and gone after it in time.''

''That's funny,'' he said slowly.

Not very, she thought, disappointed in him. He thrust the bag under her nose and tilted it.

''Look at that. Isn't that a bassoon reed?''

It was. Joan remembered Elmer's embarrassment.

''You're right,'' she said. ''While Alex was drilling the violins, George was holding forth to Elmer on the only right way to wrap a reed. She shushed them. Elmer was so embarrassed that he stuck his reed in George's bottle.'' She put her hand on his arm. ''Oh, Fred, I feel better. What if I'd seen that first and given the bottle to Elmer instead of you? He might have died, too.''

Relief swept over her. It didn't last.

"He might have been perfectly safe," Fred said. "Suppose I wanted to poison Petris's reeds. What could be easier? I grab my chance when the conductor distracts him, lean forward, and drop my reed in his bottle. A little white powder on it and I've set the trap.''

"You don't mean it." Joan shifted uneasily and hugged her elbows.

Fred leaned back so far that she thought he would surely topple over until she saw the toes hooked under his bottom drawer.

"How much do you know about Elmer Rush?" he asked finally.

"Fred, you can't imagine that sweet old man would do such a thing!"

"Have you ever seen him angry?" Fred tilted still farther back, cradling his head in his crossed hands.

"Well...once." She didn't want to consider it. There had to be a world of difference between a murderous rage and stomping around because you'd lost something. Besides, Elmer hadn't really been that angry about the lost loom. It was some slight to Julie, though he'd left before saying what it was.

"And what would you say is his chief concern?"

That was easy. "Julie. He's wonderful with her, Fred. You should see them."

"I have." Fred brought his feet down on the floor and looked her in the eye. "Tell me, what do you think would happen if he recognized George Petris as the lifeguard who nearly let Julie drown?"

"That's impossible!"

"Is it? The accident happened in California," he said. "We know Petris grew up in California. Daniel says he was a strong swimmer. If he was over eighteen, there ought to be a record."

"He wasn't, but she was," Joan said, remembering. "The babysitter he was drinking and making out with when he should have been watching Julie. Elmer said she served some time. You could find out."

It was still unthinkable. She could no more imagine Elmer poisoning George, much less cutting Wanda's throat, than she could imagine herself doing it.

"I can't believe it, Fred," she insisted. "Not Elmer."

The words echoed hollowly in her mind. Hadn't she imagined a whole town saying them about the man who had tried to force himself on her? Wouldn't she have been the first to say them about him if she had heard him accused by another?

Suddenly she could feel the letter opener in her hand again, cool and heavy. How close had she been to murder that day in the church? Close enough not to trust herself to go back, she knew. She had fled all the way to Oliver instead.

I wasn't afraid of him, she thought, even when I should have been. I was afraid of myself. How could I ever wonder what Elmer might be capable of?

"You haven't talked to him," Fred was saying.

"No."

"I don't need to tell you not to. Just remember, we're a long way from proving it. We'll give you some protection until the next rehearsal. Then you'll give the reeds to me in front of the whole orchestra."

"But I don't have them anymore."

"Only you and I know that."

"Oh." Oh.

"I'll return the bottle to you Wednesday, before the rehearsal. It will look the same, but it won't be the same. Don't worry. You'll be fine."

"And Elmer? Will he be fine?" It came bursting out of her. "Look at Julie! What George did to her was murder, too, in a way. But the law couldn't touch him. Is it so terrible if Elmer took it upon himself?"

Immediately, guilt assailed her. Who was she to value George's life so lightly? She fought back. Who was George to value Julie's so little?

"I don't want to argue that with you," Fred said quietly. "But how do the Borowskis come into your rough justice? What's their crime?"

She had forgotten Wanda, and remembering brought back her fear. Wanda's crime had consisted of being in the way. She'd known that the minute she'd found the reeds.

"Do you . . . do you think he'd really kill anybody else?"

"Anybody who gets in his way." He might have been reading her mind. "Even if you think killing Petris was an execution of sorts, it was planned. He didn't just happen to have that poison in his pocket, you know. I don't think he expected to have to kill Mrs. Borowski, though. That smacked of spur-of-the-moment improvisation. Military training, too, possibly—that silent throat cutting from behind. Has Rush ever talked about the war?"

"It never came up."

"I'll do some checking." He spoke more gently. "I'm still following some other leads, Joan. I won't forget them. But be careful. If I'm right about Rush, that sweet old man gulled Wanda Borowski into letting him into her very bedroom before he killed her. My guess is that he asked to see the oboe."

"A bassoon player might want one." Joan was trying to think rationally. "Some double reed players do play all three—oboe, English horn, and bassoon. She'd believe him if he said he was interested in buying it. He could say he'd talked to Daniel and was picking it up to try it out. After all, it wasn't Wanda's to sell. But he wouldn't know that Daniel had just called her to say he was on his way to pick it up himself. She probably blurted it out."

"Maybe even challenged his story. Could be."

"So he killed her to keep her from telling."

"And to give himself a chance to dispose of the evidence. Only by now he knows he didn't get it all."

Joan looked at the reeds again and shuddered.

She was home and in bed before it hit her that the biggest mouth in town knew who had really taken them home.

TWENTY-FIVE

FRED LUNDQUIST BUTTERED his third slice of toast and opened Tuesday morning's *Courier* to Peterson's latest story.

No longer front page news, the Borowski murder investigation rated only a few column inches and an 18–point headline. Bob had done a convincing job of portraying the police as stymied for lack of evidence. He quoted Ethel Cykler directly. Her remarks cut through his vague intimations of a phantom with a grudge against wind players.

"'You ask me, I'll tell you. I think George Petris just up and died. It beats me how you could think a sick man has anything to do with a woman who gets her throat cut in her own bedroom. The police ought to quit asking silly questions and find that maniac before he kills somebody else,' Ms. Cykler told this reporter," the article ran.

Fred winced. That should take care of Ethel, he thought, but it added one more stone to the load he felt dragging him down. Altschuler would probably chew him out again, and he didn't think explaining was likely to improve matters. He lavished strawberry jam on his toast, but he might have been eating sand.

A few days earlier he would have been crowing about the evidence he expected to find in the reed bottle Joan had brought in. Today he doubted his ability to find it, and his own speculation about Elmer Rush was beginning to seem as far-fetched to him as it had to her. Yet she had stood up to the possibility, distasteful though it obviously was to her. Hadn't seemed to hold it against him, either. So why wasn't he eager to follow through?

The heaviness in his chest told him it was because he didn't want to face Altschuler and Wade. Snap out of it, Lundquist, he preached. There's nothing new about this, except this time they said it to your face instead of behind your back. You haven't changed.

But he knew he had. The night before, he had scarcely been listening to Joan, even as he had automatically pieced together a case against Rush that had finally convinced her. He'd ordered a patrol for her house and then put the whole thing out of his mind and settled down to watch the Cubs lose one last game to Cincinnati. He no longer cared. Only the belief that the murderer might kill again was making him even go through the motions.

No ONE PENETRATED his gloom with so much as a greeting when he dragged into work late. Ketcham, shrewder than he was generally credited with being, stood silently drinking coffee. Fred flipped through his little notebook, deciding what to delegate.

"You remember I asked you the other day about a Seville," he said finally.

Ketcham gulped the last of his coffee and crumpled the cup. "Yeah."

"Just for kicks, go down the orchestra personnel list and see how many other matches you can make with these cars." He tore a page out of the notebook. "A '59 Corvette, a green Rabbit—probably at least five years old, a pink Pinto, a new red Skylark, and an old Ford pickup, also red. Start with the people and give me anything close."

"Okay. Anything else?"

"I'll let you know."

Ketcham disappeared with the list, not pushing for more than Fred wanted to tell.

The pathologist didn't answer his call, but Professor Werner invited him to bring his sample over to the lab to test it for TTX.

"I'm preparing a frog this morning anyway. If your stuff acts like my stuff, that ought to be pretty good confirmation. We can document it with photographs. Got a Polaroid?"

"I'll bring one."

The phone rang as soon as he put the receiver down. He was startled to hear Catherine's voice. Listening to her musical laugh, he wondered how it had held him and realized with some satisfaction that he had not once thought of her since she had last hung up on him. Otherwise occupied, he had managed to forget to apologize again for the sourdough debacle. It didn't matter.

"You poor dear." She had gone from furious to coy without benefit of flowers. "I read all about it. I understand completely. I want you to let me fix you a perfectly scrumptious lunch today—I know you never eat right when you're on a big case. I just won't take no for an answer. About eleven?"

"Sure, Catherine," he said. "Why not? Thanks."

"Bye, now." Her laugh tinkled in his ear again.

Where does she get that "big case" nonsense? he wondered. Only reason I have this one is that nobody else expected it to be anything but a nuisance. It had indeed been a nuisance to Catherine. The least he could do was show up and act civil.

An hour later, he was standing over Professor Werner in the lab, looking down at a frog blanketed by a wet paper towel. In his pocket Fred fingered the test tube into which he had decanted less than a teaspoonful of the water from the reed bottle. Much of the intervening time had been taken up with forms—to check out the Polaroid, to requisition film for it, even to requisition the test tube. The only thing he hadn't had to fill out in triplicate was a request for the water. He shook his head at the wonderful bureaucracy that was more concerned about pilfered test tubes than about preserving the chain of evidence. At the last minute, his innate caution had prompted him to do it right. He had interrupted Ketcham's search to have him witness the transfer of fluid and had asked him to come take notes at the lab.

The three men were cramped inside a small metal mesh enclosure. Werner explained that it screened out electrical interference from lights, motors, and recording equipment.

"The electrical signals I'm measuring here are so weak that they're covered up by anything from outside. Now let's see... I guess for your purpose, we can use plain air as a stimulant. All you want to know is the difference between how the frog responds to a puff of air before we give it some of your sample and how it responds afterwards. So, I'll aim a little puff right now. Keep your eye on the oscilloscope. It's a nice machine. I got it surplus from Purdue when they bought a fancy new model."

A wobbly line on the screen exploded into spikes and valleys, and then tapered back to what it had been.

"That's the response you get to air before you administer the TTX," Werner said. "Got your camera? We'll do it again."

Laying the print on a shelf to dry, proof that the frog had been free of tetrodotoxin when they arrived, Fred handed over the test tube.

"Will this be enough?"

"If it's any concentration at all, a drop is more than we need."

With a syringe that looked like a fever thermometer, the plunger a thin wire through the middle and the needle almost invisible, Werner injected a tiny amount of the liquid into the exposed brain tissue.

"I'm probably fussier about this than I need to be, but I always try to keep the TTX away from the afferent nerves. I want it to affect only the post-synaptic neurons, the voltage-dependent sodium channels."

Ketcham's pen had been moving steadily. Now it stopped.

"Could you spell a couple of those for me, sir?" he asked.

"Sorry," Werner said. "You don't want all that. Just write that I put some of your sample in the frog's olfactory bulb. O L and factory. One word."

The effect was rapid. By the third puff of air, five minutes after the first, the dramatic spikes on the oscilloscope had flattened out. The wobbly line rose smoothly and fell again, drawing a single gentle hill on the screen.

Werner's shoulders drooped.

"Damn," he said quietly.

"Sir?" said Ketcham.

"I'd been hoping...well, never mind. What's done is done. The stuff you have there is almost certainly from my lab."

"Couldn't anything else do that?" Fred asked.

"Not really, not in that tiny amount. I don't suppose you'll tell me where you found it."

"Not just now," Fred said.

"Figured as much. Well, let's get the picture. I'll give you some prints of results I got with TTX. You'll see that they're identical to these. You'll be able to confirm it chemically. The chemical structure of TTX is unique."

The clock in the ivy-covered bell tower struck eleven as Ketcham and Lundquist left the biology building. They walked in silence to Fred's Chevy.

"You drive, Johnny," he said, handing over the keys and climbing into the passenger seat. "Drop me at Catherine's, will you? I'll walk back after lunch."

CATHERINE DIDN'T LOOK LIKE a woman who had spent the morning slaving over a hot stove. Only her fiery hair looked anything but cool and crisp, and she had contained it sleekly with a ribbon. She had, however, gone all out. Although he had never figured out what she put into the savory dish she served him, Fred recognized its creamy sauce and resolved to do it justice. Crisp green salad with fresh herb dressing complemented the rich casserole. She hadn't wasted on him the frilly touches that made Oliver hostesses compete for her decorative platters, but the fruit bowl, he knew, had been arranged as much by color as by taste. He began to relax.

"Like it?" she asked.

"You know I do. You're a terrific cook, Catherine."

"As good as that Mrs. Spencer?" She smirked at him. "I hear you've been sampling her goodies."

With difficulty, Fred resisted the almost overwhelming temptation to hit her or stalk out. He should have known what was coming.

"Catherine, don't get started." He could feel the cream curdling in his stomach.

"Get started? What do you mean?" Her voice dripped honey. "Surely it's no secret that you've been seeing her, or is it? I heard you were turning into bosom buddies. I'd like to know where that leaves me."

Fred put down his fork.

"Since you brought it up, that leaves you sounding like a woman who wants to run my life. Maybe this is news to you, Catherine. I plan to run my own life and choose my own friends. I won't dance for a jealous woman who wants to pull puppet strings. I don't know many men who would."

"Don't you? No wonder you can't solve that murder."
Her eyes glinted.

Fred stood up, abandoning dinner entirely.

"What do you mean?" he demanded.

For a moment, he thought she was going to engage in a
childish game of "Wouldn't you like to know?" Whether she
was intimidated or couldn't resist the gossip, he couldn't tell,
but she answered him.

"For goodness' sake, Fred, I'm only saying what everyone knows, and you would, too, if you understood anything
about people at all."

"Catherine..." He stared her down.

"Oh, all right," she said. "Hasn't it ever occurred to you
that Sam Wade jumps every time Evelyn pulls a string, as
you put it? I can't see what he sees in her, but she's had him
hook, line, and sinker ever since they were kids. Of course,
a good-looking man like that is always going to have—shall
we call them admirers? And he's no saint, but Evelyn knows
just how far to let his line run out before she reels him in
again. She expects big things of him. The White House, some
say. I wouldn't put it past her to get rid of anybody Sam took
a serious interest in. You'd hardly expect him to look sideways at that boring little Mrs. Borowski, but you never
know. Still waters run deep."

Mighty deep, Fred thought. Not a word of this particular
scandal had reached him, for all the calls he'd had about the
philandering George Petris. Not that it couldn't be true.

"Catherine, are you seriously suggesting that Sam Wade
was having an affair with Wanda Borowski and that Evelyn
got jealous and killed her?"

"I didn't say she was jealous. I'd be surprised if she cared
whose bed he parks his shoes under, but if she thought he
was about to wreck his political future by messing around
with a married woman too close to home, she just might.

She's put too much time and energy into Sam to let him get away now.''

Like an investment, Fred thought. Evelyn would not be one to cut her losses. Was that what Catherine was doing? Or didn't she realize what she was revealing of herself?

He opened his mouth to contradict her, remembered the blue Seville, and shut it again.

"Fred, your dinner's getting cold," Catherine reproached him.

"I'm sorry, Catherine. I have to leave," he blurted, and did.

HE WAS GLAD TO BE on foot. Behind a wheel, he probably would have run down the first poor slob who looked at him crooked. Gradually, his jerky, angry strides began to fall into a rhythm that eased his tension. He swung along with no particular goal in mind except to get away from Catherine.

By the time he heard the college chimes strike noon, he felt ready to face another human being, if not yet Altschuler and Wade. He took a chance on finding Martha Lambert at home alone.

She came to the door smiling and wiping her hands on a dish towel.

"Why, hello, Lieutenant," she said. "Won't you come in? You just missed my father. He took Julie out for the afternoon."

She held the door for him and swiped at the dog hairs on the sofa with the towel.

"That's fine," he said, sitting down. "This time I came to see you. Are you all right?"

"Yes, thank you." She sat on the arm of the sofa. "I feel a little silly about the other day. It was one of his bad days. They don't happen often, but when they do, I lose all perspective. I'm sorry I bothered you."

"It was no bother. That's what we're here for. You kept that phone number I gave you, I hope."

Her hand flashed to her bosom.

"Yes."

Good.

"I have just a couple of questions."

"Anything, if it will help you."

WHEN HE LEFT HER, he headed directly for the hospital. Negotiating with practiced ease the maze of temporary corridors born of new construction, he found the pathologist in his laboratory.

"Good to see you, Fred," Dr. Henshaw said, stripping a pair of thin rubber gloves from his fingers and tossing them into a plastic-lined wastebasket. "I was going to send some results over to you, but this makes it easier."

"Actually, I came to ask whether you'd tested the exhibits I sent you the other day for blood."

"Funny, that's just what I was going to tell you. Is that the message you left this morning?"

"No, that's another story entirely. We seem to have found the poison that did in George Petris. Professor Werner provided pretty conclusive evidence that it's the TTX he uses."

"Good thing. I couldn't have done it so fast. Let me show you what we did find."

THE SHIFT HAD CHANGED when Fred returned to the station, whistling. So had the very air he breathed.

Kyle Pruitt, on his way out the door, grinned at him and said, "Hi ya, Lieutenant. How's it going?"

"Hello, Kyle," Fred said. "Not bad, not bad at all. Is Altschuler in?"

"Yeah, but I think he's about to take off."

"Then I'm just in time."

Fred flipped quickly through the notes on his desk. Ketcham had left one phone memo, from the San Jose police. Mrs. Petris, they said, had been housebound for more than a week with a broken leg. The police ambulance had taken her to the emergency room the previous Monday. A briefer note summarized the results of Ketcham's vehicle registration search.

Sergeant Pruitt would have been astonished to learn that the tune the lieutenant was whistling when he arrived—and when he knocked on the captain's door—was the oboe solo from the second movement of Schubert's C Major Symphony, the ''Great.''

TWENTY-SIX

JOAN DREADED Wednesday's rehearsal. She drew the line at riding with Nancy. Not wanting to explain, she talked Andrew into phoning for her after breakfast that morning. He dragged his feet.

"Why?" he asked. "What am I supposed to say?"

"You don't know why. You don't have to lie."

"Can I tell her you're coming?"

"If she asks."

He carried it off with aplomb, hung up, and turned on her.

"I thought she was your best friend."

That stung.

"I don't seem to have a best friend anymore."

"You have me." He hugged her less clumsily than usual.

"Aw," she said, hugging him back.

"Aw," he echoed, and grinned. "Gotta go, Mom. Don't wait supper tonight. I promised Mr. Werner I'd work in the lab. I'll grab something."

"Move the dirty socks off the sofa first!" But he was gone.

ALL DAY SHE FELT UNEASY. By the time Henry Skomp finally arrived to pick up his mother, Joan was leery enough of walking home alone to accept the ride he offered.

Without Andrew, the little house was quiet. She was tempted to flick on the radio, but she resisted, determined to get in half an hour's practicing before supper. Reaching into the box of music folders for the one in which she had marked her fingerings, she felt again her shock at finding the bottle of reeds there. Suddenly, Elmer's behavior at the center on

Monday made sense. She dropped the music and dialed Fred's number.

She barely recognized his cheery hello.

"Fred, is that you?"

"Sure is. What's up?"

"You—you said you'd give me back the reeds so I could give them to you at rehearsal."

"I'll stop by before you leave. Ten past seven okay?"

"I'd better go a little earlier, since I have all the music. And, Fred—I've figured out something about Elmer."

"Tell me when I get there." He hung up.

No longer in any mood to practice, or cook, either, she gave in to the radio after all, changed to jeans and sneakers, and made a meal of leftovers.

Fred arrived at seven in a suit and tie. He presented the reed bottle with a flourish.

"Want me to carry the music?" he offered.

"Yes. No. Please, won't you just sit down and listen for a minute?"

He sat, pulling up the crease in each trouser leg and straightening his tie.

"Yes, ma'am, I'm listening."

What had gotten into him? Joan plunged ahead.

"You remember asking me if I'd ever seen Elmer angry?"

"Mm-hmm."

"And I said I had, once. I didn't tell you it was only the other day. He came into the center when I should have been on my way home, and he was furious. I was stuck there waiting for one of our adult day care people to be picked up. I got the impression that someone had said something unkind about Julie. He jumped all over me about how people don't care. Finally, Henry Skomp came to pick up his mother and offered me a ride home. Elmer disappeared.

"But suppose he knew I had the bottle. Nancy might have mentioned it. He must have been expecting to find me there alone, or even walking home. If the Skomps hadn't been in the way, he would have offered me a ride and I probably would have accepted and invited him in. Now I have to go to that rehearsal. Fred, I don't want to go."

"But you're all right. And you will be, I promise. Trust me." His eyes crinkled at the edges. He leaned toward her. "Here's what I need for you to do tonight."

THE BOX OF MUSIC pulled on Joan's right arm. Her shoulder bag bumped the hand that carried the viola. Parking at the far end of the lot from the cars huddled near the entrance had seemed the cautious thing to do, especially when she had recognized Nancy's Olds and Elmer's VW side by side. Fred's Chevy was next in line, though, she saw when she came closer.

Still puzzled, she stopped to switch hands. Her role was clear. But what could have changed the morose man she had seen Monday night to this almost offensively self-confident one?

In the auditorium, she didn't see him at first. She handed the music up to Yoichi, who began setting folders out on the stands. Then she checked her strings against the tuning fork in her case. It was much easier than tuning with trumpets noodling behind her. Hugging her shoulder bag as if it contained diamonds, she climbed to the stage and looked around.

There in place of George Petris sat Fred Lundquist, holding a curved soprano saxophone, of all things. He might have told me, she thought. No wonder he looked so smug. Wherever did he find a soprano—a curved one at that?

She wondered whether he would actually try to play. In his big hands, the little sax looked more like a meerschaum pipe than a real instrument. It could probably hit the notes—she wasn't sure how high a soprano went. He'd have to transpose, though. The oboe part would be written in concert pitch, and she knew the soprano sax was a B-flat instrument.

Gradually, the other players were taking their places. Joan thought the second flutist had moved up to first. It looked as if most people had shown up, but the usual chatter was subdued.

Yoichi, handing out the last folders to the basses and cellos, saw her coming.

"Thank you for marking the bowings," he said, with his pixie smile.

"You're welcome. Do you need me now?"

"No. We are ready."

Joan sat down beside John Hocking, who was staring openly at Fred and the sax.

"What won't they think of next?" he said. "You suppose we'll tune to a B-flat?"

"No, here comes Sam," she said.

Sam Wade raised an inquiring eyebrow at Fred.

"Evening, Sam," Fred said. "I'm playing George Petris tonight."

"Play it any way you want to," Sam said. He set a shot glass full of water and reeds on the floor, sat down, ran a feather through the pieces of his oboe, and began fitting them together. Sucking on a reed, he stood the instrument on its six-legged support while he closed the case and sorted through the music on his stand. Joan watched, fascinated.

The concertmaster, whose name Joan still hadn't learned, stood, hesitated only a moment, and then pointed his bow at Sam for the long A. Sam put the reed into the top of his oboe, blew a couple of quick runs, and held the tuning fork to his ear.

Joan checked her tuning quickly. She made one small adjustment and sat back in comfort before the first brass note barged in.

Finally, Alex Campbell mounted the podium.

"You all know what happened this week," she said simply. "We have lost two fine musicians."

Thank you, Joan thought, for not pretending.

"A Requiem Mass will be said for Wanda Borowski tomorrow at St. Paul's. You may want to contribute toward the cost of flowers from the orchestra. There will be no services for George Petris. We're contributing in his memory to the Oliver College scholarship fund." She paused. "Some people have suggested dedicating this first concert of the season to George and Wanda. If you are in favor of doing so, would you please stand?"

One by one, in silence, the entire orchestra rose. Alex waited a long moment. Then she nodded, and they took their seats again. A lump swelled in Joan's throat. The formal gesture went a long way toward erasing her bitterness about the comments she had heard after George was taken away.

"We have been asked to do one thing more," Alex said. "I think we owe it to George. Detective Lieutenant Lundquist will explain what he needs. Lieutenant?"

She stepped down and Fred stood among the woodwinds.

"Thank you," he said. "You probably already know that I am in charge of investigating both these deaths. I'm at a considerable disadvantage with respect to Mr. Petris. By the time the police were called in, all of you had gone about your business and the janitor had cleaned the building. We've talked with some of you, but it would help if we could see where people were and what they were doing in the last few minutes before he was taken ill." He turned around. "Sergeant Ketcham, where are you?"

"Back here," a deep voice called from behind the basses. Looking back, Joan was surprised to see Evelyn Wade and Glenda Wallston standing at the refreshment table. Their bowl and platter were empty, but they had set out cups and stood ready to serve imaginary punch and cookies. Beside them, a middle-aged man in a dark suit and wire-rimmed glasses held a notebook and pencil.

"What if I don't want to?" asked one of the young second violinists. His voice shook.

"You don't have to," Fred answered. "This is entirely voluntary. If you aren't planning to participate, I'd appreciate it if you'd sit back in the audience for a few minutes. Unless..." He looked to the conductor.

"That should work," Alex said. "Go behind the rows where people leave their cases, Tad. No one spends the intermission back there."

"It's all right," the boy muttered. "I guess I'll do it."

"Come to think of it, you'd better all know your rights," Fred said. "Read 'em the Miranda, would you, Johnny?"

Sergeant Ketcham obliged, reading constitutional rights to silence and the advice of a court-appointed lawyer, all in a bored voice.

"Anyone else?" Fred asked. No one moved. "Then please do whatever you did at the beginning of the intermission last week. I'll represent George Petris. You'll need to tell me what to do."

Joan was puzzled. Why this game? But the others were already beginning to move.

"You put away your instrument and start over to the refreshments," Sam directed Fred.

"No, before that you must have put the lid on your reeds," Joan said. "I found them this way when I fell." She gave him the prescription bottle from her purse. He took it, put the sax in its case, and walked back toward the table.

Joan left John and Sam sitting, took an empty cup herself, wishing for real ice, spoke to Yoichi, and walked around
the orchestra pretending to put music on the stands. Out of
the corner of her eye she could see Sergeant Ketcham taking
notes. Only when she came back to her seat did she again
remember her headlong plunge into Sam Wade's lap. Even
in blue jeans, she couldn't bring herself to repeat it intentionally.

His eyes smiled at her. He, too, had remembered.

"Sam, I can't," she said.

"Sure you can," said John Hocking. "Fake it. Knock
down the stand, anyway, and whack the chairs a little."

Suddenly, it was a relief to be asked to do something de-
structive. With abandon, Joan lashed out at the stand, sent
the music flying, and skidded Fred's chair back into Elmer's, spilling the water in which Elmer's reed was soaking.
A thin stream trickled towards the pages on the floor.

"Grab the music!" Joan made a dive for it.

Fred loomed over her. "What on earth?"

"Come on, Fred, help pick it up!" She scrabbled on her
hands and knees, rescuing the precious rented pages. Sam
helped. Fred just watched, as did other orchestra members
close enough to notice the commotion.

"You're supposed to yell at her," John commented.
"That's what George did."

"Is that right?" Fred asked her. "This happened last
week, too?"

"More or less. He did shout, but I got carried away tonight. Last week most of the damage I did was to my ny-
lons. It would have been worse if Sam hadn't caught me."

"My pleasure," Sam said, with that smile that left her
weak-kneed.

"And after that?" Fred pursued it.

'And after that I put everything back and about then I think we started the second half.''

"Okay, let's do it." Fred spoke quietly to Alex, who called Yoichi. The players who had left the stage straggled back with relative speed.

The concertmaster rose to tune, but sat down in embarrassment when his stand partner reminded him that he had been too late the week before.

To Joan's right, Fred had opened the bottle of reeds and was offering it to Sam.

"Thanks," Sam said. "I can use them. Say, Elmer, this one's yours." He stretched to pass the bottle to Elmer.

"I wondered where that went," Elmer said, reaching forward to pick out the unfinished bassoon reed.

"Stop right there," said Fred, his long arm catching Elmer's hand before it touched the reed.

"I'll take that, if you don't mind." Sergeant Ketcham plucked the bottle from Sam's hand.

"What's going on?" a dozen voices demanded, Elmer's and Sam's among them.

Fred was on his feet.

"Gideon Samuel Wade, you're under arrest. Before I ask you any questions, I must advise you of your constitutional rights. You must understand your rights. You have the right to remain silent—"

"I know my rights, Fred," Sam interrupted. "What's all this?"

A wail came from backstage.

"You're crazy! Sam, stop him!"

Gone was Evelyn's reserve. Eyes blazing, hair flying, her dress catching on the music stands she shoved out of her way, she pushed to the front.

"Sam, say something!"

He put put out a hand toward her, palm down. "Calm down, Evelyn."

"Just a minute, please, ma'am," Fred said formally. "I have to do this right. I'm not going to get this one thrown out of court. Sam, you have the right to remain silent. Anything you say can be used against you in court."

"Sam, your career! You can't let him do this!" Evelyn cried.

"This is ridiculous," Sam began, but Fred cut him off.

"You know you'd be the first to insist on it," he said. "You have the right to talk with a lawyer for advice before I ask you any questions and to have him present during questioning. If you cannot afford a lawyer, one will be appointed to represent you during any questioning, if you wish."

"I can afford a lawyer."

"If you decide to answer questions now without a lawyer present, you will still have the right to stop answering questions at any time. You also have the right to stop answering questions at any time until you speak to a lawyer."

He turned to Ketcham.

"Did I leave anything out?"

"No, you got it all, Lieutenant," said Ketcham, who had been reading along from the card in his hand.

"What's the charge?" Sam asked, his public face not wavering.

"The murder of Wanda Borowski, for a start," Fred said. "And after tonight, I'm pretty sure we can add the murder of George Petris and the attempted murder of Elmer Rush."

Joan didn't hear the assorted gasps and murmurings around them. She was watching Elmer's face crumple. His head kept nodding and tears rolled down the criss-crossed lines of his cheeks. For the first time, she saw him as really

old. She was relieved to see the second bassoonist lean toward him and take his hand.

In contrast, Evelyn Wade was becoming more childish by
the moment. Sam addressed her as he might a very little girl.

"Now, Evelyn, I want you to do something for me. I'll
need a lawyer."

"You *are* a lawyer!" Her voice was petulant.

"I know, but that won't help. Get Burton." With the
pencil on his music stand, he scribbled a message on the back
of an envelope pulled from his jacket pocket. "Give him this
note."

"I don't think so," Fred said quietly. "I'll take that, Sam.
You know how we do it."

To Joan's amazement, he plucked the envelope from
Sam's hand by a corner and laid it on a white handkerchief
that Sergeant Ketcham produced from thin air.

Backing away from Evelyn and Sam, Fred lifted the flap
of the envelope with a pencil point and peered inside.

"Looks like the stuff, Johnny," he said. "That and the
knife should settle it." He let the flap close and put the
handkerchief-wrapped envelope into his pocket.

Same Wade sat utterly still.

"Come on, sir," said Ketcham. "Let's go."

Sam stood obediently, avoiding all eyes. Evelyn was staring at him, her mouth agape.

"Tell them it's not true, Sam!"

Sam was silent.

"My God, I can't believe it! You couldn't have been so
stupid." Angry tears glistened in her eyes.

"Just call the lawyer, Evelyn," he said.

Chin high, she exited upstage left.

TWENTY-SEVEN

HENRY SKOMP and Yoichi Nakamura arrived at the center almost simultaneously five minutes before closing time. Joan welcomed Henry gratefully; the board hadn't yet come to a decision on the subject of after-five adult day care. In theory, it didn't exist. In fact, she was still it.

Her chance to rest disappeared, however, when Yoichi asked her to help call an extra rehearsal to replace the one that had fallen apart the night before.

"Alex is worried about the Schubert and we have not yet read through the rest of the program. We have only three more weeks."

"What will we do for oboes?"

"For this concert, I think we must hire them. I am working on it with Alex. She is talking to the IU Music School today. Would you please call the section leaders whose names I have checked here? Ask them all to notify the members of their sections and to report to you or me if someone cannot come."

He handed her a list of players. Neat brush strokes eliminated the names George Petris, Gideon Samuel Wade, and Wanda Borowski.

Later, at home, Joan kicked off her shoes, padded to the refrigerator for ice cubes and orange juice, and started down the list.

Except for having witnessed Sam's arrest, the section leaders were little different from the people at the center who had played "Isn't it awful?" all day. To most, she said honestly, "I haven't heard any more than you already know."

Only the bare facts had made it into the *Courier*. Sam wasn't talking and Elmer's daughter had refused to let the reporter interview him.

Nancy was another story.

"Didn't I tell you?" she said. "Evelyn never cared two hoots about Sam. You know what she did this morning, of course."

"No, but I imagine you'll tell me."

"I got it from Hazel Baines, who works at the bank. Evelyn marched in there at nine sharp, cool as a cucumber, and cleaned out their joint accounts. She even brought in the key to the safe-deposit box, but of course Hazel couldn't see what she did there. It's all over town. Gil Snarr told his wife that Evelyn dropped by the funeral home and asked him to sell their double plot. She's pulled the kids out of school and Jim Hendricks says he's supposed to bring a van for her furniture tomorrow. It looks as though she isn't leaving a thing behind that isn't nailed down. Sam can't stop her. They won't let him out on bail."

"Poor Sam," Joan said.

"Poor Sam! Joan, he murdered two people!"

"Did he?"

"Well, of course he did. They don't go around arresting the county prosecutor unless they have an airtight case."

Not even a change of venue would affect that point of view, Joan thought. She wondered what Fred had turned up to change his mind and just how airtight his case against Sam was. He had sounded pretty sure of himself at the rehearsal, especially after he opened the envelope.

She was relieved when the doorbell broke into the conversation. "Gotta go, Nancy. There's someone at the door. Don't forget to call the trombones."

Fred stood on her doorstep, neither downcast nor wearing the cocky grin of the night before. She discovered that she was ridiculously pleased to see him.

"Come in, come in. I only have about a million questions to ask you."

"You and everyone else." But he smiled and settled into the one big chair in the little house.

"Would you like something to drink? Orange juice on the rocks?"

"You wouldn't have a cup of coffee, would you?"

"Sure." She started the pot and set out a couple of mugs. When she returned to the living room, she found Andrew and Fred head to head.

"What did I miss?"

"He wouldn't tell me anything, Mom," Andrew complained. "He said we had to wait for you."

"You deserve to hear it all," Fred said. "If it hadn't been for you, we might never have figured it out."

"Me?" The grin spreading across her face felt foolish even from behind. She was glad she couldn't see it. He grinned back.

"Sure, you. First you sent Yoichi to the police."

"No," she said in horror. "I sent him to Sam. If I hadn't, George would have been the only person to die. You do still think Wanda died because...because Sam was afraid of something she might say?"

"Probably," he said gently. "Especially if he told her Daniel wanted him to pick up the oboe, and she already knew that Daniel was on his way over to do it himself. But Sam wouldn't have stopped with George. And it didn't make any difference that he heard it first. He had access to all the police reports anyway. It was good we found out when we did. The first murder was so near to a perfect crime that we wouldn't have caught it if Yoichi hadn't told us about the poison. And then, when you found the reeds, you saw how easy it would be to poison an oboe player with something like TTX. If we'd identified the poison in the reeds sooner, we'd have asked Wanda where the oboe was. And that would have led us straight to Sam if she'd been alive to tell it."

"I should have found them sooner."

The bottle had been right there the whole time she had fought *Donna Diana*. Now the viola line pounded through her head in maddening perfection, as she had never yet been able to play it. She sank to the sofa, resisting with difficulty the feeling that if she covered her ears, everything would be all right again.

"You didn't," Fred said. "I wish I didn't know how you feel. It happens."

She nodded, unable to speak.

"But you did figure out what killed her, you know."

"The reed knife? Was it really?" She found it scant comfort.

"Not the one you thought. Sam used his own. When I asked him to show me what one looked like, he pulled it out of his pocket. Seems it didn't fit in his case and so he carried it in his pants most of the time. It's a handy blade and sturdy. He couldn't very well say no when I borrowed it to ask Dr. Henshaw whether George's reed knife could have been the weapon used on Wanda. I didn't happen to mention to Henshaw whose knife it was.

"On Tuesday he reported to me that he'd found blood of Wanda's type inside the handle. There's quite a good-sized opening on either side of the blade where it fits into the handle."

"So that's what made you think Wade did it?" Andrew asked.

"No, as a matter of fact, by the time I heard that, I was already sure. It will come in mighty handy in court, though."

"What did, then?"

"Well, son, your mother came to see me the other night to show me a bottle of reeds she'd found. Several oboe reeds and one big bassoon reed, all soaking in what looked like plain water. I came up with the theory that Elmer Rush, the man who played bassoon behind Petris, had killed him.

"First thing, I went to Professor Werner's laboratory to make sure the liquid in the bottle was full of his poison. To make a long story short, it was. And Rush had the opportunity to poison the bottle when he and Petris were making reeds. So did Petris, of course, but we knew by that time we were dealing with murder, not suicide. My theory was that Rush had recognized Petris from about twenty years ago, as the lifeguard who let his granddaughter almost drown. She's been in bad shape ever since."

"Why would he wait until now?" Andrew asked.

"Good question. I didn't ask it. About that time I wasn't thinking too clearly. Wade had persuaded my chief of detectives that I was wasting valuable departmental time and making a general fool of myself. I had orders to stick to my knitting and forget about the Petris business. It was supposed to be a figment of Yoichi Nakamura's imagination." He shook his head.

"I was about ready to forget about police business altogether. Now I know he was trying to make sure no one investigated that murder too carefully. He succeeded. I spun my wheels a lot." He shook his head again, slowly. "I just didn't care anymore."

"I was worried about you, Fred," Joan said. "What changed? I hardly knew you last night."

"What changed was that I found out who the lifeguard really was and I knew I'd been had."

"Sam?" asked Joan. "Not George?"

"Sam."

"How did you find out?"

"Martha Lambert, Elmer's daughter, didn't know him as Sam, but she hadn't forgotten his name. She said the lifeguard was a kid from the Bible Belt by the name of Gideon. She didn't think she'd ever forget that. It took her a while to remember the Wade part. Wade—from Fish Creek—that's how she remembered. She didn't know how close that was to Oliver. Never crossed her mind when they moved here."

"Nancy told me they called him Giddy before he left home. He went out west to train for the Olympic swim team."

"That's right. The only people back here who knew what had happened were his parents. They went out to California to see him through and take custody of him. Then they made him enlist in the marines. Mrs. Lambert knew that much. That's the last she remembered hearing about him."

"You said Wanda's killer probably had military training," Joan reminded him.

"Did I?"

"Mmm. Fred, how come this made you sure Sam was the killer? You'd already figured out that Elmer had recognized the lifeguard."

His blue eyes laughed.

"This was different. If Elmer had meant to kill Sam, then he wouldn't have poisoned George's reed bottle."

"If all this was between Elmer and Sam, then how did George get into it at all?" Joan was lost.

"Maybe partly because you fell down. I didn't know about that until last night, but I suspected something of the sort. Look, I had it all backwards. Elmer didn't recognize Sam. I've seen pictures of Sam in college and law school. You'd need a lot of imagination to pick that fellow out of a crowd today. He doesn't have any physical peculiarities. This year he doesn't even have a suntan. His hair is going gray and it's

brushed back over his ears. Elmer would remember a kid in
a crew cut.''

"I get it!" Andrew fairly shouted. "It was the old guy who
didn't change. You know, Mom, how much Grandpa looks
like the pictures of him with me when I was little? But I've
changed a lot.''

"That's it, Andrew," said Fred. "Sam Wade recognized
Elmer Rush, not the other way around.''

"But why would Wade want revenge?" Andrew asked. "It
didn't mess his life up all that much.''

"Oh," said Joan, seeing Evelyn's face clearly. "He didn't.
All Sam wanted was his wife, and all she wanted was a political career—second-hand, through him. If the word had
leaked out about his criminal youth, she'd have thrown him
over about as fast as I gather she has. He wasn't just care-
less, Andrew. He was drinking on the job and underage, too.
Julie nearly died. As it is, she'll probably never tie her own
shoes, much less read a book. He had to hide it.''

"You'd think someone would have found out by now,"
Andrew said.

"His parents died before he went into politics," Fred said.
"The legal records are sealed because of his age at the time.
They may even have been purged by now. It wasn't likely to
come up.''

"Oh, but it was," said Joan. "Nancy told me Evelyn made
him use all three names when he campaigned. That's how it
was on the orchestra list, too. Elmer would have spotted
Gideon Samuel Wade. The only reason we didn't hand those
lists out a week ago was that George died and shook us up.''

"I'm guessing that he managed to forget the whole sorry
episode until he saw Julie's grandfather in the orchestra,"
Fred said. "And I'm not sure that Sam was quite as ambi-
tious as Evelyn. He could probably have been elected to

Congress with no problem on that score—and reelected, if the local folks liked him.''

"What was that about Mom falling down?" Andrew asked.

"Now I'm really speculating," Fred answered. "Last night I asked the people to imitate what they did in the last few minutes before George Petris collapsed. I was hoping that Sam would make one last attempt on Elmer Rush and that, because we were expecting it, we'd be able to keep it from happening and catch him in the act. That's pretty much how it turned out.

"He came prepared with an ordinary white envelope. In one corner, nearly invisible, there was enough TTX to kill off most of the woodwinds. Probably from Werner's lab, though there's no way to tell. I don't know if he would have tried using it with me there, but when I offered him what looked like George's bottle of reeds, he passed it right back to Elmer and pointed out the one bassoon reed in it. When we stopped that and called him on it, he tried to get rid of the envelope of TTX by passing it to his wife with a note on it. Now we have that, too.''

"You were going to tell me about how Mom fell," Andrew reminded him.

"Sort of," Joan said. "I faked it."

"She knocked over the plastic cup Elmer was using last night to soak his reeds," Fred said. "Last week, the thing she knocked over when she fell was the prescription bottle she took home after the rehearsal. A bassoon reed hid the oboe reeds in it. When she picked things up after she fell, she saw the bassoon reed in it and put it back by Elmer's chair.''

"That could be," Joan said slowly. "There was a lid on it, and I couldn't see inside all that well. I didn't even read the label with George's name on it until I found it at home, much later. I was rushing, because he was yelling at me for falling all over his music stand.''

Does that make it my fault or his that he was killed? she wondered.

"That was the bottle Sam poisoned," Fred said. "He was after Elmer, not George. But George found his reeds in the wrong place and took one out to use. He died because Sam didn't see the oboe reeds when he dropped the TTX into the bottle.''

"That seems odd," Joan said. "Sam sat right there all through the break. Why would he wait until we all came back to do what he could have done while no one was around? I'll bet he'd already poisoned the reeds by then. After all, the bottle must have been back near Elmer while they were working on the reeds, if he put his bassoon reed into it.''

She felt better.

"Maybe," Fred said. "Either way, Sam was trying to kill Elmer, not the other way around.'' He didn't seem threatened by her arguing. "And he had to do it before Elmer saw his name on that personnel list.''

"Seems to me you should have known all along that Mr. Rush didn't do it,'' Andrew said.

"How's that?" Fred asked.

"I don't see how he'd know about the poison. They say everybody in town knew it, but Mom and I didn't. We weren't here last spring when the newspaper ran that big feature about the lab. Wasn't he new in town, too?''

Joan hugged him. "Andrew, I wish I had let you in on this the other night. I would have spared myself a lot of grief. I couldn't bear to think that Elmer had killed someone.''

He wouldn't have, she thought. And I wouldn't have. Humming, she got up to pour the coffee.

"I wonder what would have happened if the first murder had turned out the way it was supposed to,'' Andrew mused.

"Do you think Wade would have gone after the rest of the family?"

"I'm sure he thought they were still in California," said Fred. "The kids didn't know about him at all—but how could he be sure of that? You might be right, Andrew."

"We still don't know what happened to George's oboe—or his reed knife," said Joan.

"Didn't I tell you? The janitor picked up his knife the next day, figured some kid had brought it to school, and gave it to the principal." Fred shook his head. "Something in this morning's paper finally made him think it over again and call us."

"And the oboe?"

"It's gone. I imagine Sam dumped it in some abandoned quarry. He could have carried it anywhere, for that matter, and no one would have thought a thing about it. It looked just like his. I don't think we'll ever know for sure, unless he decides to confess."

"Do you think that's likely?" Joan thought Sam might have very little reason to hold back now.

"Not really. It will all depend on his lawyer. Sam doesn't seem to be making any decisions on his own. I don't think he cares."

He took a sip of his coffee and sat staring into the mug.

"It's hard to believe that just last week he had me completely buffaloed. He raked me and young Pruitt over the coals for having the gall to question his secretary about his movements on Saturday. I believed him for a long time, too. It seemed that he could have had less than ten minutes to arrive, kill Wanda, clean up, and walk back to the office.

"Then you figured out that he could have killed her before starting the washer, but the times were still too tight. For a while, I thought Evelyn Wade did it. Miss Hobbs said a light blue Seville drove past at about the right time. That's her car.''

"Oh, no," Joan said. "Evelyn spent the whole day on foot, shoe shopping. I'm sure the clerks all over town could give you a shoe-by-shoe account. She had to walk because Sam's car was in the shop. That means he was using hers."

"You mean he drove," Andrew said. "That's how he got there and back so fast."

"You two," Fred said. "We could use you both."

"You're doing the hiring these days?" Joan asked.

"Not quite, but my stock has gone up a little. Not that that's saying much, when you realize that Sam asked for me on the Petris case. He must have thought, 'Now which man can I trust not to get it right?' That's what really lit a fire under me when I heard Martha Lambert say his name."

"Oh, Fred."

"Don't 'oh, Fred' me. Captain Altschuler patted me on the back and made a little speech today. I'll know he means it if I move up from bicycles and lost dogs to stolen cars and missing persons. Next year's an election year. I can wait."

They sat in comfortable silence. Joan refilled the mugs.

"Fred," she said after a while. "I still have one question."

"What's that?"

"Could you really have played the oboe solo on that sax?"

"Heady action...and Wood's familiarity
with the Canadian terrain adds authenticity
to this worthwhile mystery."
—*Publishers Weekly*

A Reid Bennett mystery

Reid Bennett, Vietnam veteran now turned police officer, investigates the violent murder of a geologist and
finds that his presence not only triggers additional kill-
ings linked with organized crime but attempts on his
own life!

Available now at your favorite retail outlet, or reserve your copy for shipping by sending your
name, address, zip or postal code along with a check or money order for $4.25 (includes
75¢ for postage and handling) payable to Worldwide Library Mysteries:

In the U.S.	In Canada
Worldwide Library Mysteries	Worldwide Library Mysteries
901 Fuhrmann Blvd.	P.O. Box 609
Box 1325	Fort Erie, Ontario
Buffalo, NY 14269-1325	L2A 5X3

Please specify book title with your order.   FOG-1A